ADVANCES IN COMPUTATIONAL TECHNIQUES FOR BIOMEDICAL IMAGE ANALYSIS

ADVANCES IN COMPUTATIONAL TECHNIQUES FOR BIOMEDICAL IMAGE ANALYSIS

Methods and Applications

Edited by

DEEPIKA KOUNDAL
Department of Virtualization, School of Computer Science, University of Petroleum and Energy Studies, Dehradun, India

SAVITA GUPTA
Director, University Institute of Engineering and Technology, Panjab University, Chandigarh, India

ELSEVIER

ACADEMIC PRESS
An imprint of Elsevier

Academic Press is an imprint of Elsevier
125 London Wall, London EC2Y 5AS, United Kingdom
525 B Street, Suite 1650, San Diego, CA 92101, United States
50 Hampshire Street, 5th Floor, Cambridge, MA 02139, United States
The Boulevard, Langford Lane, Kidlington, Oxford OX5 1GB, United Kingdom

Notices
Knowledge and best practice in this field are constantly changing. As new research and experience broaden our understanding, changes in research methods, professional practices, or medical treatment may become necessary.

Practitioners and researchers must always rely on their own experience and knowledge in evaluating and using any information, methods, compounds, or experiments described herein. In using such information or methods they should be mindful of their own safety and the safety of others, including parties for whom they have a professional responsibility.

To the fullest extent of the law, neither the Publisher nor the authors, contributors, or editors, assume any liability for any injury and/or damage to persons or property as a matter of products liability, negligence or otherwise, or from any use or operation of any methods, products, instructions, or ideas contained in the material herein.

British Library Cataloguing-in-Publication Data
A catalogue record for this book is available from the British Library

Library of Congress Cataloging-in-Publication Data
A catalog record for this book is available from the Library of Congress

ISBN: 978-0-12-820024-7

For Information on all Academic Press publications
visit our website at https://www.elsevier.com/books-and-journals

Publisher: Mara Conner
Acquisitions Editor: Tim Pitts
Editorial Project Manager: Rafael G. Trombaco
Production Project Manager: Prem Kumar Kaliamoorthi
Cover Designer: Victoria Pearson

Typeset by MPS Limited, Chennai, India

Contents

v

SECTION III MEDICAL IMAGE CLASSIFICATION
AND ANALYSIS

SECTION IV BIOMEDICAL IMAGE COMPRESSION AND TRANSMISSION

SECTION V BIOMEDICAL IMAGE SECURITY

List of contributors

Shankar Aggarwal Chitkara University School of Computer Applications, Chitkara University, Solan, India

Eman Elsaid Alaa Department of Electronics and Electrical Communications Engineering, Faculty of Engineering, Tanta University, Tanta, Egypt

Vatsala Anand Chitkara University Institute of Engineering and Technology, Chitkara University, Rajpura, India

Amira S. Ashour Department of Electronics and Electrical Communications Engineering, Faculty of Engineering, Tanta University, Tanta, Egypt

Shoaib Amin Banday Department of Electronics and Communication Engineering, School of Engineering and Technology (SoE&T), Islamic University of Science & Technology (IUST), Jammu and Kashmir, India

Ayushi Bansal University of Petroleum and Energy Studies, Dehradun, India

D. Bhargava University of Petroleum and Energy Studies, Dehradun, India

Puja Bharti Department of Electrical and Instrumental Engineering, Thapar Institute of Engineering and Technology, Patiala, India

Parul Dutta Chitkara University School of Engineering and Technology, Chitkara University, Solan, India

Sannasi Ganapathy School of Computing Science and Engineering, Vellore Institute of Technology, Chennai, India; Centre for Distance Education, Anna University, Guindy, Chennai, India

Yanhui Guo Department of Computer Science, University of Illinois, Springfield, IL, United States

Savita Gupta Director, University Institute of Engineering and Technology, Panjab University, Chandigarh, India

Sharut Gupta Department of Mathematics and Computing, Indian Institute of Technology, Delhi, India

Bazila Hashia Department of Electronics and Communication Engineering, National Institute of Technology Srinagar, Srinagar, Jammu and Kashmir, India

Anurag Jain School of Computer Science, University of Petroleum & Energy Studies (UPES), Dehradun, India

Virender Kadyan Department of Informatics, School of Computer Science, University of Petroleum and Energy Studies, Dehradun, India

Arputharaj Kannan School of Computing Science and Engineering, Vellore Institute of Technology, Chennai, India; Centre for Distance Education, Anna University, Guindy, Chennai, India

Hossam M. Kasem Department of Electronics and Electrical Communications Engineering, Faculty of Engineering, Tanta University, Tanta, Egypt

Gurpreet Kaur Department of Computer Science and Engineering, University Institute of Engineering and Technology, Panjab University, Chandigarh, India

Jaskaranveer Kaur Terminal Ballistics Research Laboratory (TBRL), DRDO, Chandigarh, India

Deepika Koundal Department of Virtualization, School of Computer Science, University of Petroleum and Energy Studies, Dehradun, India

Shakeel Malik Department of Electronics and Communication Engineering, School of Engineering and Technology (SoE&T), Islamic University of Science & Technology (IUST), Jammu and Kashmir, India

Yogish Mallya Philips Research, Bangalore, India

Ajaz Hussain Mir Department of Electronics and Communication Engineering, National Institute of Technology Srinagar, Srinagar, Jammu and Kashmir, India

Deepti Mittal Department of Electrical and Instrumental Engineering, Thapar Institute of Engineering and Technology, Patiala, India

Balasubramanian Prabhu Kavin School of Computing Science and Engineering, Vellore Institute of Technology, Chennai, India; Centre for Distance Education, Anna University, Guindy, Chennai, India

Varun Sapra School of Computer Science, University of Petroleum & Energy Studies (UPES), Dehradun, India

Bhisham Sharma Chitkara University School of Engineering and Technology, Chitkara University, Himachal Pradesh, India

Arun H. Shastry Philips Research, Bangalore, India

Chander Shekhar Terminal Ballistics Research Laboratory (TBRL), DRDO, Chandigarh, India

Sartajvir Singh Chitkara University School of Engineering and Technology, Chitkara University, Himachal Pradesh, India

Sukhwinder Singh Department of Computer Science and Engineering, University Institute of Engineering and Technology, Panjab University, Chandigarh, India

Vishakha Sood Chitkara University Institute of Engineering and Technology, Chitkara University, Rajpura, India

Paramveer Kaur Sran Department of Computer Science and Engineering, University Institute of Engineering and Technology, Panjab University, Chandigarh, India

Pradeep Suthanthiramani School of Computing Science and Engineering, Vellore Institute of Technology, Chennai, India; Centre for Distance Education, Anna University, Guindy, Chennai, India

Shamik Tiwari School of Computer Science, University of Petroleum & Energy Studies (UPES), Dehradun, India

M.S. Vidya Philips Research, Bangalore, India

Renu Vig Department of Electronic Engineering and Communication, University Institute of Engineering and Technology, Panjab University, Chandigarh, India

S. Vyas University of Petroleum and Energy Studies, Dehradun, India

Overview

Computational techniques in biomedical image analysis: overview

Deepika Koundal[1], Virender Kadyan[2], Parul Dutta[3], Vatsala Anand[4], Shankar Aggarwal[5] and Sharut Gupta[6]

[1]*Department of Virtualization, School of Computer Science, University of Petroleum and Energy Studies, Dehradun, India* [2]*Department of Informatics, School of Computer Science, University of Petroleum and Energy Studies, Dehradun, India* [3]*Chitkara University School of Engineering and Technology, Chitkara University, Solan, India* [4]*Chitkara University Institute of Engineering and Technology, Chitkara University, Rajpura, India* [5]*Chitkara University School of Computer Applications, Chitkara University, Solan, India* [6]*Department of Mathematics and Computing, Indian Institute of Technology, Delhi, India*

Chapter Outline

Advances in Computational Techniques for Biomedical Image Analysis. DOI: https://doi.org/10.1016/B978-0-12-820024-7.00001-3

1.1   Introduction

Medical imaging is a part of biomedical imaging that incorporates radiology to detect diseases. Scanning of organs is very common with other laboratory tests such as blood tests or specimen tests to make decisions for diagnosis. Imaging modalities are used by radiologists to take images of the organs in order to detect any abnormal tissue (Kasban et al., 2015; Spahn, 2013). It is an imperative tool that helps in learning about the human body for both diagnoses and therapeutic purposes.

Medical images are formed by an imaging system that sends an energy source, which when penetrated into humans in return different tissues help in creating various signals, absorb it. These signals are detected by a particular detector, which is then manipulated into an image. Nowadays, medical imaging systems generally play an important role in completely clinical applications which vary from medical scientific research to diagnostics as well as treatment planning. However, implementation of medical imaging processes are quite computationally high because of existence of three-dimensional (3D) medical corporation which needs to be practiced in real life clinical applications. Over a period of time, the advancement in graphics processors motivate researchers to perform computational tasks with lower pricing for high demanding operation of various medical image applications.

The key objective of the study is to offer brief overview to new researchers who wish to explore and need to study comprehensively the impact of medical image processing approaches such as classification, image preprocessing, segmentation, and fusion. Apart, this study includes the survey of various technological advancement using computational techniques with respect to existing conventional applications in key areas of medical image processing such as segmentation, visualization, registration, and security. The current challenges and issues related with medical images are also presented with a perspective that it can inspire future applications in medicine. Many different techniques can be used to glance inside a human body viz. X-ray, computed tomography (CT), ultrasound, scintigraphy, positron emission tomography (PET), magnetic resonance imaging (MRI), elastography, single photon emission computed tomography (SPECT), fundus, etc. Nowadays, 3D and 4D representation of organs are common for diagnosis purposes (Acharya et al., 1995; Jaiswal, 2018). This chapter presents a relative learning between diverse medical imaging techniques, benefits, risks, and applications in detail.

The rest of the sections are formulated as below: Section 1.2 presents different categories of medical imaging modalities. Section 1.3 discusses computational methods using medical images. Section 1.4 summarizes the discussion and conclusion.

1.2 Medical imaging modalities

There are various kinds of medical imagery modalities. Some of them are discussed below.

1.2.1 X-ray

X-ray was discovered by Röentgen in 1895. These are high power electromagnetic rays that can infiltrate solids (Xu and Tsui, 2013). Ionizing emission is sent into the person's body that is absorbed by tissues to get an image of the internal structure. Generally, practitioners performed X-rays for diagnosis of chest diseases and fractured bones/joint dislocation, bone cancer, blocked blood vessels, cysts, breast tumors, calcifications, heart problems, situations affecting the lungs such as asthma, infections such as osteoporosis, pneumonia, arthritis, digestive problems, dental issues and to recover swallowed objects. Apart, multiple types of X-rays are available nowadays that are used to investigate multiple conditions and diseases (Xu and Tsui, 2013). Distinct categories of X-rays exist which are used for diagnosis, monitoring and treating different medical conditions such as mammogram to examine breast cancer (Xu and Tsui, 2013). Barium enema is employed to get a closer look at gastrointestinal tract. CT is another type of X-ray that combined with computer processing helps in creation of comprehensive images (scans) for cross sections of each body part, which are later joined to form a 3D X-ray image. Fluoroscopy employed a fluorescent screen and X-rays that help study moving as well as real-time structures of the body such as a real-time view of a heart beating. It is also beneficial in providing a view of digestive or blood flow processes through combination of swallowed or injected contrast agents.

1.2.2 Computed tomography

CT helps in collection of different X-ray projections through diverse angles that are pooled to generate comprehensive cross-sectional imagery of a body (Pranata et al., 2019). It allows doctors to view certain parts of the body in a three-dimension perspective. Apart, noise (quantum noise) in CT is influenced by the amount of distinct X-ray photons which are reached using a detector. Noise in a CT is mostly beneficial in search of a large space covering tumors, metastasis, and lesions admit their existence, as well as their spatial location, size, and intensity of the tumor. It can also help in detecting the presence of blood vessels, blood clots, and tumors on the head and brain. It also displays the presence of enlarged ventricles (occurred due to building of cerebrospinal fluid) and their image with few abnormalities which occurs due to the nerves or muscles of an eye. It is also helpful in detection of short scan timing (500 ms to limited seconds) which makes use of anatomic regions, and includes susceptible patient motion as well as their breathing. For example, thorax CT is used for infiltrations of fluid, visualization of nodular structures, effusions, and fibrosis. It has the ability to act as an origin for interventional work for minimally invasive therapy and CT-guided biopsy. Its image can be used equally as a ground for outlining treatment of radiotherapy cancer, and to track the process for cancer treatment and determined the behavior of tumor during treatment. It also provides an imaging of good soft tissue resolution (contrast) along with high spatial resolution. Furthermore, it facilitates the usage of CT in orthopedic medicine along with imaging of the bony structures, which involves fractures, complex joints imaging like tip of shoulder or hip, prolapses (protrusion) of vertebral discs. It also involves specially those that affect the spine. Apart, image postprocessing capacity of CT such as multiplanar reconstructions and 3D display, the further increment values of CT imaging specially for surgeons. It is a type of 3D CT scan that acts as helpful tool that aids in facial trauma followed by surgical reconstruction.

1.2.3 Magnetic resonance imaging

In MRI, magnetic field and radio waves are used for creating meticulous imagery of body organs. An MRI scanner comprises of three important mechanisms: magnetic field gradient system, radio frequency scanner, and main magnet (Sauwen et al., 2016). It is a painless and noninvasive procedure that is used to determine the anomalies that are presented inside the brain or the spinal cord, tumors, cysts, musculoskeletal disorders, injuries, abnormality of the joints like the knee and back, a few kinds of heart issues, some degenerative diseases, and liver related issues.

1.2.4 Functional magnetic resonance imaging

Functional magnetic resonance imaging (fMRI) is used to evaluate cognitive activity by observing blood flow to definite brain areas with an increase of blood flow in some areas of active neurons. It results in activity of some insight that was caused due to neurons in the brain. This method has dominated in brain mapping which helps scientists to retrieve the spinal cord and brain without going into drug vaccine or invasive method. It also supports researchers by helping them study the basic function of a diseased, normal, or abnormal brain. It can be employed in some important practice of clinic. Normal MRI scans can also be important for noticing irregularities in the structure of tissue. Also, an fMRI can identify certain irregularity in some action of the body. fMRI acts as a test for the functionality of tissues rather than how they are actually represented. Similarly, doctor's employs fMRI to obtain the basic risks related to brain surgery by determining the place of the brain that is involved in some serious functionality such as speaking, planning, movement, or sensing of basic activities. fMRI can diagnose impact of stroke, brain injuries, tumors, head injuries, or neurodegenerative diseases like Alzheimer's (Chyzhyk et al., 2015; Tang et al., 2018).

1.2.5 Magnetic resonance spectroscopy

It is a variant of traditional magnetic resonance (MR) imaging that provides an overview of the amount of concentration for each chemical compound that is known as metabolites—inside the body. It aids in the investigation as well as diagnosis of cancer and metabolic issues, which affects the brain. Most of the researchers believe that MR spectroscopy can also prove to be helpful in detecting recurring cancer. It acts as a guide for radiation therapy and helps in identifying malignant from a healthy tissue that lies inside a breast and prostate. Magnetic resonance spectroscopy MR imaging also employs radio waves, magnetic field, and a computer which helps in creating detailed images of the body. It also used MR which helps in measuring metabolites. Metabolites are generated in the brain and other parts of the human body by reaction of chemicals. It gives some details on the position of particular chemicals that lie inside the human body or on biochemical activity in particular cells (Feldman et al., 2012).

1.2.6 Ultrasound

Ultrasound is also known as ultra-sonography or medical-sonography. To produce medical imagery, high-frequency sound waves are used, which results in echoes that are received back. An ultrasound machine has different components, like the transducer used for generating high-frequency sound waves, the transmitter used to generate pulse, the control unit used for focusing, digital processors and systems used to display the image of human anatomy and compensating amplifiers. Ultrasound imagery technique is very useful in biomedical imagery to detect and diagnose different abdominal, urological, cardiac, gynecological, breast diseases, etc. (Koundal et al., 2018). Ultrasound transducer needs to be positioned against the skin of a patient. Diverse tissues in the body reproduce sound waves to generate a picture of the human anatomy. These high-frequency sound waves are derived by ultrasound machine and further curved into images.

1.2.7 Elastography

A medical imaging modality helps in mapping of elastic property and rigidity of body tissues. The current impact of diseases can be investigated from the status of whether that tissue is basically rigid or elastic. However, a cancerous tissue is harder than surrounding normal tissues (Tyagi and Kumar, 2010). Various techniques are employed by tactile imaging and tactile sensors using ultrasound, stress sensors, and MRI. A function that applies pressure on the resilient tissues surface below functional deformation generates a tactile image. It strictly mimics physical palpation. It is widely used for detecting diseases or organs such as prostate cancer, thyroid, or breast cancer (Tyagi and Kumar, 2010). There are different types of ultrasound elastographic techniques such as acoustic radiation force impulse imaging, quasistaticelastography/strain imaging, optical coherence tomography, supersonic shear imaging (SSI), and shear-wave elasticity imaging (SWEI).

1.2.8 Nuclear medicine

Nuclear medicine comes under molecular imaging. It included molecular imaging through a measureable label such as a radiotracer with a molecule of physiological significance for assessing several cellular function parameters (Li and Nishikawa, 2015). Molecular imaging is a kind of diagnostic imaging that is used to provide detailed information of the body's interior at cellular and molecular level, whereas other medical imaging techniques mostly show anatomical illustrations. It assists the doctors to determine the functioning of the body as well as measuring its biological and chemical processes. It also helps in offering unique insights into the human body, which enable doctors to personalize patient care (Parker and Holman, 1981). It can be conducted using various types of techniques such as scintigraphy, PET, and SPECT (Rahmim and Zaidi, 2008). This diagnostic technique shows the biological function of the tissue being investigated, as it is organ- or tissue-specific for viewing specific organs such as the brain, heart, or lungs. If the agent used target-specific cellular receptors then it can also be whole-body based (Catana et al., 2006) such as the metaiodobenzylguanidine scan, PET/CT scan, the indium white blood cell scan, the octreotide scans, and the gallium scan. However, other modalities such as MRI and CT scans show only the anatomy of a specific organ to visualize the abdominal or chest cavity. Molecular imaging techniques are safe, noninvasive, and painless; they are utilized for the diagnosis of gastrointestinal, bone, kidney, brain disorders, heart disease, lung disorders, thyroid disorders, cancer, and more. These (nuclear medicine and molecular) imaging techniques can assist in diagnosing a wide scope of diseases. Traditionally, ultrasound is used to produce images of the body interior with high-frequency sound waves which are directed through the body and bounced back if diverse tissues are encountered, and then echoes are determined and are transformed to images with the help of the computer. Whereas molecular ultrasound imaging utilized the contrast agent as targeted microbubbles, which are extremely small and hollow structures during an ultrasound.

1.2.8.1 Scintigraphy

Scintigraphy helps in capturing radiation, which creates 2D images. It is also known as gamma scan. Radioisotopes, which are attached to drugs, are made to move to a specific organ and gamma radiation is emitted which is captured by exterior detectors to form images (Elfarra et al., 2019). Gamma cameras are employed for capturing the images by detecting internal gamma radiation. Functional display of skeletal metabolism is provided by it and is highly sensitive for detecting cancer as well as providing rapid evaluation of the total skeleton. It is primarily used in the detection of primary hyperthyroidism, osteomalacia, osteoporosis, and hyperthyroidism diseases. This technique is also helpful in identifying the fractures, coexistent pathology in osteoporosis, and causes of pain (Worth et al., 2019).

1.2.8.2 Single photon emission computed tomography

SPECT is an imaging scan that is utilized to determine how blood flows to various organs. In this, radiations are emitted to form 3D images with gamma cameras that are used for capturing internal radiations. It is a type of nuclear tomographic medical imagery technique that employs gamma rays for the creation of images (Ma et al., 2019). In this, gamma-emitting radioisotope is injected into the patient's bloodstream which gives cross-sectional slices of the patient's tissues. SPECT scan imaging acquires multiple 2D images from different angles and then tomographic reconstruction method is employed to yield 3D images with the computer. It is utilized for viewing the blood flow through arteries and veins in the brain. It has been concluded that SPECT is able to detect reduction in the blood flow to injured tissues more easily and is more susceptible to brain injury as compared to CT or MRI scan (Ma et al., 2018). It is also useful in the diagnosis of stress fractures, seizures, tumors, infections, and strokes in the spine.

1.2.8.3 Positron emission tomography

PET is a noninvasive and painless imaging procedure of nuclear medicine, also known as PET scan or PET imaging. It utilizes a small quantity of a radioactive substance for the diagnosis, evaluation, or treatment of several types of diseases. It generates 3D images instead of 2D and radiotracer is swallowed, injected, or inhaled as a gas based on the type of disease examination such as cancers, gastrointestinal, heart disease, neurological, and endocrine disorders (Li et al., 2018). It has the potential to recognize the disease in an earlier stage as nuclear medicine examination can locate the molecular movement. It also has the capability to determine whether the patient is responding to treatment or not. These tests aid physicians for the diagnosis and evaluation of medical conditions. Nuclear medication exams pinpoint molecular activity; therefore, these are able to identify diseases on its onset (Matsukura, 2019).

1.2.8.4 Nuclear magnetic resonance

Nuclear magnetic resonance (NMR) is an imaging process that is employed for monitoring the local magnetic fields around nuclei. It helps in determining content and purity of a sample as well as its molecular structure (Siu and Wright, 2019).

1.2.9 Optical imaging

Optical imaging utilizes visible light as well as exclusive characteristics of photons for obtaining images in detail of various tissues or organs (Singla et al., 2019; Lu et al., 2010). Optical coherence tomography (OCT) is a type of optical imaging that obtains the subsurface images of the body. Ophthalmologists use the OCT scan in order to obtain the images in detail within a retina. Cardiologists use it for the investigation of coronary artery diseases. In optical imaging, light-producing photons are developed to encompass particular molecules like brain chemicals which stay on the peak of cancer cells. It utilizes very sensitive detectors that can identify low levels of light emission by these molecules that form the body interior. Optical imaging can be bioluminescent and fluorescence imaging. Bioluminescent imaging utilizes a natural light-emitting photon by following the progression of particular cell types or by retrieving the position of a specific type of chemical reactions within the body. Whereas, fluorescence imaging utilizes photons that generate light which are triggered by an external source of light such as a laser.

1.2.10 Fundus imaging

Fundus imaging employs eye drops to dilate the pupil which can be done through ophthalmic fundus photography using a particular type of camera known as a fundus camera. It is also used to point on the fundus. The resulting imagery can be impressive, viewing the optic nerve through which visual "signals" are transmitted to the brain (Maheshwari et al., 2019; Saha et al., 2019).

1.2.11 Histopathological images

Histopathology is the process of examining the invasive or noninvasive sample under microscope by the pathologist to locate, analyze, and classify diseases like cancer. It includes a biopsy in which a small tissue is taken onto glass-slide by a pathologist for the diseases diagnoses. Nowadays digitization of pathology is becoming a popular trend for automatic analysis of visual data by the visualization and interpretation of pathologic cells and tissue samples in high-resolution images using some computerized tools. Therefore image analysis methods are required to develop which will aid pathologists for making automated diagnosis of diseases. The manual analysis of histopathological image by the pathologist for the detection of diseases leads to subjective diagnosis of the sample and varies with the expertise level of the examiner. The structure of the tissue, cells' distribution in tissue, and cell shapes regularities are examined by pathologists to determine the benign and malignant tissue in the image. The number of detection, segmentation, and classification algorithms using histopathology images have been presented (Saha et al., 2019). Automated histopathological examinations have been performed for several cancer detection applications such as breast, prostate, renal cell carcinoma, lung cancer grading, and pediatric tumor neuroblastoma (Kawalkar and Talmale, 2015; Aksac et al., 2019). Histopathologic images have been the gold standard for the evaluation of some cancers using various segmentation, feature extraction, and classification techniques. Though, analysis of such images has been a challenging task even for expert pathologists, due to inter and intra observer variabilities as well as resources and time constraints.

1.2.12 Comparison and risks of medical imaging modalities

Various medical imaging modalities discussed in the above sections are compared in terms of history, applications, and benefits in Table 1.1. Each of the above discussed modalities has some risks associated with them. Some of them are discussed in this section in Table 1.2.

1.3 Computational techniques in medical image analysis

Medical image analysis is a process of retrieving relevant information from various medical images by means of computational techniques. In recent years, there has been tremendous growth in computational techniques for medial image analysis. New computational techniques have been employed to analyze and process images which include graph theoretical methods,

Table 1.1 Comparison of biomedical imaging modalities.

S. no.	Name of modality	Used to evaluate/applications	Benefits
1	X-ray	Broken bones, cavities, swallowed objects, lungs	Noninvasive and painless
2	CT	Used to investigate blood clots and blood vessel defects in the head	It is fast and simple
3	MRI	Irregularity of brain and spinal cord, tumors and cysts	Noninvasive and harmless method
4	Ultrasound	Deformities in skin, muscle tissues, and cracks in bones	Painless, patients are not exposed to ionizing radiation
5	Elastography	Detect and assess how severe the liver disease is and guide or replace a liver biopsy	Painless and fast
6	Scintigraphy	Evaluate kidneys, bones, heart	Fast
7	SPECT	Tumor imaging, infection imaging, and thyroid imaging	Monitor disorders in the body
8	PET	Cancers, heart diseases, endocrine disorders	Painless and relatively low radiation exposure
9	NMR	Structural elucidation and drug discovery	NMR spectra are unique, well-resolved, analytically tractable
10	Optical imaging	Visualizing soft tissues in the body	Noninvasive, reduces exposure to harmful radiations
11	Fundus imaging	Optic disc, eye retina, and blood vessels	Noninvasive and painless

Table 1.2 Risks associated with different modalities.

S. no.	Name of modality	Risk(s)
1	X-ray	May develop cancer later in life
2	CT	Increased risk of developing leukemia, brain tumors, and other cancers
3	MRI	Headaches, nausea, and pain or burning at the point of injection in some people
4	Ultrasound	Ultrasound waves can heat the tissues slightly
5	Elastography	Slight risk of allergic reaction in some patients
6	Scintigraphy	Risk of some disorders in patients
7	SPECT	Bleeding, pain, or swelling where the needle is inserted
8	PET	Allergic reactions
9	NMR	Danger associated with high magnetic fields
10	Optical imaging	Least threat as compared to other imagery modalities such as X-ray

dynamic programming for optimization, fuzzy set theory, machine learning, and soft computing methods. Additionally, deep learning is an emerging area for medical image analysis and classification. This chapter emphasizes on innovative computational methods to image analysis and processing (Oliveira and Tavares, 2014; Bankman, 2008). The main objective of this chapter is to provide a comprehensive study of various techniques of medical image processing and their analysis which have been investigated through high-performance computing solutions (Rundo et al., 2019; Shen et al., 2017). For the analysis of images, image preprocessing, segmentation, and classification have been performed.

1.3.1 Image denoising

In medical science, several types of digital images are utilized to analyze the human body anatomy. Different sources of medical images are X-rays, MRI, CT scan, ultrasound, etc. These sources are very susceptible for generating noise in medical images (Turkheimer et al., 2008). Unfortunately, in medical images, the sources can be the reason for the noise. They produce noise in medical images during the image capturing of the human anatomy. These types of noises in medical images are very critical because noises in images corrupt the image quality and in the corrupted image, disease identification is a tough task. Another reason for noise in medical images is radiation. Different sources of digital images use radiation to take images of the human anatomy. But, high radiation is very harmful for the human body. Hence, the amount of radiation that is used to take the image of the human body is minimal, which increase the noise in the medical image (Koundal et al., 2016). Hence, to detect the accurate disease of the human anatomy, denoising of medical images is necessary. For proper analysis of medical image, denoising is very important by machines and humans as well. Many researchers identify this problem of medical images and they provide multiple solutions or techniques for denoising medical images (Jifara et al., 2019). Different techniques have been used that depend on the noise model. Different types of noises occur in an image while taking the image of human anatomy. Each noise has its properties and affects an image in a different manner. Their exist multiple noises in medical images: salt and pepper, Gaussian, and speckle noise. Gaussian noise commonly affects the gray pixels in medical digital images. It arises in medical images at image acquisition time, and reasons for such are warm radiations, thermal vibration, sensors sound, etc. Another name of Gaussian noise is electronic noise. Generally, it has been found in all types of medical images. Salt and pepper noise is also a type of noise which is mostly found in medical images of X-rays, MRI, and CT. This noise affects the quality of the medical image by replacing the light pixels values with dark pixels values and dark pixels values with light pixels values. Salt and pepper noise is caused by bit errors during transmission, alive pixels values, and error in analogue to digital image conversion (Manjón et al., 2008). In this noise only low-value and high-value pixels are possible, and the probability of every pixel is $<.1$. Salt and pepper noise is also known as spike, impulse, and shot noise. Speckle noise is found in ultrasound images. This noise corrupts the quality of the medical image. In nature, it is multiplicative. Speckle noise is an intrinsic characteristic of ultrasound images, and this is the reason for low contrast and resolution of medical images. It is a granular noise which is found in the digital image, and degrades the quality of the MRI and active radar images (Katiyar and Katiyar, 2019). Speckle noise is an error in the transmission of data. Brownian noise is a type of fractal noise, also known as fractal, colored, flicker, pink, or 1/f noise. Brownian motion, and this motion seen in the medical image, is due to suspended particles available in the fluid of the human body or white noise. The type of this process is nonstationary-stochastic. Image denoising is a process by which one can remove noise from existing noisy image, in order to extract the real image. Nowadays, the overall recovery of relevant information from noisy images is a challenging problem to obtain a high quality images (Hiremath et al., 2013). In medical images, reduction of noise is a very important step while processing an image as well as in computer vision. It is a preprocessing task of image processing. Therefore it is necessary to choose an efficient denoising algorithm that can help in retrieval of actual medical images.

Denoising is an image processing technique that focuses on removing various types of unwanted noise available in digital images. In image processing, there are multiple denoising techniques. The choice of the denoising technique used in digital images depends on the type of noise available in digital images. Fundamental methods for denoising digital images are basically classified into two approaches: transform domain and spatial domain filtering as presented in Fig. 1.1.

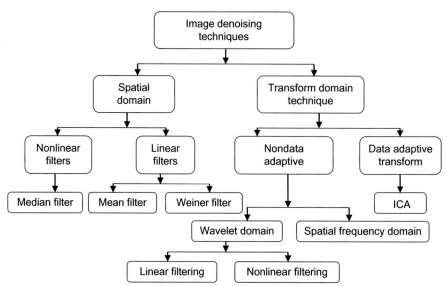

Figure 1.1 Hierarchical representation of various types of image denoising techniques.

1.3.1.1   Spatial domain technique

Spatial domain technique is a long-established denoising method. It is a technique that is directly applied to digital images in the form of spatial filters to remove noise. Spatial filter technique is grouped into two filtering techniques, linear filter and nonlinear filters (Sanches et al., 2008). In the area of image processing, filtering is a method that is used to do many preprocessing and other tasks like interpolation, re-sampling, denoising, etc. Selection of filter method depends on the type of the task done by the filter method and the kind of digital image. In digital image processing, to maintain the original image, filter methods are used to remove the unwanted noise from digital images (Priya et al., 2018; Agostinelli et al., 2013). *Nonlinear filters* have several different applications, mainly for the removal of a specific type of unwanted noise from digital images. In this method, there is no inbuilt method to recognize the noise in the digital image first. Usually, nonlinear filters remove noise to a specific point, and makes images blurry and edges hidden. In the last decade, different types of median (nonlinear) filters have been developed by various researchers to remove this problem. The most popular nonlinear filters are median filter, partial differential equations, nonlocal mean, and total variation. *Linear filter* is a denoising technique in which output results of an image change linearly. Denoising results depend on the input of the image. As the input in the image change, results of the image change linearly. Processing time of linear filters for denoising of an image depends on the input signals and that those give output signals. To remove Gaussian noise from digital medical images, mean linear filter is the most favorable filter for mean square error. This technique is the easy technique for denoising digital images (Wieclawek and Pietka, 2019). In mean filter, first calculate the average or mean pixels values of the neighbor pixels and then replace it with every pixel of the digital image. It is a very useful linear filtering technique to remove noise from a digital image. Another linear filter technique is the Wiener filter. This technique needs all information of additive noise, noise spectra, and signals of the digital image; and this technique works perfectly if all given input signals work smoothly. This method is for removing noise and reducing mean square error of the desired process and estimated random process.

1.3.1.2 *Transform domain*

Technique includes methods those are based on wavelet based noise filtering methods. It is basically depends on functions. It can be grouped in data adaptive filters and nondata adaptive transforms. Generally transform domain techniques are categorized as wavelet, contourlet, and curvelet. Data adaptive transforms have ICA (independent component analysis) transformations methods in which many components like projection detection and analysis of factor are included. It is a method that has mostly been used for partition problem of blind source type. It is beneficial to remove Gaussian and non-Gaussian noise from digital medical images. The main problem of ICA methods is the computational time, and it takes significant time for computation because it requires a minimum of two frames of an image to remove noise (Kaur et al., 2012). Nondata adaptive transforms technique can be grouped into two subgroups, wavelet and spatial domain. Spatial methods of filtering are a type of transform domain. Spatial methods use LPF (low-pass filter) and FFT (fast-Fourier transform). In this, removal of noise can be performed by discontinuing frequency. This method of frequency takes too much time to denoise. Wavelet domain nondata transforms filtering technique can be grouped into two subgroups, linear filtering and nonlinear filtering methods. Linear filter method between both two methods of Weiner filter is the best filter to remove noise because it gives better results. This method is mostly used to remove Gaussian noise, and a criterion of noise removal is mean square error. If in this method, output results are not up to the mark, then the wavelet transform method is used which maps the noise with the signal method. In nondata adaptive transforms, soft and hard thresholding methods are used. Hard thresholding method is used when input is greater than the thresholding value, else it is 0. Where input arguments of a digital image decreased to 0, soft thresholding method is used. In this digital image output may be noisy. Large threshold values produced maximum zero coefficients signal and selection of appropriate threshold value is performed very carefully (Leal and Paiva, 2019).

1.3.2 Image segmentation

Image segmentation plays a crucial role in the process of various biomedical imaging analyses which helps in better understanding its type, location, and detection of numerous diseases in them. It is generally used to trace the presence of tumors and other pathologies. It also helps in measuring tissue volumes for a computer-guided surgery and its diagnosis. Further, it tries to support treatment planning, and finally provide a study of anatomical structure, which helps in finding, simplification, classification, and recognition region of interest (ROI).

Image segmentation in medical image has suffered due to various issues such as variant shapes of ROI, confusion in the limits of ROI, quality of an image, lack of a ground truth, proper selection of technique for its application and their drawbacks in medical imaging devices. The different approaches for executing segmentation vary broadly depending on precise application, imaging modality, anatomical structure, size measurement, etc. For example, the segmentation of the thyroid nodule is different compared to the liver nodule segmentation. In the case of medical images, no single segmentation method exists, in which shows suitable results (Koundal et al., 2018). General methods exist that can be employed to different data. Though, methods that are designed for specific applications can attain better performance by taking previous knowledge of the tissue. However, selecting a suitable approach for segmentation is difficult. Different types of image segmentation techniques are shown in Fig. 1.2.

Edge-based methods are actually based on edge's detection. Segmentation is basically performed by identifying the gray level gradients. In this, different objects are separated by edges. By using edge detecting, operator's edges can be found in an

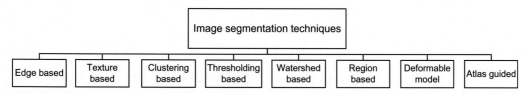

Figure 1.2 Image segmentation techniques.

image. Usually, edge is detected on basis of algorithms like Laplacian of Gaussian operator, Sobel algorithm, and Prewitt algorithm (Tang et al., 2000)

Texture-based method consists of mutually linked elements. It might be smooth, grained, or fine which depends on its structure and tone. Here structure is a spatial relationship in between the pixels and the tone is centered on intensity properties of pixels (Tesař et al., 2008).

In clustering based method, the main purpose is to develop decision boundaries that are based on unlabeled training data. This task is not easy as different size clusters and shapes occur in multidimensional feature space. Patterns in between a cluster are the same with each other as compared to patterns that belong to different clusters (Frigui and Krishnapuram, 1999).

Clustering techniques are divided into partition and hierarchical algorithm. Although, hierarchical methods show only single output, these are more accurate. On the other hand, partition methods are used in applications involving large datasets (Tseng and Yang, 2001).

Thresholding-based methods are used to find threshold values. Shubham et al. developed Masi entropy using multilevel thresholding method. In this method the author had focused on colored image multilevel thresholding by employing various entropies on satellite and natural images (Shubham et al., 2019).

Watershed algorithm has been applied on cancerous thyroid images and it makes image segmentation using morphological operations and helps to attain ROI. In this algorithm, segmentation of the image is done by divided areas that are drained by different systems. To obtain watershed lines internal markers are used (Ponraj et al., 2015). Region-based techniques are based on partitioning an image into homogeneous regions. This technique employs the seeded region, growing and choice of optimal seed value/s are a critical issue.

Deformable models support a robust segmentation approach that relies on bottom-up image-based and top-down necessities from its previous information. These generally represent curves or surfaces of a higher dimension which is used for a temporal segmentation process. Deformable models include parametric and geometric deformable models that have been extensively used for segmenting and identifying anatomic structures in medical image analysis (Metaxas and Yan, 2019). Active contour and level set are deformable models used for segmenting medical images. *Atlas guided* is a commonly used approach and it's popular among image segmentation technique in terms of biomedical. It has the tractability to capture anatomical deviation efficiently, thus providing an efficient segmentation accuracy (Wu et al., 2019). Thus, in a medical application, the automatic interpretation of images can also be extracted through clinicians with respect to labor-intensive work which enhanced their output, stability, and replicability of its judgment. On other side, it also helped in allowing them to target the other aspect of their task.

Machine learning provides the system a capability to learn automatically and improve it with the help of experience. Machine learning is a type of technique for identifying patterns, which can further be applied on medical images. Machine learning starts with algorithms of machine learning which helps in figuring image features. With the help of these features diagnosis or prediction can be done. Nowadays, machine learning is applied in different fields. In the coming future, machine learning will change many of the characteristics of healthcare with medical imaging supported domains like pathology and radiology (Fu et al., 2019).

In *deep learning*, computers learn directly from the raw data all the useful demonstrations and features automatically (Moeskops et al., 2016; Wang et al., 2018; Lee et al., 2017). The main characteristic of deep learning model is feature learning that is automatic learning representations of data. *Convolutional neural networks (CNNs)* are also beneficial for the process of image segmentation which provides input in the form of various chunks of segmented images that are further labeled in pixels (Kayalibay et al., 2017; Minnema et al., 2018). It not only compiled an overall image at once but also tried to scan them by focusing on a small "filter" of various smallest units of it, that is, pixel by pixel, which need to be mapped for a whole image. Further, fully convolutional networks (FCNs) have been introduced over conventional CNNs that have fully-connected layers in it which are not able to handle various input sizes. FCNs employ convolutional layers to compile input sizes and further fastly process it (Bi et al., 2018; Yaguchi et al., 2019). The end output layer has a large favorable field, which carries with respect to its height, width of an image on other hand the number of channels refer to various classes related to it. The convolutional layers divide each pixel to analyze the aspect of every image just like its location corresponding to various objects. Apart, ensemble learning synthesizes output into two or more relevant analytical approach into a single spread. It can help in prediction of its accuracy and also tried to lower its generalization error (Sourati et al., 2019; Jia et al., 2018; Fraz et al., 2012; Gu et al., 2013). This further helps in its exact classification and segmentation with respect to images. The method of segmentation using ensemble-learning approach tried to produce various types of weak base-learners which help in organizing various chunks of an image, and which are later combined with respect to its output. Later, it helps in obtaining a single optimal learner. However, convolutional residual networks are focused on deeper networks that generally have larger proficiency to learn, but on the other side deeper networks faced the challenge of gradient vanishing and issue of degradation (Alom et al., 2018a,b; Chang, 2016). The *recurrent neural networks (RNNs)* are endowed with recurrent connections that permit the network for remembering the patterns from last inputs. The ROI in medical images are distributed over several adjoining slices such as in CT resulted in correlations in successive slices. Therefore RNNs are used to obtain inter-slice contexts from input slices as a form of sequential data (Alom et al., 2018a,b). The RNN structure is comprised of two sections; intra-slice information extraction can be done by CNN models and the RNN can do inter-slice information extraction. Long short-term memory (LSTM) is one of the types of RNN (Cai et al., 2017a,b; Gao et al., 2018). In a standard LSTM network, the inputs should be vectorized inputs which is a drawback of segmenting a medical image, as spatial information can be lost. Therefore, in convolutional LSTM, vector multiplication has been replaced with the convolutional operation. Contextual LSTM is performed to the output layer of deep CNN to obtain segmentation by gaining the contextual information across the adjoining slices (Hesamian et al., 2019; Cai et al., 2017a,b).

1.3.3 Image registration and fusion

Image fusion (IF) is an emerging field for generating an informative image with the integration of images obtained by different sensors for decision-making. Image registration is the first step of fusion in which the source image is mapped with respect to the reference image (Viergever et al., 2016).

Various techniques of IF can be categorized as pixel level, decision level, and feature level. IF methods can be classified as spatial and frequency domain. The spatial technique deals with pixel values of the input images in which the pixels values are manipulated to attain a suitable outcome. The entire synthesis operations are evaluated using Fourier transform (FT) of the image and then Inverse Fourier Transform (IFT) is evaluated to obtain a resulting image. Other IF techniques are PCA, his, and high pass filtering and Brovey method (James and Dasarathy, 2014; Dolly and Nisa, 2019). Discrete transform fusion techniques are extensively used in IF as compared to pyramid based fusion technique. The spatial-based technique is a simple IF method consists of max-min, minimum, maximum, simple average, and simple block replace techniques. *Frequency domain*: These techniques decomposed the multiscale coefficients from the input images. Spatial distortion can be handled by the frequency methods such as Cosine, wavelet, and contourlet (Rajalingam and Priya, 2018).

1.3.4 Medical image classification

Classification of medical images plays a vital role in automated diagnosis. It is defined as the process to identify different features that are occurring in an image. It is an important part of digital image analysis which is a big issue in image analysis tasks. The main goal of classification of medical images is not only to get high accuracy but also to identify benign or malignant tissues (Deepa and Devi, 2011; Nanni et al., 2012; Sudharshan et al., 2019). Classification techniques are generally categorized as supervised and unsupervised techniques. Various types of classification techniques are shown in Fig. 1.3.

Commonly used linear classifiers in the case of breast cancer detection are logistic regression and linear discriminant analysis. Linear classifiers have not shown good performance for the nonlinear separable data and adaptability for the complex problem. *Naïve bayes* has been based on Bayes rule of conditional probability. This model has shown itself as consistently vigorous to desecration of a conditional independence hypothesis. It assumes that all features of the database are unconstrained to each other given the context of the class. *Decision tree* is a simple tree structure in which nonterminal nodes denote tests on one or more attributes and terminal nodes reveal results of assessment. Each nonterminal node has a threshold associated with one or more features to distribute the data into its descendants, and the procedure halts when each terminal node only

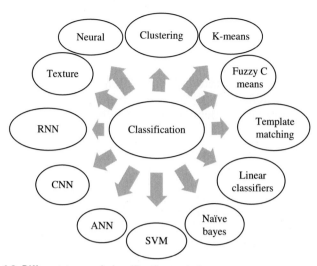

Figure 1.3 Different types of classification techniques.

encompasses one class. Therefore decision tree can be employed as a classification tool after setting the thresholds in the training practice (Ahn et al., 2019). *Neural networks* are also utilized as a key tool for medical images classification. The first neural network is based on data driven self-adaptive methods whereas the second neural networks are based on universal functional approximation which are utilized in various applications like MRI, ultrasound, etc. A *support vector machine* is a supervised technique that is based on binary classifier. In this, a hyperplane is used for separating the two classes of samples. It is utilized for classifying the two classes of instances by determining the maximum separating hyperplane between two. Support vector machines are also called as linear classifiers. *Artificial neural network (ANN)* is a self-learning system based on a mathematical model that varies its parameters based on internal or external information. It is comprised of an output layer, input layer, and hidden layers (Kozegar et al., 2019). ANN is dependent on initial value, suffered from long training time, and unrepeatable. These networks have also the issue of over-parameterization and over-training. *CNNs* are a type of neural network that involves a stack of layers, which performs a particular operation. Each intermediate layer accepts the output of the prior layer as its input (Lakshmanaprabu et al., 2019; Khan et al., 2019). This permits it to show temporal dynamic performance. *RNNs* are connectionist paradigms that seize the dynamics of sequences via cycles in the network of nodes. These are able to select passing the information across sequence steps, while processing sequential data one element at a time (Yan et al., 2019; Pandya et al., 2019). Hence, these can model input/output sequences of elements that are dependent. Unlike feed forward neural networks, RNNs can utilize their own internal state (memory) to process input sequences. Additional, RNN can simultaneously model the sequential and time dependences on multiple scales.

1.3.5 Medical image compression techniques for transmission

Image compression has performed a valuable role in medical imaging as massive information hording and exchange of data for diagnosis purpose is the necessity. Numerous compression techniques are used as a part of medical progression as critical medical data may be life threatening. These pioneering developments have performed an extreme role in medical imaging. Nowadays, there is a tremendous amount of increase in medical images on the Internet. Therefore the need for secure and quick analysis is essential in the medical domain. The goal behind the medical image compression is to display medical images with only important information so that the medical images could be stored effectively and transmitted efficiently. Compression techniques are generally categorized as lossy compression technique and lossless compression techniques. Lossy compression techniques are those techniques in which some information may be lost which is not recommendable in the medical domain. Examples of such techniques are vector quantization, transform coding, and wavelet compression techniques. Whereas, lossless compression techniques are those in which important information is attempted to be retained which is very useful in the case of medical imaging. In medical imaging, SPIHT, JPEG, and wavelets are generally used. Nowadays, content-based image compression is used in medical image storage applications. An integration of both lossless and lossy compression methods is used for such application. Wavelets technique and codebook-based approach is among them which is simple and efficient.

1.3.6 Security in communication

The security of images is a critical issue in the medical domain for the transmission through communication networks and storage in the archive. The security assurance in a medical image can be characterized in terms of privacy which refers to the denial of access to information by unauthorized individuals; authenticity is that which validated the source of the image and integrity that assured that the images have not been modified or deleted. Traditional security methods include encryption, network firewall, and data embedding which can only assure that each data packet of the image sent has not been compromised during image transmission, but still there is lack of work on how to know whether the image received or sent is actually the original data. Therefore, these methods only provide solutions for privacy and authenticity, but not for image integrity. The two types of methods to secure medical images are hiding information in some carrier image and encryption. The information can be hid as watermarking and stegnography. Other methods can be employed for the protection of biomedical images such as those that consist of several types of important information, which could be useful for the diagnosis. A number of improved approaches have been developed for the enhancement of security and reduction for the intrusion chances.

1.4   Discussion and conclusions

Medical image analysis is a challenging task that requires several types of computational methods in various imaging applications such as image preprocessing, classification, segmentation, compression, and security. In medical science, detecting and diagnosing the different types of diseases is a challenging task without examining the interior of human body. The external diseases of the human body can be easily identified with human eyes but detecting internal diseases of human anatomy is a challenging task. Hence, detecting different diseases of the human anatomy, visual images of body organs and tissues are required. Medical images help us to solve this problem. Different types of techniques are used for capturing the human anatomy images which are called medical imaging. When medical imaging devices capture the human anatomy images, captured images are noisy and require preprocessing of images to make images meaningful. This chapter presented the various medical imaging modalities with diverse computational techniques for their analysis. The computational techniques based on soft computing, machine learning, and deep learning are discussed. Still there are many issues, which are required to be solved such as classification efficiency, computational complexity, and practical feasibility. These issues are associated with computational methods to solve real-time problems in medical image analysis. Preprocessing is a technique that is used for enhancing the quality of the medical images. Various techniques of preprocessing of medical images are denoising, segmentation, classification, IF, image registration, etc. These techniques help to analyze medical images. To perform all these preprocessing operations on medical images, various computational techniques like fuzzy sets, deep learning, machine learning, CNN, etc. on medical images have been used. An overview of different computational techniques and imaging modalities such as MRI, medical radiation, fundus, ultrasound, elastography as well as computational techniques such as machine learning, deep learning, and fuzzy techniques are used for removing the challenges that face analyzing medical images based on the concepts, benefits, risks, and applications provided. The discussions have shown that none of the modalities can be alone reliable in all medical applications. These discussions will be beneficial for beginners and researchers in this field.

References

Acharya, R., Wasserman, R., Stevens, J., Hinojosa, C., 1995. Biomedical imaging modalities: a tutorial. Comput. Med. Imaging Graph. 19 (1), 3−25.

Agostinelli, F., Anderson, M.R. and Lee, H., 2013. Adaptive multi-column deep neural networks with application to robust image denoising. Advances in Neural Information Processing Systems, 1493−1501, Twenty-seventh Conference on Neural Information Processing Systems held in Harrahs and Harveys, Lake Tahoe from 5th to 10th December 2013.

Ahn, E., Kumar, A., Feng, D., Fulham, M. Kim, J., 2019. Unsupervised feature learning with k-means and an ensemble of deep convolutional neural networks for medical image classification. arXiv preprint arXiv:1906.03359, pp. 1−8.

Aksac, A., Demetrick, D.J., Ozyer, T., Alhajj, R., 2019. BreCaHAD: a dataset for breast cancer histopathological annotation and diagnosis. BMC Res. Notes 12 (1), 82−84.

Alom, M.Z., Hasan, M., Yakopcic, C., Taha, T.M. Asari, V.K., 2018a. Recurrent residual convolutional neural network based on u-net (R2U-net) for medical image segmentation. arXiv preprint arXiv:1802.06955.

Alom, M.Z., Yakopcic, C., Taha, T.M. Asari, V.K., 2018b. Nuclei segmentation with recurrent residual convolutional neural networks based U-Net (R2U-Net). In: NAECON 2018-IEEE National Aerospace and Electronics Conference, IEEE, pp. 228−233.

Bankman, I. (Ed.), 2008. Handbook of Medical Image Processing and Analysis. Elsevier.

Bi, L., Feng, D., Kim, J., 2018. Dual-path adversarial learning for fully convolutional network (FCN)-based medical image segmentation. Vis. Comput. 34 (6−8), 1043−1052.

Cai, J., Lu, L., Xie, Y., Xing, F. Yang, L., 2017a. Pancreas segmentation in MRI using graph-based decision fusion on convolutional neural networks. In: International Conference on Medical Image Computing and Computer-Assisted Intervention. Springer, Cham, pp. 674−682.

Cai, J., Lu, L., Xie, Y., Xing, F. Yang, L., 2017b. Improving deep pancreas segmentation in CT and MRI images via recurrent neural contextual learning and direct loss function. arXiv preprint arXiv:1707.04912.

Catana, C., Wu, Y., Judenhofer, M.S., Qi, J., Pichler, B.J., Cherry, S.R., 2006. Simultaneous acquisition of multislice PET and MR images: initial results with a MR-compatible PET scanner. J. Nucl. Med. 47 (12), 1968–1976.

Chang, P.D., 2016. Fully convolutional deep residual neural networks for brain tumor segmentation. International Workshop on Brainlesion: Glioma, Multiple Sclerosis, Stroke and Traumatic Brain Injuries. Springer, Cham, pp. 108–118.

Chyzhyk, D., Savio, A., Graña, M., 2015. Computer aided diagnosis of schizophrenia on resting state fMRI data by ensembles of ELM. Neural Netw. 68, 23–33.

Deepa, S.N., Devi, B.A., 2011. A survey on artificial intelligence approaches for medical image classification. Indian J. Sci. Technol. 4 (11), 1583–1595.

Dolly, J.M. Nisa, A.K., 2019. A survey on different multimodal medical image fusion techniques and methods. In: 2019 1st International Conference on Innovations in Information and Communication Technology (ICIICT), IEEE, pp. 1–5.

Elfarra, F.G., Calin, M.A., Parasca, S.V., 2019. Computer-aided detection of bone metastasis in bone scintigraphy images using parallelepiped classification method. Ann. Nucl. Med. 33 (11), 866–874.

Feldman, M.D., Viswanath, S., Tiwari, P., Toth, R., Madabhushi, A., Tomaszeweski, J. et al., 2012. Rutgers State University of New Jersey and University of Pennsylvania. Computer assisted diagnosis (CAD) of cancer using multi-functional, multi-modal in-vivo magnetic resonance spectroscopy (MRS) and imaging (MRI). U.S. Patent 8,295,575.

Fraz, M.M., Remagnino, P., Hoppe, A., Uyyanonvara, B., Rudnicka, A.R., Owen, C. G., et al., 2012. An ensemble classification-based approach applied to retinal blood vessel segmentation. IEEE Trans. Biomed. Eng. 59 (9), 2538–2548.

Frigui, H., Krishnapuram, R., 1999. A robust competitive clustering algorithm with applications in computer vision. IEEE Trans. Pattern Anal. Mach. Intell. 5, 450–465.

Fu, G.S., Levin-Schwartz, Y., Lin, Q.H., Zhang, D., 2019. Machine learning for medical imaging. J. Healthc. Eng. 1–3.

Gao, Y., Phillips, J.M., Zheng, Y., Min, R., Fletcher, P.T. Gerig, G., 2018. Fully convolutional structured LSTM networks for joint 4D medical image segmentation. In: 2018 IEEE 15th International Symposium on Biomedical Imaging. IEEE, pp. 1104–1108.

Gu, Y., Kumar, V., Hall, L.O., Goldgof, D.B., Li, C.Y., Korn, R., et al., 2013. Automated delineation of lung tumors from CT images using a single click ensemble segmentation approach. Pattern Recognit. 46 (3), 692–702.

Hesamian, M.H., Jia, W., He, X., Kennedy, P., 2019. Deep learning techniques for medical image segmentation: achievements and challenges. J. Digital Imaging 32 (4), 582–596.

Hiremath, P.S., Akkasaligar, P.T., Badiger, S., 2013. Speckle noise reduction in medical ultrasound images. Advancements and Breakthroughs in Ultrasound Imaging. Intechopen, pp. 201–241.

Jaiswal, S., 2018. Applications and comparison of medical imaging modalities. Int. J. Eng. Sci. Invent. 7 (1), 94–100.

James, A.P., Dasarathy, B.V., 2014. Medical image fusion: a survey of the state of the art. Inf. Fusion 19, 4–19.

Jia, H., Xia, Y., Song, Y., Cai, W., Fulham, M., Feng, D.D., 2018. Atlas registration and ensemble deep convolutional neural network-based prostate segmentation using magnetic resonance imaging. Neurocomputing 275, 1358–1369.

Jifara, W., Jiang, F., Rho, S., Cheng, M., Liu, S., 2019. Medical image denoising using convolutional neural network: a residual learning approach. J. Supercomput. 75 (2), 704−718.

Kasban, H., El-Bendary, M.A.M., Salama, D.H., 2015. A comparative study of medical imaging techniques. Int. J. Inf. Sci. Intell. Syst. 4 (2), 37−58.

Katiyar, A., Katiyar, G., 2019. Denoising of images using neural network: a review. Advances in System Optimization and Control. Springer, Singapore, pp. 223−227.

Kaur, J., Kaur, M., Kaur, P., Kaur, M., 2012. Comparative analysis of image denoising techniques. Int. J. Emerg. Technol. Adv. Eng. 2 (6), 296−298.

Kawalkar, P. Talmale, G., 2015. Review paper on histopathological image analysis approach for automatic detection of glandular structures in human tissue. In: International Conference on Pervasive Computing. IEEE, pp. 1−5.

Kayalibay, B., Jensen, G. van der Smagt, P., 2017. CNN-based segmentation of medical imaging data. arXiv preprint arXiv:1701.03056, pp. 1−24.

Khan, S., Islam, N., Jan, Z., Din, I.U., Rodrigues, J.J.C., 2019. A novel deep learning based framework for the detection and classification of breast cancer using transfer learning. Pattern Recognit. Lett. 125, 1−6.

Koundal, D., Gupta, S., Singh, S., 2016. Speckle reduction method for thyroid ultrasound images in neutrosophic domain. IET Image Process. 10 (2), 167−175.

Koundal, D., Gupta, S., Singh, S., 2018. Computer aided thyroid nodule detection system using medical ultrasound images. Biomed. Signal. Process. Control. 40, 117−130.

Kozegar, E., Soryani, M., Behnam, H., Salamati, M., Tan, T., 2019. Computer aided detection in automated 3-D breast ultrasound images: a survey. Artif. Intell. Rev. 1−23.

Lakshmanaprabu, S.K., Mohanty, S.N., Shankar, K., Arunkumar, N., Ramirez, G., 2019. Optimal deep learning model for classification of lung cancer on CT images. Future Gener. Comput. Syst. 92, 374−382.

Leal, A.S., Paiva, H.M., 2019. A new wavelet family for speckle noise reduction in medical ultrasound images. Measurement 140, 572−581.

Lee, J.G., Jun, S., Cho, Y.W., Lee, H., Kim, G.B., Seo, J.B., et al., 2017. Deep learning in medical imaging: general overview. Korean J. Radiol. 18 (4), 570−584.

Li, Q., Nishikawa, R.M. (Eds.), 2015. Computer-Aided Detection and Diagnosis in Medical Imaging. Taylor & Francis.

Li, S., Jiang, H., Wang, Z., Zhang, G., Yao, Y.D., 2018. An effective computer aided diagnosis model for pancreas cancer on PET/CT images. Comput. Methods Prog. Biomed. 165, 205−214.

Lu, S., Cheung, C.Y.L., Liu, J., Lim, J.H., Leung, C.K.S., Wong, T.Y., 2010. Automated layer segmentation of optical coherence tomography images. IEEE Trans. Biomed. Eng. 57 (10), 2605−2608.

Ma, L., Ma, C., Liu, Y., Wang, X., Xie, W., 2018. Diagnosis of thyroid diseases using SPECT images based on convolutional neural network. J. Med. Imaging Health Inform. 8 (8), 1684−1689.

Ma, L., Ma, C., Liu, Y., Wang, X., 2019. Thyroid diagnosis from SPECT images using convolutional neural network with optimization. Comput. Intell. Neurosci. 1−11.

Maheshwari, S., Kanhangad, V., Pachori, R.B., Bhandary, S.V., Acharya, U.R., 2019. Automated glaucoma diagnosis using bit-plane slicing and local binary pattern techniques. Comput. Biol. Med. 105, 72−80.

Manjón, J.V., Carbonell-Caballero, J., Lull, J.J., García-Martí, G., Martí-Bonmatí, L., Robles, M., 2008. MRI denoising using non-local means. Med. image Anal. 12 (4), 514–523.

Matsukura, Y., 2019. Development of a CNN-based computer-aided diagnosis system for Lugano classification of malignant lymphoma by using whole-body FDG PET-CT. J. Nucl. Med. 60 (Suppl. 1), 2002.

Metaxas, D.N., Yan, Z., 2019. Deformable models, sparsity and learning-based segmentation for cardiac MRI based analytics. Handbook of Medical Image Computing and Computer Assisted Intervention. Academic Press, pp. 273–292.

Minnema, J., van Eijnatten, M., Kouw, W., Diblen, F., Mendrik, A., Wolff, J., 2018. CT image segmentation of bone for medical additive manufacturing using a convolutional neural network. Comput. Biol. Med. 103, 130–139.

Moeskops, P., Wolterink, J.M., van der Velden, B.H., Gilhuijs, K.G., Leiner, T., Viergever, M.A., et al., 2016. Deep learning for multi-task medical image segmentation in multiple modalities. International Conference on Medical Image Computing and Computer-Assisted Intervention. Springer, Cham, pp. 478–486.

Nanni, L., Lumini, A., Brahnam, S., 2012. Survey on LBP based texture descriptors for image classification. Expert. Syst. Appl. 39 (3), 3634–3641.

Oliveira, F.P., Tavares, J.M.R., 2014. Medical image registration: a review. Comput. Methods Biomech. Biomed. Eng. 17 (2), 73–93.

Pandya, M.D., Shah, P.D., Jardosh, S., 2019. Medical image diagnosis for disease detection: a deep learning approach. U-Healthcare Monitoring Systems. Academic Press, pp. 37–60.

Parker, J., Holman, B., 1981. Computer-Assisted Cardiac Nuclear Medicine. Little Brown, Boston, MA.

Ponraj, N., Saviour, L. Mercy, M., 2015. Segmentation of thyroid nodules using watershed segmentation. In: 2nd International Conference on Electronics and Communication Systems. IEEE, pp. 1098–1102.

Pranata, Y.D., Wang, K.C., Wang, J.C., Idram, I., Lai, J.Y., Liu, J.W., et al., 2019. Deep learning and SURF for automated classification and detection of calcaneus fractures in CT images. Comput. Methods Prog. Biomed. 171, 27–37.

Priya, A., Sinha, K., Choudhary, S. Pridarshini, S., 2018. Image denoising technique using various filters models: a survey. In: International Conference on Computing, Power and Communication Technologies (GUCON). IEEE, pp. 919–923.

Rahmim, A., Zaidi, H., 2008. PET versus SPECT: strengths, limitations and challenges. Nucl. Med. Commun. 29 (3), 193–207.

Rajalingam, B. Priya, R., 2018. Multimodal medical image fusion based on deep learning neural network for clinical treatment analysis. Int. J. Chem Tech Res. 11(6), pp. 160–176, 2018. CODEN (USA): IJCRGG, ISSN, 0974–4290.

Rundo, L., Tangherloni, A., Nobile, M.S., Militello, C., Besozzi, D., Mauri, G., et al., 2019. MedGA: a novel evolutionary method for image enhancement in medical imaging systems. Expert. Syst. Appl. 119, 387–399.

Saha, O., Sathish, R. Sheet, D., 2019. Fully convolutional neural network for semantic segmentation of anatomical structure and pathologies in colour fundus images associated with diabetic retinopathy. arXiv preprint arXiv:1902.03122, pp. 1–4.

Sanches, J.M., Nascimento, J.C., Marques, J.S., 2008. Medical image noise reduction using the Sylvester–Lyapunov equation. IEEE Trans. Image Process. 17 (9), 1522–1539.

Sauwen, N., Acou, M., Van Cauter, S., Sima, D.M., Veraart, J., Maes, F., et al., 2016. Comparison of unsupervised classification methods for brain tumor segmentation using multi-parametric MRI. NeuroImage: Clin. 12, 753–764.

Shen, D., Wu, G., Suk, H.I., 2017. Deep learning in medical image analysis. Annu. Rev. Biomed. Eng. 19, 221–248.

Shubham, S., Bhandari, A.K., 2019. A generalized Masi entropy based efficient multilevel thresholding method for color image segmentation. Multimed. Tools Appl. 78 (12), 17197–17238.

Singla, N., Dubey, K., Srivastava, V., 2019. Automated assessment of breast cancer margin in optical coherence tomography images via pretrained convolutional neural network. J. Biophoton. 12 (3), e201800255.

Siu, A.G. Wright, G.A., Sunnybrook Research Institute, 2019. System and method for detection of collagen using magnetic resonance imaging. U.S. Patent Application 10/307,076.

Sourati, J., Gholipour, A., Dy, J.G., Tomas-Fernandez, X., Kurugol, S., Warfield, S.K., 2019. Intelligent labeling based on fisher information for medical image segmentation using deep learning. IEEE Trans. Med. Imaging 2642–2653.

Spahn, M., 2013. X-ray detectors in medical imaging. Nucl. Instrum. Methods Phys. Res. Sect. A 731, 57–63.

Sudharshan, P.J., Petitjean, C., Spanhol, F., Oliveira, L.E., Heutte, L., Honeine, P., 2019. Multiple instance learning for histopathological breast cancer image classification. Expert. Syst. Appl. 117, 103–111.

Tang, H., Wu, E.X., Ma, Q.Y., Gallagher, D., Perera, G.M., Zhuang, T., 2000. MRI brain image segmentation by multi-resolution edge detection and region selection. Comput. Med. Imaging Graph. 24 (6), 349–357.

Tang, X., Zeng, W., Shi, Y., Zhao, L., 2018. Brain activation detection by modified neighborhood one-class SVM on fMRI data. Biomed. Signal. Process. Control. 39, 448–458.

Tesař, L., Shimizu, A., Smutek, D., Kobatake, H., Nawano, S., 2008. Medical image analysis of 3D CT images based on extension of Haralick texture features. Comput. Med. Imaging Graph. 32 (6), 513–520.

Tseng, L.Y., Yang, S.B., 2001. A genetic approach to the automatic clustering problem. Pattern Recognit. 34 (2), 415–424.

Turkheimer, F.E., Boussion, N., Anderson, A.N., Pavese, N., Piccini, P., Visvikis, D., 2008. PET image denoising using a synergistic multiresolution analysis of structural (MRI/CT) and functional datasets. J. Nucl. Med. 49 (4), 657–666.

Tyagi, S., Kumar, S., 2010. Clinical applications of elastography: an overview. Int. J. Pharma Bio Sci. 1, 1–8.

Viergever, M.A., Maintz, J.A., Klein, S., Murphy, K., Staring, M., Pluim, J.P., 2016. A survey of medical image registration – under review. Med. Image Anal. 33, 140–144.

Wang, G., Li, W., Zuluaga, M.A., Pratt, R., Patel, P.A., Aertsen, M., et al., 2018. Interactive medical image segmentation using deep learning with image-specific fine tuning. IEEE Trans. Med. Imaging 37 (7), 1562–1573.

Wieclawek, W., Pietka, E., 2019. Granular filter in medical image noise suppression and edge preservation. Biocybern. Biomed. Eng. 39 (1), 1–16.

Worth, C., Hird, B., Tetlow, L., Wright, N., Patel, L., Banerjee, I., 2019. Thyroid scintigraphy differentiates subtypes of congenital hypothyroidism. Arch. Dis. Child. .

Wu, J., Zhang, Y. Tang, X., 2019. A multi-atlas guided 3D fully convolutional network for MRI-based subcortical segmentation. In: 16th International Symposium on Biomedical Imaging. IEEE, pp. 705–708.

Xu, J., Tsui, B.M., 2013. Quantifying the importance of the statistical assumption in statistical X-ray CT image reconstruction. IEEE Trans. Med. Imaging 33 (1), 61–73.

Yaguchi, A., Aoyagi, K., Tanizawa, A. Ohno, Y., 2019. 3D fully convolutional network-based segmentation of lung nodules in CT images with a clinically inspired data synthesis method. In: Medical Imaging 2019: Computer-Aided Diagnosis, vol. 10950. International Society for Optics and Photonics, p. 109503G.

Yan, R., Ren, F., Wang, Z., Wang, L., Zhang, T., Liu, Y., et al., 2019. Breast cancer histopathological image classification using a hybrid deep neural network. Methods 1–9.

Further reading

Erturk, S.M., Johnston, C., Tempany-Afdhal, C., Van den Abbeele, A.D., 2009. Imaging tools in human research. Clinical and Translational Science. Academic Press, pp. 87–104.

Kaur, J., Kaur, R., 2014. Digital image de-noising filters a comprehensive study. Int. J. Res. Comput. Appl. Robot. 2 (4), 55–62.

Koundal, D., Gupta, S., Singh, S., 2013. Survey of computer-aided diagnosis of thyroid nodules in medical ultrasound images. Advances in Computing and Information Technology. Springer, Berlin, Heidelberg, pp. 459–467.

Seshamani, S., Cheng, X., Fogtmann, M., Thomason, M.E., Studholme, C., 2014. A method for handling intensity inhomogeneities in fMRI sequences of moving anatomy of the early developing brain. Med. Image Anal. 18 (2), 285–300.

Shubham, S., Bhandari, A.K., 2019. A generalized Masi entropy based efficient multilevel thresholding method for color image segmentation. Multimed. Tools Appl. 78 (12), 17197–17238.

Stylianou, A., Talias, M.A., 2013. Nanotechnology-supported THz medical imaging. F1000Research 2 (1), 100.

Image Preprocessing and Segmentation Techniques

Multimodal medical image fusion using deep learning

Jaskaranveer Kaur and Chander Shekhar
Terminal Ballistics Research Laboratory (TBRL), DRDO, Chandigarh, India

2.1   Introduction

In recent years, with significant development in technology and instrumentation, medical image processing has become a hot area of research due to its pivotal role in the health sector. In the area of medical imaging various modes of medical images like positron emission tomography (PET), single photon emission computed tomography (SPECT), computed tomography (CT), magnetic resonance imaging (MRI) (James and Dasarathy, 2014, pp. 4–19), etc. depict the information from different perspectives regarding human organs. CT portrays the contour of bone structure. It describes dense bone structures

Advances in Computational Techniques for Biomedical Image Analysis. DOI: https://doi.org/10.1016/B978-0-12-820024-7.00002-5

but lacks characterization of soft tissues, that is, cannot detect physiological changes (Maes et al., 2003, pp. 1699−1721). CT has advantages such as a short scan time, and it gained popularity as a three-dimensional (3-D) imaging technique, and its prominent use is for 3-D tumor imitation (Zacharaki et al., 2003, pp. 686−689). On the other hand, MRI can better visualize the normal and pathological soft tissue structures in brain, heart, and eyes with better accuracy. PET images contain organ metabolism's functional information and the blood flow in brain tissues. PET is often combined with CT and MRI to provide anatomical and metabolic information. SPECT reveals information about blood vessels' structure. So each individual category has its own features and in order to get all the relevant information in a single image the best possible solution is fusion of different modality images (Dasarathy, 2012, pp. 1−9). The focus of research in this domain is on fusion algorithms to get better quality fused images while preserving featured details of the input image. So the objective of multimodal image fusion is to retrieve corresponding information from individual modalities and divulge information which is otherwise imperceptible to human beings. The process of amalgamating different modality images is termed as multimodal medical image fusion and that covers a vast variety of methods dealing with medical concerns reflected by images of body organs and cells.

Medical image fusion is generally applied at three stages viz., pixel level, feature level, and decision level. Fusion at pixel level is concerned with information linked with pixels (Piella, 2003, pp. 259−280; Yang and Li, 2012, pp. 10−19). Feature level is the next stage which extracts various attributes like intensity, edges, and textures and then fuses these to get the final image (Calhoun and Adali, 2009, pp. 711−720). Decision level is top level of fusion; where input to the fusion algorithm comes from the initial level recognition and categorization (Yunfeng et al., 2008, pp. 2411−2414).

The study of image fusion has been the talk from the last three decades. It has great benefits for society, but the major concern of image fusion algorithms is calculation of weight map which further incorporates pixel level information from different modality input images and produces the final fused image. In conventional fusion methods, this task is based on handcrafted features which are quite vulnerable and easily gets affected by noise and mis-registration. Hence, it cannot establish its candidature as a robust method to extract and fuse activity-level information.

In contrast to this, several deep learning (DL) techniques exist that tend to learn constructive representations and characteristics directly and automatically from the raw data without the use of manually designed traits. Moreover, in today's scenario the data from healthcare is increasing drastically and for analysis and prediction of the same DL-based methods can prove quite useful. DL methodology ascended to outstanding rank, when neural networks started doing better than other techniques on various image analysis standards of high priority in the research field of computer vision.

In medical imaging particularly, significance of DL has been commenced by introduction of convolutional neural networks (CNNs) (LeCun et al., 1998), a useful approach to learn important characteristics of images and other structured information. DL-based image fusion has its applications in the areas of digital photography, multimodal image fusion, and remote sensing imagery as depicted in Fig. 2.1.

In addition to the importance and trend of DL techniques in the area of image fusion, several other factors are there which further promote the deployment of DL for diverse image fusion applications. Thus the conventional system of multimodal medical image fusion has been summarized in Section 2.2 to give the reader an overview on how spatial and transfer domain methods work in order to produce the final fused image and which components of the system need modification for greater

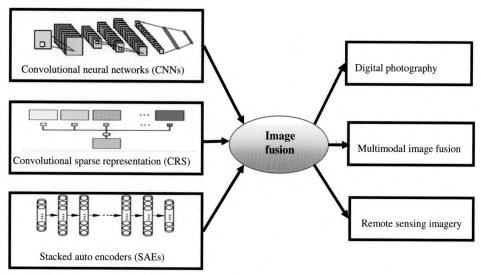

Figure 2.1 A deep learning (DL) based image fusion (schematic diagram).

efficacy. In Section 2.3, the challenges of traditional methods and benefits of DL-based system are demonstrated. Furthermore, Section 2.4 presents the commonly used DL models to achieve multimodal image fusion. Section 2.5 elaborates a detailed review of DL-based multimodal medical image fusion. At last, Section 2.6 presents the final concluding comments.

2.2   Conventional multimodal medical image fusion system

Multimodal medical image fusion is the procedure of amalgamating manifold pictures from multiple or single imaging modalities, for example, PET, SPECT, CT, MRI, etc. into a distinct image with more detailed anatomical and spectral information. The main focus of fusion practice is to improve the quality of an image while preserving the most desirable and relevant characteristics of each. Therefore the final fused image, that is, output of fusion procedure, has a more accurate depiction of pictorial information than individual input images, which in turn increase the medical images' clinical applicability for diagnosis.

In order to deal with medical issues that got reflected by the body's organs and cell's images captured with the help of advance medical imaging technologies, there is one umbrella term known as medical image fusion that consists of various images and general information fusion methodologies. The areas of chronological documentation, medicinal diagnostics, and examination have been greatly benefitted by emerging significance and application of cutting edge medical imaging technologies. Due to advancement in computing and high end images provided by advanced imaging methodologies, it is possible to assess the medical images quantitatively. This in turn not only improves the efficiency of doctors to diagnose and provide accurate decisions, but also reduces the decision making time.

2.2.1   Imaging modalities

The art, procedure, and process of generating visual demonstrations of the internal body organs and cells for medical diagnostic and treatment is known as medical imaging. Medical images provide anatomical/structural and functional information of the body's organs and cells that further ease the process of clinical treatment (Ammari, 2008). There are various modalities that are used in the medical field to gain insight of organ, but each modality has its own advantages and limitations. Each

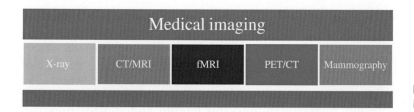

Figure 2.2 Various medical imaging modalities.

modality corresponds to specific information presented. Fig. 2.2 shows various imaging modalities and some of these are described below:

2.2.2 Components of medical image fusion system

The system of multimodal image fusion is comprised of three main components: decomposition and reconstruction methods, fusion rule to fuse different input images, and the most important one is assessment methods to verify and validate the image quality as described by James and Dasarathy (2014, pp. 4−19).

2.2.2.1 Image decomposition and reconstruction methods

The very first level in image fusion process is decomposition of input image and the output image of the whole process has to be obtained by applying reconstruction method. A number of image decomposition and reconstruction methods have been projected and categorized in literature as follows:

1. Color space methods: In this space the most used medical image fusion methods are luminance/chrominance (YUV), intensity hue saturation (IHS), and lightness/color (lab). So source images (Red-Green-Blue, RGB) are converted into one of these above stated color spaces by RGB-IHS conversion, RGB-YUV conversion, and RGB-lab conversion schemes. Operations are done on the processed image and the final output image is recreated with inverse transform corresponding to decomposition scheme.
2. Pyramid methods: Pyramid representation is applied to decompose the source input image into multiscale representation which provides a series of residual images and one approximate image. Pyramid methods can use Laplacian pyramid, ratio pyramid, and gradient pyramid for decomposition purpose. This scheme provides direct access to the enhanced image features of various sizes. Final fused image is recovered with inverse of pyramid transform used for decomposition.

3. Wavelet methods: Wavelet transformation-based medical image fusion methods are considered as multiscale geometric analysis implements. Initially, the low and high-frequency components need to be separated because of the nature of the information provided by them and to achieve this the source input image is decomposed. Then, the role of image fusion rules comes into the picture and diverse rules are selected to fuse different frequency components. At last, the inverse wavelet transform reconstructs the final fused image. Various extension of wavelets are present to fuse the input images; for example, discrete wavelet transform (DWT) is applied to preserve and localize the information related to different frequency components in spatial frequency domain and time domain, but DWT lacks the property of shift-invariance. To overcome its limitations, redundant discrete wavelet transform (RDWT) removes downsampling operation of DWT to fulfill shift invariance requirements. Furthermore, multiwavelet (MWT) succeeds to preserve greater details and texture information as its filters do not strongly segregate between low pass and high pass category. Lifting wavelet is the second generation of wavelets which has lesser computation. The other wavelet transforms are non-subsampled contourlet transform (NSCT) and contourlet transform (CT). These represent the images in a better way than wavelets because it has contour segments that understand the geometrical structure of images. Shearlet (ST) is another transform under the wavelet family which has a special place in the image fusion process because of the unlimited number of directions for shearing. It is best suited for sparse directional image representation.

4. Methods based on salient features: Fusion methods of this category are quite different from the other image fusion methods. These methods offer several key features and advantages as compared to others such as low computational complexity, shift-invariance, and retained saliency features. Guided filtering (GF) (Li et al., 2013, pp. 2864−2875)-based image fusion is an example of a salient feature-based method. In this method base and detail layers are obtained by Laplacian filters and then fusion rules are applied on these layers to get final fused image.

2.2.2.2 Image fusion rules

The algorithms that emphasize the attributes of interest and hold down the characteristics of irrelevance are termed as rules to fuse the significant information during the process of image fusion. These rules are the key concept in fusion process as selection of good fusion rules leads to better results of the fusion process. It is impossible to design one fusion rule for all the applications. Customarily, there are four components of an image fusion rule: (1) activity-level measurement, (2) coefficient grouping, (3) coefficient combination, and (4) consistency verification.

1. Activity-level measurement: This kind of measurement scheme quantifies the saliency of each and every coefficient at different levels. The levels to measure saliency are categorized into three groups based on the way they operate. Their names are: coefficient-based activity, region-based activity, and window-based activity as described in literature.

2. Coefficient grouping: This mechanism provides the information about association of pixels belonging to different images, but present at the same decomposition level. As after application of multiscale decomposition (MSD) each coefficient will have similar property coefficients present in various other levels of decomposition and frequency bands. So, there is also categorization of grouping schemes. These can be no-grouping, that is, coefficients are not associated with each other, single-scale grouping and multiscale grouping to efficiently serve the purpose of grouping mechanism.

3. Coefficient combination: Coefficient combination means how the individual image coefficients are combined to get coefficients of a merged image. The categories of this method comprises: (1) maximum rules (MR), (2) average rules (AR), and (3) weighted average rules (WAR). These rules are generally applied on a source image's coefficient to get final fused pixel via maximum, average, or WAR.

4. Consistency verification: This makes sure that every single pixel in a defined neighborhood is fused with the same fusion rule for a more accurate outcome. It exploits the property of the good fusion rule that it will fuse the coefficients of a neighborhood in a similar fashion.

There are various fusion rules based on fuzzy logics and statistics, for example, HMT-hidden Markov tree model and principal component analysis (PCA) which reveal the hidden saliency features. Another group of fusion rules is based on the human visual system (HVS).

2.2.2.3 *Image quality assessment*

The most critical component of multimodal medical image fusion process is the image quality assessment which assesses the fusion algorithm and validates the final fused image for clinical usage. The research in the field of quality assessment intends to design specific algorithms that assess the quality of the final fused image taking into account the various features that need to be present in the final image for greater clinical usability. Broadly there are two types of assessment rules: subjective evaluation and objective metrics. Due to the criticality and expertise required to analyze a medical image, subjective methodology always emerges as the most reliable method. However, this approach is impractical due to stringent tests and other organizational overheads. On the other hand, objective assessment metrics are specifically designed algorithms to assess only one kind of information without the human intervention. In addition to this, objective methods produce single numerical value corresponding to algorithm which gives a clear depiction of information and also makes it easy for conducting the comparative studies.

2.2.3   Need of multimodal image fusion in medical sector

There are many such cases where medical images contribute for the prognosis, diagnosis, and treatment of several diseases. Image guided surgery and radiotherapy is one good example in this context. Several medical imaging technologies are present that give different kinds of information about the body's organs and cells. However, the selection of specific imaging modality for targeted study requires medical knowledge about the organ of interest. Furthermore, each imaging technology has its limitations and provides only certain details about the organ. They do not provide complete behavioral, anatomical, and functional information, and such limited information might lead to inaccurate clinical analysis.

So, the more feasible approach is to combine information from multiple modalities for more accurate clinical assessment. However, there is a set back because, to do so it needs an expert who can dig the useful yet complementary information from different individual modalities and later on can use or suggest this information for treatment purpose. Solutions to this problem are:
- Invent new imaging modalities that provide more information like both functional and anatomical in one single modality.
- Develop new image fusion methods that can merge the complementary information extracted from both the input images in one single fused image.

Obviously the latter approach is better to deal with the problem as it is cheaper as compared to the other one which needs new hardware for generating new imaging modality.

2.2.3.1 *Objectives of medical image fusion using multiple modalities*

- The fusion process of multimodal medical images is used to retrieve complementary information from individual modalities.
- It improves image quality while preserving specific features.
- Fusion of multimodal images produces a fused image, which is free from random and redundant information which is otherwise present in the input visual representations.
- Fusion process cuts the storage space, instead of storing two individual images only one fused image will be stored.
- As the fusion process of multimodality medical offers information of complementary nature from both the sources, it increases the efficacy of medical personnel to reach at equitable decision with greater accuracy.
- It divulges information in the final fused image that is otherwise imperceptible for HVS.
- Information from individual modalities leads to accurate localization of abnormalities.

2.3 Inspiration to use deep learning for image fusion

2.3.1 Complexities associated with conventional approaches of image fusion

The key challenging factors in the context of image fusion are the datasets of medical images, imaging techniques, and human beings. These are discussed below:

1. The most challenging and nontrivial task is the correct arrangement of the rightly selected imaging modalities that would depict the maximum information regarding the subject. Next in this list is extraction and processing of desirable features that contribute to the final fused image. Last but not the least is selection of fusion rules that divulge the individual information to produce features for the output image.
2. The accessibility of a dataset itself poses a restriction for researchers. The dilemma occurs because a patient's medical data is usually kept private due to its sensitive nature, hence

accessibility is restricted. Consequently, such hindrance hampers the enhancement, progress, and the evaluation of the projected mechanism with the other researcher's mechanism.

3. Apart from dataset and modalities the methods used for image fusion impose another sort of challenges due to its limitations. The general forms of restrictions are quality of final fused image and computation effort, which are generally deciding factors on whether to use the method to solve real time problems or not.

4. The reason for hindrance in the development of fusion techniques is behavioral and structural complexity of certain body organs such as brain and heart. Apart from this, obtaining a good quality image of human body organs is restricted by unavoidable movements of the subject under study.

5. The demanding task is still the accurate permutation of salient feature extraction, processing, and appropriate fusion rules to get the desired quality output image.

6. Many complex decomposition methods and activity level measurement or weight assignment policies have been proposed, but the core issue is related to the design of a universal method that could take into account all the crucial aspects related to calculation of accurate activity level and fusion rule to amalgamate the key features from corresponding input images.

7. Furthermore, both the tasks of activity level calculation and fusion rules are defined and designed separately and manually without establishing a relationship between them. This further limits the performance of fusion algorithms.

8. The image transform domains present a great challenge in image fusion, as most of the successful approaches depend on image decomposition methods for desirable results. However, the decomposition method like pyramid-based decomposition, wavelet-based methods, sparse representation (SR), and multiscale geometric decomposition still suffer from several artifacts (Liu et al., 2015, 2016; Zhang et al., 2018).

9. One of the major challenges is the lack of broadly accepted objective quality assessment metrics. This part of the fusion process has received much less consideration as compared to research on transform methods in spite of its critical importance.

2.3.2 Advantages of deep learning in image fusion

As a primary provider to enhance the diagnosis, the approaches which have positively affected the research area of computer vision come under the techniques of machine learning. Image processing has a key role in several research fields such fusion of multifocus images, image registration, segmentation, and medical image fusion as a part of computer aided diagnostics to assist clinical practitioners. Other various applications include remote sensing images, face recognition, and content-based image retrieval research areas. DL, which is a subset of machine learning, is a more robust approach and best suited for these research regions. Among its several models, CNN has presented its usage in medical image fusion. In this subsection, it has been illustrated that image fusion can also be benefitted from DL strategies.

Firstly, the major feature of DL methods is the ability to build hierarchical demonstrations by extracting high-level traits from characteristics that are of low-level nature as demonstrated by Guo et al. (2016, pp. 27−48). The model with the greatest benefit for an area of image fusion research, that is, would be CNN due to its power and profound structural design. The architecture permits digging out of the salient features at multiple levels of abstraction with great effectiveness for the inputs which consist of grid like topologies (images and videos fall under this category because of their structure as 2-D/3-D matrix).

In addition to this, conventional methods require experts to develop certain features that need to be extracted by models. However, the CNN has the ability to learn useful representations of images and assign weights accordingly, which excludes the usage of handcrafted features and bring uniformity in using CNN because the model needs to be trained with labeled and annotated data once without explicitly mentioning the features to be learned. The tasks of image transformation, measurement of activity level, and fusion rules are implemented as one implicit process that further reduces the complexities arisen due to interdependencies in prior arrangement.

Furthermore, the design of image transforms and fusion strategies impose a great deal of challenge to obtain state-of-the-art results. Li et al. (2002, pp. 985−997) presented that CNN models have a greater ability to simplify the issues related to the procedure of image fusion which can be viewed as classification problem. Furthermore, usage of CNNs for fusing the multifocus images is a classic example of fusion as classification problem as claimed by Liu et al. (2017a, pp. 191−207), which not only outperforms the existing methods but also results in better computation.

Interestingly, some CNN designs used for other image processing applications can be used as feature extraction and representation method for image fusion task. To exemplify, the model described in the paper (Dong et al., 2016, pp. 295–307) for super resolution has been extended to use for image fusion as demonstrated by Yang et al. (2017, pp. 1–15).

To delve deeper, CNN models have marked their superiority also in the domain of quality assessment as presented in literature (Zagoruyko and Komodakis, 2015, pp. 4353–4361). It has been evident that most of the objective quality assessment metrics have their foundation on local similarity measuring and the CNN model given in Zagoruyko and Komodakis (2015, pp. 4353–4361) which was proposed to measure local similarity between two input image patches, and quite astonishingly investigational results proved the supremacy of CNNs for the given task. Hence, CNNs can be considered as a candidate to establish new quality assessment metrics.

2.4 Frequently employed deep learning models in the field of medical image fusion

There are several models of DL that are generally applied to fuse the various medical modality images. As already shown in Fig. 2.1, there are three broad categories of models named: (1) convolutional neural networks (CNNs), (2) convolutional sparse representation (CSR), and (3) stacked auto encoders (SAEs).

2.4.1 Convolutional neural networks

In most of the DL-based methods input is generally in vector form, but in the case of medical images structural information among neighboring pixels is important to further establish the relationships where vectorization can destroy the relationship information. So, CNNs are designed to accept 2-D or 3-D image data to be fused. CNNs exhibit multilayer architecture that comprise of several convolutional layers with pooling layer in-between and the final outcome is delivered by fully connected layers generally referred to as the last layer of architectural design. The basic schematic diagram as shown in Fig. 2.3 clearly depicts the usage of CNNs for multimodality image fusion.

1. Convolutional layer:

    The central focus of the CNN's foremost layer, that is, convolutional is to identify the local attributes at different positions. Generally, the feature detection is done at each

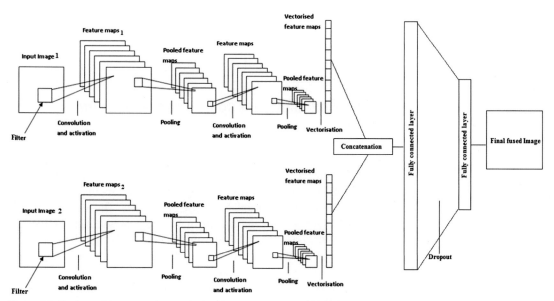

Figure 2.3 Basic architecture of convolutional neural networks (CNNs) for multimodal image fusion.

layer by convolving a filter, frequently of size 3×3, with activation values from previous layer to present the *feature map.*

2. Activation layer:

    The outcome of convolutional layers, that is, feature map is used to fed through nonlinear activation function to further improve the expressiveness of the network. Generally used activation functions are Relook, exponential linear units, sigmoid, and tanh.

3. Pooling:

    Pooling layers follow the convolutional layers and mainly contribute to achieve downsampling of feature maps produced by preceding convolution layer. A small entity of the feature map in the convolutional layer is used to produce corresponding feature map unit in the pooling layer by selecting a representative on the basis of max-pooling or average-pooling.

4. Dropout:

    Dropout is an averaging technique where stochastic sampling of neural networks is used. This results in performance boost of respective network.

5. Fully connected layer:

    There is a group of layers in CNN that are the very last layers in the architectural design of network and often called classification layers. As the name signifies the neurons of the preceding layer are fully connected to these layers. These layers are responsible for taking higher-order features and producing scores and probabilities of different classes.

2.4.2 Convolutional sparse representation

CSR is used in the name of convolutional sparse coding (CSC) when applied in the field of image representation. Zeiler et al. (2010, pp. 2528–2535) has developed a unique concept of deconvolutional networks which acts as base for CSC. Deconvolutional networks are trained in layer-wise fashion in an unsupervised manner. In addition to this, the output of the previous layer is used as an input for the subsequent layer and the main motive of passing information through layers is to obtain SR as output from each layer. Moreover, as the name specifies the deconvolutional network is opposite of the convolutional network which maps features to pixels while processing images, and this quality makes it possible to get images as output. CSR is better than conventional SR; traditional method sparse decomposition is performed with sliding window over the image that results in multivalued output. In contrast to this, CSR captures the whole image as input to process and produce optimal SR.

2.4.3 Stacked auto encoders

SAEs are well established and accepted class of DL networks in the field of visual classification and image restoration. The basic idea underline the working of SAEs is inclusion of two training phases, one is called unsupervised pretraining and another is supervised fine tuning. In its simplest form auto encoder (AE) is a double layer network of neurons that tends to learn the representation of input by reducing the reform error. As it is very evident that representation power of two-layer network is limited and in order to sort this issue along with increasing the representational power to a greater extent, a number of AEs are grouped together called SAEs.

2.5 Review of deep learning-based image fusion techniques

A new approach was presented by Liu et al. (2017a, pp. 191–207), which is implementing CNNs for an image fusion

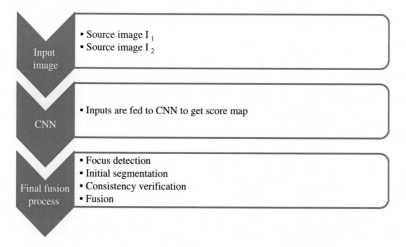

Figure 2.4 Schematic flow of proposed fusion algorithm taking into account the multifocus images.

task for the very first time that eventually out-perform the conventional methods to produce better results measured on the basis of standard objective quality assessment metrics and visual quality. The critical issues of image fusion process are measuring activity levels and deciding to choose right fusion rules for effective results. In order to implement the measurement of activity levels, several filters have been designed for all fusion methods belonging to transform domain or spatial domain to extract contained high-frequency information. Above stated crucial issues are difficult to avoid for obtaining an acceptable level of fusion. To deal with this dilemma a new technique is presented in this paper based on the concept of DL. This new technique has a different concept, which advocates the use of direct mapping between the output of the convolutional layer, that is, feature map and corresponding input image. The proposed method is shown in Fig. 2.4 and the chief component of the scheme is the use of CNN to calculate the focus property of input images. To delve deeper, the whole fusion process is basically divided into four parts: first and foremost is detecting focus information and the next step is executing segmentation at the initial level. After successfully getting the segmented image, consistency verification procedure has to be carried out and the last phase is fusion.

As shown in Fig. 2.5, the two input images have been fed to CNN to get the score map of input images which has all the desired information for instance in the context of multifocus visual representations, the main concern is that the focus property and map represent the same. The CNN network has several models (Zagoruyko and Komodakis, 2015, pp. 4353−4361) like:

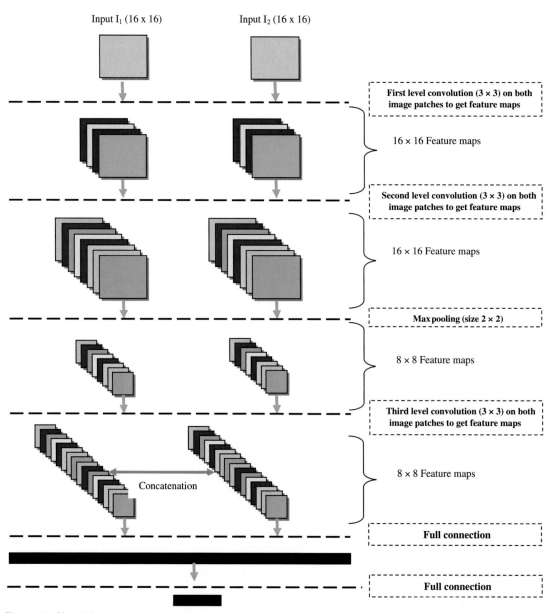

Figure 2.5 Pictorial representation of the convolutional neural network (CNN) model used in the projected technique [18]. Spatial size of the patch shows the training process of CNN only; in test/fusion process system is capable of processing the images of arbitrary size.

Siamese, pseudo-Siamese and two-channel; however, in this paper authors have chosen to use the basic version known as Siamese neural network because of two reasons. Firstly,

Siamese network presents a more natural approach to showcase the fusion process. The moreover, equal weights corresponding to each branch indicate the equal contribution of both the source images for the final value of activity level measurement and feature extraction. Furthermore, the Siamese network model is easy to train as compared to other CNN models. The next step is selecting the input patch size to train the system, the optimal size selected in this particular paper is 16×16. This is based on the number of max pool layers, as too large or too small patch sizes result in block artifacts with no guarantee of neural network model's accuracy.

Training of CNN model has been done with DL framework known as Caffe (Jia et al., 2014, pp. 675−678) and the corresponding weights of each convolution layer has also been initialized by Xavier algorithm (Glorot and Bengio, 2010). The training examples are created from ILSVRC 2012 validation image set, which consists of 50k high-quality images derived from a dataset named ImageNet (Stanford Vision Lab, Stanford University, Princeton University 2016). Now after successful training of CNN, the system has been deployed to provide fused images. Here the main features have been given by neural network in the form of the focus map. Furthermore, to improve the effectiveness the focus map needs to be processed further and this processing task has been accomplished by using a threshold value of 0.5. The final outcome is the binary map with more clear and precise representation. The final binary segmented map contains some miss-classified information although the binary segmented map provides and preserves maximum information. Guided filter has effective edge preserving properties and converts the structural knowledge of a guidance image into the filtering outcome of the source image. The sequence of segmentation and consistency verification processes convert the focus map into decision map and further application of WAR produces the ultimate fused image. The results have been compared with other state of art multifocus image fusion techniques like: GF, multiscale weighted gradient, dense scale-invariant feature transform (DSIFT), NSCT, sparse representation (SR), and NSCT-SR on the basis of selected objective quality assessment metrics: (1) normalized mutual information, (2) human perception-based metric, (3) gradient-based metric, and (4) structural similarity. The algorithm demonstrated in this paper provides better results. The main attraction of this algorithm is that its extension can be taken into account for performing fusion on other types of images for example-multimodal and multiexposure.

Liu et al. (2017b, pp. 1−7) extends the work presented in Liu et al. (2017a, pp. 191−207) for the purpose of fusing multimodality medical images, but with some modifications that are suitable for multimodality source images. The basic architecture of CNN used for training and testing phase has been kept same. However, fusion scheme proposed in this literature exhibits some differences in fusion algorithm which is carried out after generating the feature map from the CNN. The multipurpose fusion scheme explained by Liu et al. (2017a, pp. 191−207) operates in spatial domain which is usually unsuitable for medical imaging fusion because of artifacts in the final fused image.

Hence the alternations made to the method discussed (Liu et al., 2017a, pp. 191−207) are: (1) use of transform domain methods and (2) slighter model that not only lessens the memory utilizations, but also enhances the computational efficiency. The schematic representation of the proposed technique to ensure the fusion of medical images belonging to multiple modalities is depicted in Fig. 2.6. During the execution this

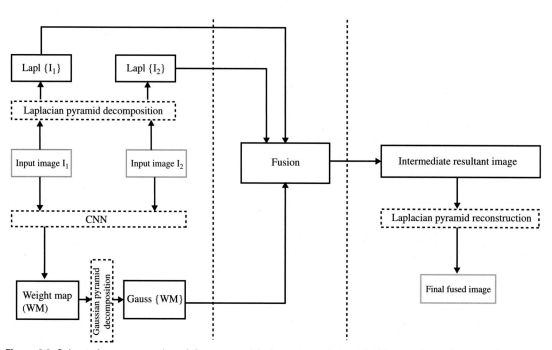

Figure 2.6 Schematic representation of the proposed fusion scheme for medical images belonging to multiple modalities [7].

scheme two source images, which are definitely of different modalities, are fed to CNN network to generate the weight map. Furthermore, the same input images are decomposed by Laplacian pyramid decomposition which is MSD method and much more suitable for human visual perception. Made clear from Fig. 2.6, the Gaussian pyramid has been deployed to decompose the outcome of CNN which is the weight map. The next step after decomposition of images and weight map is to fuse the coefficients based on some fusion strategy. The authors have described a local energy-based coefficient fusion method to obtain the final outcome image after fusion. The Laplacian pyramid reconstruction has been applied to produce the final fused image with all the complementary information from two source images belonging to different medical modalities. The five pairs of CT, MR, and SPECT images used in this study have been obtained from the whole brain atlas database (Johnson and Becker) created by Harvard medical school, each image exhibiting 256×256 pixel size. The related clinical case is metastatic bronchogenic carcinoma of a 42-year old woman with an extended record of tobacco utilization. The YUV color space has been deployed while fusing the colored image with grayscale image. While evaluating the planned fusion algorithm with other state of the art fusion techniques, the prior one shows better results on the basis of standard objective quality assessment metrics used in this literature: information entropy, mutual information, Xydeas–Petrovic's gradient-based metric, Piella–Heijmas's similarity based metric, and visual information fidelity fusion metric.

Hermessi et al. (2018, pp. 2029–2045) demonstrated a new method for the fusion of medical images in ST domain based on CNN with similarity learning. This method takes into account the advantages of ST transform which provides more directional features and is shift invariant. Furthermore, there is a lack of annotated data in the medical image domain which limits the benefits of CNN. So to overcome this limitation the concept of transfer learning has been deployed to transfer features from the spatial domain to frequency domain. The basic CNN network explained in Liu et al. (2017, pp. 985–997) has been used as a pretrained model that needs to be fine-tuned for better results. To delve deeper, the fusion process illustrated in this literature is performed at decision level with multiscale geometric analysis extracting the salient features and deep CNN producing feature maps. The input images has been taken from the whole brain atlas dataset (Johnson and Becker, 1999) and a pair of preregistered CT and MR images are considered as source images. The input images are decomposed into higher frequency and lower frequency sub-bands with non-subsampled ST transform. The high-frequency sub-bands of both the source input scans is fed to trained CNN and new feature maps have been obtained because of fine-tuned parameters. The output from CNN is 256 feature maps corresponding to each input image and these in turn are fused via weighted normalized cross-correlation. Consecutively, low-pass coefficients have been fused on the basis of local energy value because, the low-frequency sub-bands possess the energy of the image. At last, the inverse non-subsampled ST transform is performed to obtain the resultant fused image. Performance of the intended technique is evaluated on the basis of various quality assessment metrics and in this paper mutual information, structural similarity, entropy, and standard deviation have been used for this purpose.

2.6 Conclusion

The popularity of DL techniques in multimodal medical image fusion domain has been advancing at a quick pace in recent years. The main contribution of this chapter can be summarized as follows:

1. The complications that are associated with conventional image fusion research domain are explored and the advantages of DL methods in the field of image fusion have been elaborated in Section 2.3.
2. A detailed study of various DL-based image fusion techniques has been presented in the last section of this chapter, which covers base concept, central and key steps, several applications and major traits of DL based recently presented image fusion techniques including SAE, CNN, and CSR.

To conclude, the recent growth accomplished in DL-based image fusion demonstrates a promising inclination in the area of image fusion with an enormous potential for future improvement. It is greatly predicted that further associated investigators would continue in the future to encourage the development of image fusion.

References

Ammari, H., 2008. An Introduction to Mathematics of Emerging Biomedical Imaging. Springer, Berlin.
Calhoun, V.D., Adali, T., 2009. Feature-based fusion of medical imaging data. IEEE Trans. Inf. Technol. Biomed. 13 (5), 711—720.

Dasarathy, B.V., 2012. Information fusion in the realm of medical applications—a bibliographic glimpse at its growing appeal. Inf. Fusion 13 (1), 1–9.

Dong, C., Loy, C., He, K., Tang, X., 2016. Image super-resolution using deep convolutional networks. IEEE Trans. Pattern Anal. Mach. Intell. 38 (2), 295–307.

Glorot, X., Bengio, Y., 2010. Understanding the difficulty of training deep feed forward neural networks. J. Mach. Learn. Res. 9, 249–256.

Guo, Y., Liu, Y., Oerlemans, A., Lao, S., Wu, S., Lew, M.S., 2016. Deep learning for visual understanding: a review. Neurocomputing 187, 27–48.

Hermessi, H., Mourali, O., Zagrouba, E., 2018. Convolutional neural network-based multimodal image fusion via similarity learning in the shearlet domain. Neural Comput. Appl. 30, 2029–2045.

ImageNet. Retrieved from: <http://www.image-net.org/>, 2016.

James, A.P., Dasarathy, B.V., 2014. Medical image fusion: a survey of the state of the art. Inf. Fusion 19, 4–19.

Jia, Y., Shelhamer, E., Donahue, J., Karayev, S., Long, J., Girshick, R., et al., 2014. Caffe: convolutional architecture for fast feature embedding. In: Proceedings of ACM International Conference on Multimedia, pp. 675–678.

Johnson, K.A., Becker, J.A., 1999. The Whole Brain Atlas. Retrieved from: <http://www.med.harvard.edu/AANLIB/>.

LeCun, Y., Bottou, L., Bengio, Y., Haffner, P., 1998. Gradient-based learning applied to document recognition. Proc. IEEE 86 (11), 2278–2324.

Li, S., Kwok, J., Wang, Y., 2002. Multifocus image fusion using artificial neural networks. Pattern Recognit. Lett. 23 (8), 985–997.

Li, S., Kang, X., Hu, J., 2013. Image fusion with guided filtering. IEEE Trans. Image Process. 22 (7), 2864–2875.

Liu, Y., Liu, S., Wang, Z., 2015. A general framework for image fusion based on multi-scale transform and sparse representation. Inf. Fusion 24 (1), 147–164.

Liu, Y., Chen, X., Ward, R., Wang, Z., 2016. Image fusion with convolutional sparse representation. IEEE Signal Process. Lett. 23 (12), 1882–1886.

Liu, Y., Chen, X., Peng, H., Wang, Z., 2017a. Multi-focus image fusion with a deep convolutional neural network. Inf. Fusion 36, 191–207.

Liu, Y., Chen, X., Cheng, J., Peng, H., 2017b. A medical image fusion method based on convolutional neural networks. In: Proceedings of 20th International Conference Information Fusion, pp. 1–7.

Maes, F., Vandermeulen, D., Suetens, P., 2003. Medical image registration using mutual information. Proc. IEEE 1699–1721.

Piella, G., 2003. A general framework for multiresolution image fusion: from pixels to regions. Inf. Fusion 4 (4), 259–280.

Yang, B., Li, S., 2012. Pixel-level image fusion with simultaneous orthogonal matching pursuit. Inf. Fusion 13 (1), 10–19.

Yang, B., Zhong, J., Li, Y., Chen, Z., 2017. Multi-focus image fusion and super-resolution with convolutional neural network. Int. J. Wavelets Multiresolut. Inf. Process. 15 (4), 1–15.

Yunfeng, Z., Yixin, Y., Dongmei, F., 2008. Decision-level fusion of infrared and visible images for face recognition. In: Chinese Control and Decision Conference (CCDC), pp. 2411–2414.

Zacharaki, E., Matsopoulos, G., Nikita, K., Stamatakos, G., 2003. An application of multimodal image registration and fusion in a 3D tumor simulation model. In: Proceedings of 25th Annual International Conference of IEEE Engineering in Medicine and Biology Society. IEEE, pp. 686–689.

Zagoruyko, S., Komodakis, N., 2015. Learning to compare image patches via convolutional neural networks. In: Proceedings of IEEE Conference on Computer Vision and Pattern Recognition, pp. 4353–4361.

Zeiler, M., Krishnan, D., Taylor, G., Fergus, R., 2010. Deconvolutional networks. In: Proceedings of IEEE Conference on Computer Vision and Pattern Recognition (CVPR), pp. 2528–2535.

Zhang, Q., Liu, Y., Blum, R., Han, J., Tao, D., 2018. Sparse representation based multi-sensor image fusion for multi-focus and multi-modality images: a review. Inf. Fusion 40, 57–75.

3

Medical image fusion framework for neuro brain analysis

Gurpreet Kaur[1], Sukhwinder Singh[1] and Renu Vig[2]
[1]*Department of Computer Science and Engineering, University Institute of Engineering and Technology, Panjab University, Chandigarh, India*
[2]*Department of Electronic Engineering and Communication, University Institute of Engineering and Technology, Panjab University, Chandigarh, India*

3.1 Introduction

Digital image processing has been encompassed into various areas of synthesis ranging from human activities to technological expertise. We deliberate on the medical domain, for better interpretation of clinical data acquired from topographical modalities. The medical health care is primarily dominated by the involvement of imaging scans for disease diagnosis and monitoring. The underlying bone, organ, or the tissue can well be captured using a radiological modality for clinical evaluations and further classification and processing. This leads to masses of imaging data being generated in the form of repeat scans to evaluate the disease progress or to capture the affected region or lesion by more than one modality. Considerable advancement in technology, higher attainable resolutions, and faster scanning times are a few attributes toward this added

Advances in Computational Techniques for Biomedical Image Analysis. DOI: https://doi.org/10.1016/B978-0-12-820024-7.00003-7

dependency. The medical image fusion mechanism can be ably implemented to constrict managing volumes of medical data being generated. Moreover, without the presence of an automated mechanism, the radiologist needs to fuse the image slices from one or more modalities in mind. This is not always practically viable. The acquired clinical images can be combined together into a single fused image to reinforce diagnosis. Medical image fusion unites patient images of the organ or the lesion into a single fused image (Wang et al., 2005)

The patient imagery from complimentary modalities are combined for visual irrefutable information. Medical images are categorized into anatomical and functional image modalities (Hasegawa and Zaidi, 2006; Jingzhou et al., 2009). The anatomical modality magnetic resonance imaging (MRI) and functional nuclear medicine modality as single photon emission computed tomography (SPECT), positron emission tomography offer only partial investigative information (Angenent et al., 2006). MRI creates section slices to describe high decree structural data while the core essential metabolic changes are sketched and examined using SPECT. Multimodal medical fusion collaborates attributes of anatomical structures, physical function, and metabolic content under study outlining, one fused outcome from both the modality sources for precise diagnosis (James and Dasarathy, 2014). But in neuro diagnosis the spatial information is lost, the analysis is limited by geometric misalignments, and the resultant fused image is dim, with loss of original clinical information due to high disparity in both the modalities.

The basic fusion model can be defined by simple averaging technique to amalgamate clinical data. As overlie happens while merging the image data the fused image in averaging is smoothened and not very clear. The statistical techniques as principal component analysis (PCA) and independent component analysis well disclose the saliency of structures and signify the input vector as a sum of orthonormal basis function (Hao-quan and Hao, 2009; Chen, 2017). The transform domain multiscale techniques reveal resemblance to the human visual system, to well seize the spatial frequencies from images (Solanki and Patel, 2011). These can be mostly categorized into pyramids, basic wavelets, and advanced wavelet techniques. Pyramid models are not adopted in the proposal as these grossly suffer from artifacts, poor results, and not holding the diagnostic information well in the fused image (Shutao, 2017). The wavelets have localized properties and preserve structures from anatomical images and color information from functional inputs (Hill and Hawkes, 1994; Liu, 2010; Hasegawa et al., 2002; Yang et al., 2010; Teng et al., 2010;

Calhoun, 2009). There are limitations associated with each wavelet base as pseudo Gibbs effects, shift invariance, and limited detail information. The techniques as discrete wavelet transform (DWT), stationary wavelet transform (SWT) (Jiang et al., 2017), discrete fractional wavelet transform (DFRWT) (Mendlovic et al., 1997; Shi et al., 2012; Xu et al., 2016) are extended to curvelet transforms (Ali et al., 2008), shearlets (STs) transforms, and non-subsampled contourlet transforms (Wang et al., 2013b) which form the advance wavelets. These produce superior results but at a higher associated cost and complexity. Also finer results are reported in literature for images from a multi focus domain. Medical image fusion has a poor outcome due to intricacy in the heterogeneous structure of medical data (Bhatnagar et al., 2015).

A two phase fusion method to encompass the strengths of existing techniques and to overcome the limitations in literature is proposed using fractional Fourier transform (FRFT) and seven benchmark techniques. The mechanism involves processing medical images using FRFT prefixed with averaging, PCA, DWT, SWT, curvelets, and DFRWT for clinical clarity and improvised diagnostic credit. The proposal is well evaluated subjectively to further confirm the findings with finer visual output by comparisons with original benchmark techniques. The metrics results coincide with superior outcomes, signifying more clarity in analysis and better preserving diagnostic information with superior quality from original images.

3.2 Fractional Fourier transform

Wavelet transform is extensively used in literature in medical image fusion. Wavelets are localized transforms and perform time-frequency analysis. It effectively represents time resolution but is insignificant where input energy is not dominant in the frequency domain (Shi et al., 2014). Therefore they are limited in their ability to deal with inputs not in the frequency domain and also endure setback due to shift invariance.

For an input function $f(x)$ the scaling function is given by $\varphi(x)$ and the narrowband function by $\psi(x)$, derived from the parent scaling function. Alternatively, the high and the low pass filter banks on the principles of multiresolution analysis formulate the approximation and the three directional detail components (Li, 2017). As per the correlation, the Fourier transform (FT) of the input function $f(x)$ is multiplied with mother wavelet, followed by inverse transform. FT forms Hilbert transform pair given as:

$$ej\,\omega\,n = \cos(\omega\,n) + j\,\sin(\omega\,n) \qquad (3.1)$$

where $\omega > 0$. It is based on complex-valued oscillating sinusoids. Wavelets are shifted by m amount and using n as scale parameter the $h(x)$ is multiplied with a modulation term to obtain the daughter wavelet $h_{n,m}(x)$ in the time-frequency plane. Hence, the basic orthogonal DWT function is represented by:

$$\varphi_{n,m}(x) = \begin{cases} 1 & \text{when } n = m \\ 0 & \text{otherwise} \end{cases} \qquad (3.2)$$

A transform with m variable as continuous and n as discrete is a hybrid wavelet. There are various hybrid wavelet transforms proposed in literature Anoh et al. (2014); Ezhilarasan et al, (2018) but they suffered from overlapping of the mother wavelet, the requirements of large spatial regions for wavelet replications and spatially coherent illumination of different wavelets (Teng et al., 2010). The conventional wavelet is generalized based on FT to obtain transforms in fractional domain as short time fractional Fourier transform (STFRFT) (Wang et al., 2013), Fractional wavelet packet transform (FRWPT) and FRFT (Wang et al., 2005).

STFRFT performed segment wise spectral analysis on a time localized window. This transform suffered from poor resolution and was governed by the selected window size. The FRWPT (Xu et al., 2016) is based on the parent impulse filter property of wavelets and aims to combine the merits of both wavelets and FRFT, but being computationally expensive and short of substantial analysis was not widely adopted.

The wavelet is limited in time-frequency plane, for which FRFT overcome and represent the input in fractional domain. FRFT is a localized global transform with important properties. It has unique properties to identify the input in fractional domain, due to the rotation of FT by an angle α. This exemplifies the energy density in time and frequency plane. The fractional frequencies are notified across the whole analysis duration (Yang et al., 2010). It is associated with chirp universal function and can handle the fractional shifts in chirp function. These are ably separated using FRFT, but FRFT cannot obtain the local signal properties. It provides spectral content with lacking time localization. The global kernel in FRFT requires additional representation in time domain. The FRFT is made to coalesce with wavelet transform to obtain the discretizing factor and the discretized mother wavelet with integers m and n are thus given by:

$$W_{r,s} = \frac{1}{\sqrt{2^m}} \Psi\left(\frac{t - n2^m}{2^m} t\right) \tag{3.3}$$

where the multiplicative of m and n are represented by r and s and are the scale and shift parameters. The FT with argument scaled by cosec θ is computed as:

$$\Psi^*(k\ cosec\ \alpha) = \mathrm{FT}(\Psi(t)) \tag{3.4}$$

The linear transformation from FRFT without cross term interference aids in seeking multiresolution analysis representation signal in transform domain. It exploits the wavelet transform for its advantage of time-frequency–based multiresolution analysis and combines it with the benefits acquired from FRFT to elaborate the input in fractional scale multiresolution analysis.

3.3 Material and method

In order to attain intrinsic geometrical structure from the original images we aim to exploit properties of fractional decomposition and multiresolution analysis. The technique is implemented at pixel level in the transform domain. The implementation has been done in MATLAB Version 2018a. The proposed fusion framework is depicted in Fig. 3.1.

In Phase 1, the original source image is selected from anatomical and function modality. A modality selection parameter "k" is incorporated, with the value of k varying from $\{1 \cdot n\}$. When k is prefixed to 1, the input images are acquired from the same modality of the same underlying organ.

This is termed as single modal fusion (S^M). With $k = 2$, bimodal (Bi^M) fusion is defined and for $k \geq 2$ fusion is multimodal. In the proposed method, k is prefixed to 2, with inputs from anatomical and functional modality.

3.3.1 Gray and color neuro images

The images for different neuro ailments are acquired from an online benchmark database. The gray anatomical MRI and color functional SPECT are procured for analysis. MRI image has a different base as T1-weighted, T2-weighted, and density weighted images. These are formed due to the inhomogeneities of the microscopic magnetic interaction

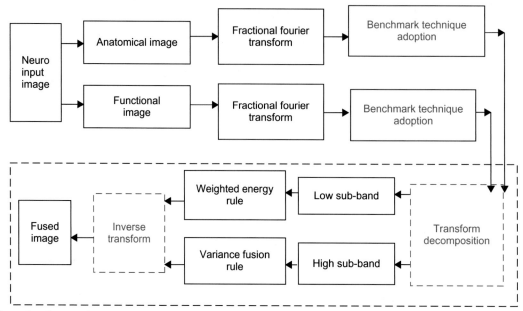

Figure 3.1 Proposed neuro image fusion framework.

amongst the particles. T1 is as good as tissue characterization while T2 is high on tissue discrimination and both differ in tissue contrast. The artifacts in MRI are generated due to the chemical shifts. The preliminary analysis reveals relevant dissimilarities amongst the acquired data. These dissimilarities are in terms of acquisition of clinical data, the variation in terms of structural details, physiological functions, patient movements, distortions, scalar and vector spare representations (Johnson Keith and Becker Alex, 1999). The SPECT image is represented in red-green-blue (RGB) color space. RGB is an additive color space and excites three visual cones. The spatial masks of gray scale image and RGB color image is given by Fig. 3.2.

The chromacity value in the RGB plane is represented by

$$R + G + B = 1 \qquad (3.5)$$

and the intersection relationship for each component red R^C, green G^C, and blue B^C is given by

$$R^C(x, y) = \frac{R}{R + G + B} \qquad (3.6)$$

$$G^C(x, y) = \frac{G}{R + G + B} \qquad (3.7)$$

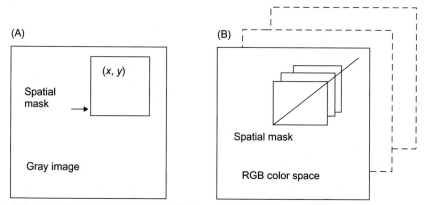

Figure 3.2 Spatial mask. (A) Gray scale image. (B) Red-green-blue (RGB) color image.

$$B^C(x,y) = \frac{B}{R+G+B} \qquad (3.8)$$

The gray scale MRI image is a scalar image and is represented by

$$f^{GI}(x,y) = \left[f_i(x,y)\right]^T \qquad (3.9)$$

The color SPECT is a vector image function. The tri-stimulus values obtained with explicit combination are represented in color image f^{CI} (x,y) by

$$f^{CI}(x,y) = \left[R^C(x,y), G^C(x,y), B^C(x,y)\right]^T \qquad (3.10)$$

With an increase in dimensionality, the computational processing complexity and memory requirement enhances. The spatial density of the image is determined by spatial frequency.

3.3.2 Neurological data

The input images are acquired from http://med.harvard. edu/AANLIB/home.html (Johnson Keith and Becker Alex, 1999), Med Harvard website of benchmark database images. Anatomical and functional modality images of the same organ under study are procured. The data is normalized for processing. Four cases from cerebrovascular disease, neoplastic disease, degenerative disease, and inflammatory neurological brain images are used in the study. The images used in the study are enclosed in Fig. 3.4. The medical aspects of all the four ailment categories are enclosed in Table 3.1.

Table 3.1 Neuro ailment case details.

Case	Case 1	Case 2	Case 3	Case 4
Study	Cerebrovascular disease	Neoplastic disease	Degenerative disease	Inflammatory disease
Ailment	Stroke aphasia	Hemianopia tumor	Alzheimer's	Lyme encephalopathy
Modality	MRI T2-SPECT	MRI T2-SPECT T1	MRI T2-SPECT	MRI T2-SPECT
Age	48 M	51 M	74 F	35 M
Medical remarks	Hypertension-transcortical motor aphasia with right central seventh nerve palsy	Hemianopia and right weakness, suspected for recurrent tumor	High arterial blood pressure and a history of hysterectomy	Reported erythema migrans with oligoarticular arthritis

3.3.3 Fractional process domain

In order to attain intrinsic geometrical structure from original images we aim to exploit properties of FRFTs and multiresolution analysis. A fractional Fourier technique is applied on the original source images to extract salient features. This method of feature extraction, its count and quality are directly correlated to the analysis and synthesis mechanism. As the transform uses fractional convolution derivative from different scales, it iteratively captures singularities at various scales. FT as a linear sum of partial spectra of a two-dimensional image, provides a spatial frequency spectrum of independent spatial variables a, b given as

$$F_I(a, b) = \mathrm{FT}(f(x, y)) \tag{3.11}$$

The medical images possess a finite number of discontinuities. This realizes the existence condition associated with FTs. FT is an invertible transform function given by

$$f(x, y) = \mathrm{FT}^{-1}(f(x, y)) \tag{3.12}$$

to yield into a perfect reconstruction image in the original domain. For higher readability of medical image inputs, linear point operators are applied, mathematically representing the transform as

$$g(x, y) = O^p(f(x, y)) \tag{3.13}$$

(A)

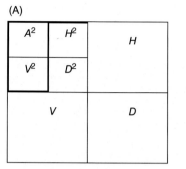

(B)

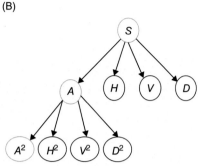

Figure 3.3 (A) Image quadrant decomposition representation. (B) Quad tree decomposition.

where $g(x, y)$ forms the image output and O^p as the point operator. As depicted the output is analogous to input representing spatial variability. Colors have a considerable effect on readability and interpretation of medical data, feature identification and analysis, substantially on diagnostic value.

In phase 2, the processed image obtained from previous phase is fed to the analysis section of the benchmark technique block to choose from averaging, PCA, DWT, SWT, curvelets, and DFRWT. One of these benchmark processes is adopted and implemented. The image quadrant decomposition representation on processing with discrete transform is represented in Fig. 3.3.

The level of decomposition is represented by J where $J \in [1, n]$. Here J is restricted at level 2, in order to control detail coefficient spreading (Shen et al., 2013). In order to combine the neuro multimodal images, the activity level measures in the fusion combination rules are adopted. Fusion rules exploit the distinctiveness of input images. The approximation band coefficients are fused by weighted energy based rule. This represents the measure of the homogeneous component and captivates the important coefficients. The detail band coefficients detain exclusive salient information of sharp features, edges, and contour structures. These are fused using the weighted variance rule. The inverse transform is applied to formulate the final fused image.

3.4   Result and discussion

The diagnostic segments from brain images visible in an anatomical modality may be missing in the functional modality. Single examination of each medical modality separately for neuro diagnosis is intricate for the medico due to the brain structure. In order to reinforce clinical analysis, the field of view is enhanced by consist overlap of multiple modalities. Each image is associated with a variation factor. A composite image is obtained with a new enhanced quality. The benchmark source anatomical and functional images are represented in Fig. 3.4 with the computed fused images.

The metrics used for evaluation include subjective and objective metrics. The objective metrics used are entropy (EN), mutual information (MI), and structure similarity index (SSIM).

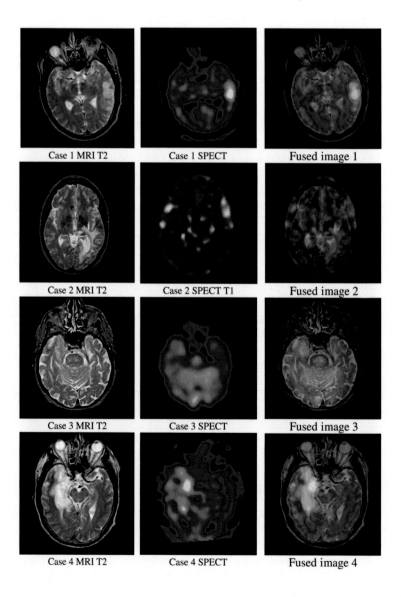

Figure 3.4 Neurological fusion images.

The averaging technique results in a dull output repressing imperative clinical output. In the preliminary result analysis the techniques are limited in their ability to represent diagnostic aspects in a clinically thriving manner. As in PCA leads to loss of function content. Curvelets disclose only an undersized segment with clarity and do not confine the functional content ably. DWT has superior representation but also has loss in diagnostic content with blurring and false coloring. SWT transform has poor illustration. The objective results are consolidated in the Table 3.2.

The original images are from different modalities and heterogeneous in content and depict less details. The functional input is further dim, low in resolution and dynamic range. The existing techniques result in a dull output repressing imperative clinical data in neuro imaging domain. Augmentation in result parameters in each adopted technique is visible through the result parameters. The proposed mechanism results refine the fusion mechanism to depict the clinical aspects. The metric of EN indicates good fusion quality and content. Structural similarity measures the loss of correlation in inputs. A high similarity is depicted with more spatial elements observable in the fused image.

Table 3.2 Neuro ailment case results.

Objective	Evaluation	Discrete wavelet transform (DWT)	Principal component analysis (PCA)	Stationary wavelet transform (SWT)	Curvelet	Fractional wavelet transform (FRWT)
Case 1	SSIM	1.2182	0.750	1.3089	1.1546	1.3104
	EN	5.7765	5.040	5.7613	5.2971	5.8240
	MI	2.2544	1.32 0	2.3084	2.7498	2.2955
Case 2	SSIM	1.3274	0.693	1.4024	1.2781	1.4035
	EN	4.2754	5.491	4.1517	4.4946	4.1533
	MI	0.3270	3.180	0.4448	0.1415	0.4437
Case 3	SSIM	0.7843	0.801	0.8100	0.6501	0.8611
	EN	5.7453	5.034	5.2721	5.3023	5.3240
	MI	1.7891	2.330	1.8637	1.644	1.8572
Case 4	SSIM	0.7722	0.630	0.8013	0.8571	0.7840
	EN	5.5441	6.101	5.5209	6.0753	6.1751
	MI	3.1334	2.570	2.6521	2.0261	2.5801

SSIM, Structure similarity index; EN, entropy; MI, mutual information.

A few artifacts are generated due to disturbances in teams of detection efficiency, attenuation, and slice thickness variations. Most artifacts are rectified by performing enhancement after image acquisition. Thus these are not taken into account in the proposal. The dual process extracts the salient features applying fractional Fourier technique and the multiscale benchmark technique.

3.5   Conclusion

There are a lot of technological advancements in the human image acquisition devices. Scans are procured of the same lesion or tissue using multiple modalities. As the clinical component visible in one image may be missing in the other, multiple images are put together to help reinforce the associated diagnostic value. There are various benchmark techniques devised in literature to perform multimodal image fusion but lag in vital aspects. We propose to process the benchmark images using FRFT to represent the input in fractional domain and exemplify the energy density in time and frequency plane to better aid fusion. Four multimodal imaging cases of neuro ailments are used to validate the proposal. The evaluation has a higher clinical performance and better preserved spatial content for further processing.

References

Ali, F.E., Saad, A.A., El-samie, F.E.A., 2008. Curvelet fusion of MR and CT images. Electromagnetics 3, 215–224.

Angenent, S., Pichon, E., Tannenbaum, A., 2006. Mathematical methods in medical image processing. Bull. Am. Math. Soc. 43 (3), 365–396.

Anoh, K.O.O., Abd-Alhameed, R.A., Jones, S.M.R., Ochonogor, O., Dana, Y.A.S., 2014. Novel fractional wavelet transform with closed form expression. Int. J. Adv. Comput. Sci. Appl. 5 (1), 182–187.

Bhatnagar, G., Wu, Q.M.J., Liu, Z., 2015. A new contrast based multimodal medical image fusion framework. Neurocomputing 157, 143–152.

Calhoun, V.D., 2009. Feature-based fusion of medical imaging data. IEEE Trans. Inf. Technol. Biomed. 13 (5), 711–720.

Chen, C.I., 2017. Fusion of PET and MR brain images based on IHS and log-Gabor transforms. IEEE Sens. J. 17 (21), 6995–7010.

Chetan, K., Narendra, S., Patel, M., 2011. Pixel based and wavelet based image fusion methods with their comparative study. In: National Conference on Recent Trends in Engineering and Technology, pp. 13–14.

Ezhilarasan, K., Jayadevappa, D., Pushpa Mala, S., 2018. Performance analysis of image compression based on fast fractional wavelet transform combined with spiht for medical images. IVTAVT J. Image Video Process. 8 (3), 1722–1729.

Hao-quan, W., Hao, X., 2009. Multimode medical image fusion algorithm based on principal component analysis. In: IEEE Symposium on Computer Network and Multimedia Technology, pp. 1−4.

Hasegawa, B.H., Iwata, K., Wong, K.H., 2002. Dual-modality imaging of function and physiology. Acad. Radiol. 9, 1305−1321.

Hasegawa, B.H., Zaidi, H., 2006. Dual-modality imaging: more than the sum of its components. Quantitative Analysis in Nuclear Medicine Imaging. Springer, Boston, pp. 35−81. Available from: http://doi.org/10.1007/0-387-25444-7-2.

Hill, D.L.G., Hawkes, D.J., 1994. Medical image registration using voxel similarity measures. In: AAAI Spring Symposium Series Applications of Computer Vision in Medical Image Processing, pp. 34−37.

James, A.P., Dasarathy, B.V., 2014. Medical image fusion: a survey of the state of the art. Inf. Fusion 19, 4−19.

Jiang, Q., Xin, J., Lee, S.-J., Yao, S., 2017. A novel multi-focus image fusion method based on stationary wavelet transform and local features of fuzzy sets. IEEE Access 5, 1.

Jingzhou, Z., Zhao, Z., Jionghua, T., Ting, L., Zhiping, M., 2009. Fusion algorithm of functional images and anatomical images based on wavelet transform. In: 2nd International Conference on BioMedical Engineering and Informatics). IEEE, pp. 1−5.

Johnson Keith, A., Becker Alex, A., 1999. The Whole Brain Atlas. Lippincott Williams and Wilkins, South Asia. Retrieved from: <http://www.med.harvard.edu/AANLIB/home.html>.

Li, S., 2017. Pixel level image fusion: a survey of the state of art. Inf. Fusion 33, 100−112.

Liu, C.-L., 2010. A Tutorial of the Wavelet Transform.

Mendlovic, D., Zalevsky, Z., Mas, D., García, J., Ferreira, C., 1997. Fractal wavelet transform. Appl. Opt. 36 (20), 4801−4806.

Shen, R., Cheng, I., Basu, A., 2013. Cross-scale coefficient selection for volumetric medical image fusion. IEEE Trans. Biomed. Eng. 60 (4), 1069−1079.

Shi, J., Zhang, N., Liu, X.P., 2012. A novel fractional wavelet transform and it's applications. Sci. China Inf. Sci. 55 (6), 1270−1279.

Shi, J., Liu, X.P., Zhang, N., 2014. Multiresolution analysis and orthogonal wavelets associated with fractional wavelet transform. Signal Image Video Process. 9, 211−220.

Shutao, L., 2017. Pixel Level Image Fusion: A Survey of the State of Art. Inform. Fusion 33, 100−112.

Teng, J., Wang, X., Zhang, J., Wang, S., 2010. Wavelet-based texture fusion of CT/MRI images. In: 3rd International Congress on Image and Signal Processing (CISP), vol. 6, pp. 2709−2713.

Wang, Z., Ziou, D., Armenakis, C., Li, D., Li, Q., 2005. A comparative analysis of image fusion methods. IEEE Trans. Remote Sens. 43 (6), 1391−1402.

Wang, P., Tian, H., Zheng, W., 2013. A novel image fusion method based on FRFT-NSCT. Math. Probl. Eng. 2013, 1−9.

Wang, J., Peng, J., Feng, X., He, G., Wu, J., Yan, K., 2013b. Image fusion with nonsubsampled contourlet transform and sparse representation. J. Electron. Imaging 22 (4), 043019.

Xu, X., Wang, Y., Chen, S., 2016. Medical image fusion using discrete fractional wavelet transform. Biomed. Signal. Process. Control 27, 103−111.

Yang, Y., Park, D.S., Huang, S., Rao, N., 2010. Medical image fusion via an effective wavelet-based approach. EURASIP J. Adv. Signal. Process. 2010, 579341.

4

Automated detection of intracranial hemorrhage in noncontrast head computed tomography

M.S. Vidya, Arun H. Shastry and Yogish Mallya
Philips Research, Bangalore, India

Chapter outline

Advances in Computational Techniques for Biomedical Image Analysis. DOI: https://doi.org/10.1016/B978-0-12-820024-7.00004-9

4.1 Introduction

An intracranial hemorrhage (ICH) is a type of bleeding that occurs inside the skull. ICH could be life-threatening and has a high mortality and low recovery rate. Approximately half of this mortality occurs within the first 24 hours (van Asch et al., 2010), highlighting the critical importance of early and effective treatment in the emergency department (ED). Noncontrast head CT scan is the most commonly used imaging modality for assessment of neurological emergency cases.

With improvements in technology, and the increasing availability of medical imaging equipment, the application and usage of digital imaging-based procedures in the field of medicine is increasing considerably. This has led to a growing problem where a trained radiologist may not be available for interpretation of these digital images, or has a large workload, raising the need for the creation and implementation of solutions for automation of screening, classification, and localization of diseases to aid the clinical experts.

This chapter examines the state-of-the-art methods for the task of automated assessment with a focus on ICH.

4.2 Intracranial hemorrhage

ICH refers to any bleeding that has occurred inside the skull cavity (cranium). Such bleeding could occur within the brain tissue (also called brain parenchyma), or inside the fluid filled brain cavities (called ventricles), or within the surrounding spaces (epidural, subdural, and subarachnoid). ICHs are thus categorized into intra-parenchymal (IPH), intra-ventricular (IVH), subdural (SDH), subarachnoid (SAH), and epidural hemorrhages (EDH). Overall, ICH has a worldwide incidence of about 25 out of 100,000 people, with a mortality rate reaching 40% within 1 month of presentation (van Asch et al., 2010). Further, only 20% of survivors are expected to have full functional recovery at 6 months (Aguilar and Freeman, 2018).

Direct injury causing a bleed, followed by the edema and inflammatory response can disrupt or compress adjacent normal brain tissue, leading to neurological dysfunction. Further substantial displacement of brain tissue can raise the pressure within the brain and lead to life-threatening brain herniation syndromes. This manifests as various symptoms in patients based on the type and location of the bleed. The manifestations include (but are not limited to) headache, vomiting, seizures (fits), and focal or generalized neurologic symptoms (coma), etc. Only neuroimaging provides a definitive diagnosis of an ICH.

4.3 Neuroimaging techniques for intracranial hemorrhage

Neuroimaging techniques provide an insight into the anatomical structure, providing information of a wide range of pathological conditions of the brain and skull such as hemorrhage, ischemic stroke, hydrocephalus, cerebral edema, bone fractures, etc. In addition, other characteristics of the bleed such as location, extension to the ventricular system, presence of surrounding edema, development of mass effect, and midline shift can also be identified. The neuroimaging modalities incorporated in detection of ICH include:

4.3.1 Noncontrast computed tomography

Noncontrast CT (NCCT) is the most rapid and readily available tool for the diagnosis of ICH. Its wide availability and relatively low acquisition time makes it the imaging study of choice in patients with acute neurological complaints visiting an ED (Khan et al., 2013).

4.3.2 Magnetic resonance imaging

Magnetic resonance imaging (MRI) is the preferred modality of investigation for further characterization of ICH and evaluation of its cause. MRI offers greater sensitivity than computed tomography (CT) for micro hemorrhages, as well as across all stages of ICH evolution.

4.3.3 Computed tomography angiography

CT angiography (CTA) has been gaining acceptance as a diagnostic tool in the acute setting primarily for ruling out vascular abnormalities as secondary causes of ICH.

4.3.4 Dual energy computed tomography

Dual energy CT (DECT) is a novel technique, also known as spectral CT. It has demonstrated benefits in detecting regions of hemorrhagic transformation following reperfusion therapy (Gupta et al., 2010).

Given the common and global usage of noncontrast head CT (NCHCT) in the ED for detection of intracranial pathologies, the current chapter focuses specifically on CT with respect to ICH.

4.4 Presentation of intracranial hemorrhage on noncontrast head computed tomography and need for automation

The presentation of ICH on NCHCT can be described in terms of the morphology of the bleed as well as the density on CT images. Based on the elapsed time since the onset of bleed, ICH can be classified as hyperacute (<6 hours), acute (6–72 hours), early subacute (3–7 days), late subacute (1 week to 1 month), and chronic (>1 month) bleeds. On a NCHCT, the hyperacute and acute bleeds appear as regions of increased density compared to the gray and white matter i.e. brighter or whiter than the brain (Fig. 4.1, all CT images used in this chapter are from the public CQ500 dataset). During the first 48–72 hours after the bleed, the increasing relative density of the bleed enhances the density on CT. Thus the hyperacute, acute, and early subacute bleeds appear hyperdense on CT. Following this, the progressive changes in the clot leads to CT attenuation and the bleeds appears isodense (to brain tissue)

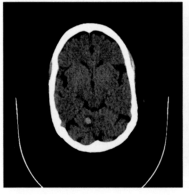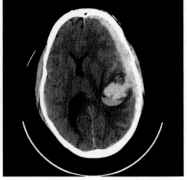

Figure 4.1 Appearance of different types of hemorrhages on a noncontrast head CT (NCHCT).

on CT in the late subacute phase. The chronic bleeds appear hypodense and typically resolve completely by about 2 months (Saad et al., 2018). The morphology of ICH on CT also varies based on the subtype and the location of the bleed, for example, EDH typically appear biconvex while subdural hemorrhages typically appear crescentic overlying the cerebral convexity. Readers can refer to a recent review Saad et al. (2018) for further details on radiological features of ICH.

The above scenario paints a picture in which making a radiological diagnosis of ICH and its subtypes requires a fair degree of clinical expertise and thus may be a daunting task to the inexperienced eyes. To illustrate this, it was noted that during an out of hour period, when radiologists are not available, physicians in the ED often perform the initial interpretation of the images. A study conducted in Australia showed that senior ED medical staff are only correct two-thirds of the time in interpretation of NCHCT (Khoo and Duffy, 2007). Though NCHCT scans can be acquired quickly, any delay in interpretation, owing to a multitude of factors, including the lack of expertise, could result in adverse patient outcomes. It is to be borne in mind that in critical cases, time to treatment is of utmost importance and the physician must identify the pathologies accurately and initiate treatment at the earliest. In recent years, radiological imaging has considerably grown due to improvements in technologies and ease of access to such technologies. This poses a unique challenge where there is both a relative lack of trained experts, as well as the presently available radiologists are burdened with a considerable workload. These challenges raise the need for the creation and implementation of solutions for automated interpretation of medical images for screening, classification, and localization of diseases to aid clinicians.

4.5 Automation techniques in medical imaging

Machine learning and pattern recognition deal with the automated identification of patterns and regularities in data and are widely used to make decisions across various fields including medical imaging (Maier et al., 2019). The automated analysis of medical images using machine learning and computer vision techniques has grown over the last couple of years.

Large expansions in the volume of data and its associated challenges have led deep learning (DL) methods to supersede the traditional machine learning techniques, which were manual, tedious and biased. DL methods, which exploit the hierarchal structure of artificial neural network for decision-making, are becoming increasingly common. The ability of these systems to automate the identification of key factors needed to make decisions can unravel insights not discernable to a human. Deep convolutional neural networks (DCNNs) have thus become the dominant machine learning approach for medical image classification tasks.

DL methods in medical imaging can be broadly divided in to three classes:

1. the three-dimensional (3D) models, which use multiple slices or all the slices in the volume together to provide scan (or volume) level prediction;
2. the two-dimensional (2D) models, which use each slice in the volume independently to make slice level prediction and combine these predictions to provide a scan level prediction and;
3. the hybrid models, which combine various aspects of 2D and 3D models.

Detection of ICH has been a widely studied topic. Prior solutions in the automated interpretation of NCHCT primarily focus on traditional methods or 3D whole scan analysis and slice level (2D) prediction as an intermediate for a scan level prediction. There has been a shift from these widely used algorithms to hybrid methods, which combine the advantages of several techniques.

4.6   Traditional machine learning

The stages involved in machine learning models (Fig. 4.2) can be broadly classified into a preprocessing phase (to clean, enhance the image, and optionally identify a region of interest [ROI]), a feature extraction and selection phase (the input for the identification of descriptors that would aid in making the final decision), and a classification phase (using extracted features for decision-making).

Figure 4.2 Components of creating a machine learning model.

4.6.1 Preprocessing

The first stage is the preprocessing in order to remove noise, enhance the quality of the input, identify of the object of interest, etc. There are several challenges in the automated processing of medical images. These images are often affected by noise, blurriness, and may have low contrast, resulting in difficulty in the observation and detection of diseases (Vasuki et al., 2017). Medical images also vary in terms of brightness, contrast, sharpness, and visibility of structures across medical imaging system parameters and manufacturers. Hence, the first and vital step would be image enhancement and standardization. Commonly used image enhancement and standardization methods can be broadly categorized into spatial and frequency domain methods. Spatial domain methods refer to the image plane itself and involve the direct manipulation of the pixels in an image. Frequency domain methods are based on the transformation of the image to the frequency domain using the Fourier transform and manipulation in this space.

4.6.2 Feature extraction and Selection

Feature extraction is the process of identification and extraction of meaningful, complete, and distinctive identifiers with respect to the question in context. Features need to be designed to contain sufficient and complete information in order to characterize each class to make the specific decision and also be robust to the variability in the input data. Once designed, a feature vector is then created by extracting these features from the input data point. The process by which these features are manually identified, tailored, and selected are often referred to as hand-crafted features. These hand-crafted features are often challenging to generalize and the features need to be reengineered for every new task in hand.

In image processing, algorithms are used to identify and detect various vital components or desired parts and features of the image. Commonly used features in medical imaging can be categorized into:
- Intensity-based such as first and second order statistics.
- Shape-based including shape descriptors such as circularity, convexity, blobs, corners, etc.
- Texture-based.
  - Statistical measures such as features from the (1) gray-level co-occurrence matrix (GLCM) (entropy, energy, correlation, contrast, variance), (2) gray-level run length

matrix features (gray-level nonuniformity, high/low gray-level run emphasis, long/short run emphasis, run percentage, run length, nonuniformity), (3) local binary patterns (LBP), (4) histogram of gradients/phase, (5) edge density and (6) autocorrelation features;

• Transform based such as Gabor filters, wavelet features, and laws texture masks.

Once the hand crafted features have been extracted, the next step is to identify which of them are relevant. This is necessary as having irrelevant features could add noise and hence lead to a decline in performance or accuracy of the models. Feature selection is the process by which only relevant features that largely contribute to the output variable in question, are selected either manually or by automatic methods. The aim of feature selection is to improve model performance, reduce complexity, reduce overfitting and enable faster training.

Feature selection methods can be broadly classified into three classes (Guyon and Elisseeff, 2003), namely,

• Filter methods (such as correlation coefficients, information gain), that assign a score (for ranking) to each feature based on a statistical measure.

• Wrapper methods (such as recursive feature elimination), which consider the selection of an input feature set as a search problem, where various combinations are identified. These subsets are evaluated and compared using a predictive model's accuracy.

• Embedded methods (such as LASSO, ridge regression), which learns which features contribute maximally to the model performance during creation.

4.6.3 Classification

In the classification step, the final value or class needs to be predicted based on the feature vector x extracted, by estimating the function f defined by $y_{pred} = f(x)$, where y_{pred} is the predicted output and the goal would be to minimize the error or what is called the cost function, that is, variations between corresponding pairs of y_{pred} and y_{gt} (the ground truth). In linear regression, the function $f(x)$ is represented by $y_{pred} = Wx + B$, where W is the set of weights associated with each feature in x and B is the bias. The process of finding the optimal f is done using an optimization algorithm (such as gradient descent), in order to minimize the cost function in the field of machine learning. The function is determined during the training phase and then evaluated during testing.

Some of the classical methods include linear regression, logistic regression, naive Bayes classifiers, and clustering methods such as nearest neighbor, support vector machines (SVMs), decision trees, and random forests.

4.7 Challenges in using traditional methods

The process of hand-crafted feature engineering is a tedious task. Some of the key design considerations are, what are the important features, how does one determine exhaustively all the features required, how many additional features can be generated from a start set of features, and how does one determine and model the various interactions with multiple combinations of the parent features. Additionally, there is also an influence due to human bias, where an individual may be inclined toward re-using certain features that have worked for prior problem statements.

4.8 Deep learning

Neural networks, which are the basis for most DL methods, are comprised of several layers—an input layer, one or more hidden layers and an output layer, each containing a number of neurons as shown in Fig. 4.3. Each neuron captures the set of parameters, that is, weights (w) and biases (b), and an activation (a) given by $a = \sigma(Wx + b)$ where σ is a nonlinear element-wise transform referred to as the transfer function.

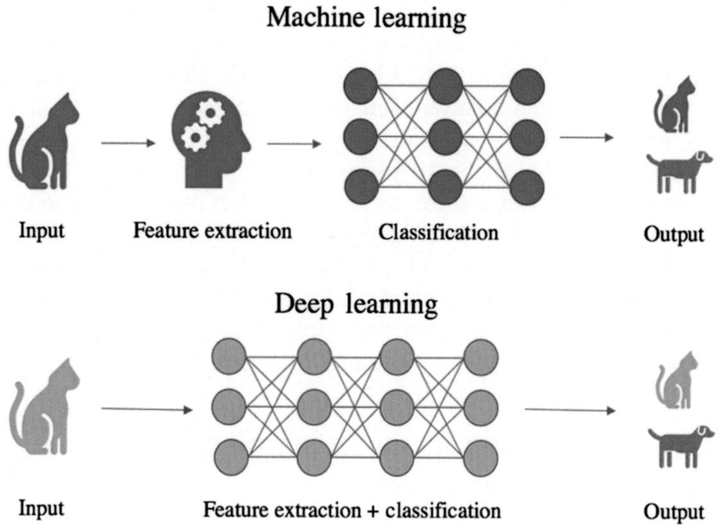

Figure 4.3 Machine learning versus deep learning (DL).

The activations of each neuron from the previous layer are combined iteratively to generate exhaustive and complex feature representations. In the final layer of the network, the final activation is mapped to an output distribution over the classes by applying an activation function such as sigmoid or softmax to generate the set of probabilities for each class. Similar to the traditional approaches, the network parameters are tuned with respect to a cost function, in order to determine the optimal parameters for the full feature extraction and classification pipeline.

A deep neural network is one in which there are multiple hidden layers. DCNN are a class of deep neural networks widely and successfully used for image processing and analysis. In contrast to generic DL networks, DCNNs learn common convolutional operations or kernels, which are used for detecting the same object or pattern across the image. This reduces the number of parameters that need to be learnt and makes the network robust to variance of object location in the image. Additionally, in DCNNs, pooling layers are used, where values of nearby pixels are aggregated usually using a permutation-invariant max or mean operation. Similar to the generic neural networks, DCNNs consist of one or more fully connected layers (i.e., regular network layers described above) at the end of the convolutional/pooling layers. Finally, the activations of the last layer are passed through a nonlinear transform to obtain the distribution over the output classes.

The generic neural network is limited by fixed size inputs, which limits its capabilities to process series data. Recurrent neural networks (RNNs) are a class of neural networks where the connections between neurons of the network form a directed graph along a temporal sequence, which allows it to exhibit temporal behavior. These networks remember the past, allowing them to take into consideration prior information of the same input while making a decision. The outputs of an RNN are not just dependent on the activations of the previous layers as in NNs, but also a hidden state vector (h), which represents the current input and the context from previous input data processed. The hidden state vector of a neuron at time t is given by, $h_t = (Wx_t + Rh_{t-1} + b)$ where, W and R are the weight matrices, x_t is the vector of features from the current input data, and h_{t-1} is the hidden state vector from the previous time state.

4.8.1 Visualization for deep learning

One of the primary drawbacks of DL methods is comprehending what the DL model has learnt and how it comes to a certain decision. With traditional machine learning, since the features are manually designed, the models are easy to understand. However, because of the design of a DL model, it is extremely challenging to understand the factors that contribute to a certain decision, since the whole process of feature extraction and classification is combined. It is extremely important to understand this for multiple reasons. Firstly, the confidence on a black box approach is very low in life-dependent applications such as in healthcare. If the user does not understand the reason for the decision, he or she is unlikely to trust it. Additionally, the network is bound to make errors, however unlikely. If the ROI is highlighted in the image, the end clinician can quickly review and accept/reject the final finding. Lastly, interpreting these networks is the one primary component to truly understand where they fail, why they fail, and how to improve them.

Visualization of CNNs is a vital component in understanding the network itself and interpreting the same. There have been several efforts to understand the predictions of CNNs. Several methods such as deconvolution (to highlight specific location in the image that strongly activate each neuron), guided backpropagation (which helps in understanding the effect of each neuron within the whole network), class activation maps, gradient based class activation maps (GradCAM), and the more recently introduced GradCAM++ have been widely used for this purpose.

4.9 Automated detection techniques in intracranial hemorrhage

4.9.1 Preprocessing

4.9.1.1 Resampling

The parameters with which the CT scans are acquired vary across hospitals, instrument models, and manufacturers. The thickness of each slice and number of slices may also vary across these sources. Resampling is an image interpolation technique used to create a new image with the desired voxel spacing and image extent. Resampling is mainly used to achieve uniform dimensionality when the slice thickness and size varies. Resampling can be of two types, anisotropic (the final voxel spacing across the x, y, and z-axis are different) and isotropic (the final voxel spacing across the three axes are the same). Isotropic resampling is specifically utilized in scenarios where

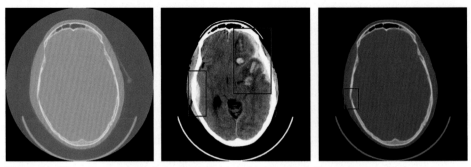

Figure 4.4 Effect of windowing (left to right: no window, brain window, bone window) on a noncontrast head CT (NCHCT) containing a subdural hemorrhage (SDH) and a fracture.

the inter-slice pixel spacing is significantly larger than that of the in-plane spacing.

The resampling strategies that have been applied are, isotropic in-plane resampling of 1 mm × 1 mm and 250 mm × 250 mm field-of-view in-plane (Grewal et al., 2018) and through-plane resampling of 5 mm and the size of each slice 224 × 224 (Chilamkurthy et al., 2018). As noted through these examples, the techniques for resampling are essentially need based and may vary based on the algorithm used.

Although standardization of size by down sampling could have benefits, up sampling adds to intensity noise due to interpolation. For example, interpolation between two slices where a specific pixel location in-plane in one slice is bone and in the next slice is soft tissue, results in a pixel that has intensity value between soft tissue (isodense) and bone (hyperdense) which could mimic a hemorrhage (hyperdense compared to soft tissue).

4.9.1.2 Contrast enhancement and windowing

In CT imaging, the density of a tissue is represented in Hounsfield units (HU). In this scale, water has a value of 0 HU, materials with greater density such as bone, have positive values and the materials with lower density such as air have negative values. Windowing is a gray-level mapping method widely used for contrast enhancement of CT scans, in which the tissues of interest are highlighted by assigning the HU intensity values of these tissues to a narrow visible intensity range (Carley, 2012). A window is specified with a window level (WL) which is the mean point of the window and a window width (WW) which specifies total width of the window. Pixels with HU values outside of the specified window (i.e., <WL-WW/2 or >WL+WW/2) are clipped.

Fig. 4.4 shows the effect of windowing on a scan containing a SDH. As shown, without any window applied, it is difficult to visualize the structures of brain. By applying a brain window, the hemorrhage along with its effect on the structures within the cranium is clearly seen. The bone window shows a fracture as highlighted, likely to have caused the hemorrhage near this location.

There are certain standard windows used for highlighting hemorrhagic regions, most commonly noted across the publications is the brain window (WL = 40, WW = 80) (Arbabshirani et al., 2018; Chilamkurthy et al., 2018; Desai et al., 2017; Grewal et al., 2018; Vidya et al., 2019). Since the effect of hemorrhage is often seen on the surrounding structures as well, application of multiple windows for the same slice to obtain multiple images have also been demonstrated across publications. These windows (and their corresponding ranges) could be predefined, custom selected, or dynamically defined as described in the examples below.

Chilamkurthy et al. (2018) have used the brain (WL = 40, WW = 80), bone (WL = 500, WW = 3000), and subdural (WL = 175, WW = 50) window. The bone window could highlight possible extra axial bleeds in the brain window while the subdural window enhances the difference between the skull and extra axial bleed. Desai et al. (2017) have used three different windows as well namely, brain (WL = 35, WW = 80), acute blood (WL = 95, WW = 220), and stroke window (WL = 33, WW = 27).

Ye et al. (2019) on the other hand have employed three custom ranges (−50 to 150, 100−300 and 250−450) in order to highlight differences between hemorrhage and normal tissue, intensity changes between the skull and the inner skull boundary and to reduce the influence of the skull on the hemorrhage predictions respectively.

Tong et al. (2011) proposed a method to dynamically define the range of the window. The smoothed curve of the image histogram is transformed into absolute first difference. The upper and lower limit (I_U and I_L) are automatically detected by the closest peak on the right and left respectively. The obtained limits are then used for linear contrast stretching as below:

$$F(i,j) = I_{max} \frac{\left(I(i,j) - I_L\right)}{I_U - I_L} \tag{4.1}$$

Maduskar and Acharyya (2009) utilized a gamma correction and a sigmoid shaped mapping function to the input scan and

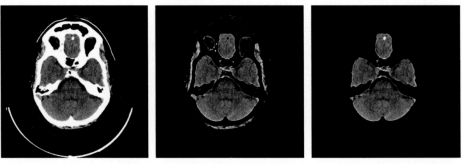

Figure 4.5 Importance of suppressing background. Left to right: Original image, skull stripped image, and brain region extracted using method described by Vidya et al. (2019).

in order to enhance contrast, the pixels having intensities above a certain value are lightened while those below are darkened.

4.9.1.3 Skull and background removal

The skull and the surrounding soft tissue can contribute to noise in the study, when the ROI lies only within the cranial cavity. In such scenarios skull stripping and background removal may be performed. The HU intensity of bone structures is significantly greater than other structures and hence can be easily suppressed by setting the pixel values over a given threshold to a minimum value (e.g., 0) as shown in Fig. 4.5.

These thresholds may be either predefined (Liu et al., 2008; Tong et al., 2011), or obtained from the skull peak noted in the histogram of the image (Maduskar and Acharyya, 2009; Shahangian and Pourghassem, 2013). Further, a standard FCM clustering (of three groups—the skull, the intracranial region, and dark regions outside the skull and within the brain) may also be employed to aid skull removal (Sun et al., 2015).

Following skull stripping, additional soft tissue background artifacts such as edema/other structures may still exist and hence need to be removed once again (Shahangian and Pourghassem, 2013). As shown in Fig. 4.5, the lower brain region specifically contains many background artifacts that need to be removed. Extraction of intracranial structures from skull stripped images also poses a challenge (e.g., edema outside the skull can have same density as the brain tissue). Masking out the nonbrain region has been demonstrated in our prior work (Vidya et al., 2019), where, from the background removed scan, we identified the slice containing the largest soft tissue island across all slices (s_{max}). For all slices in the cranial

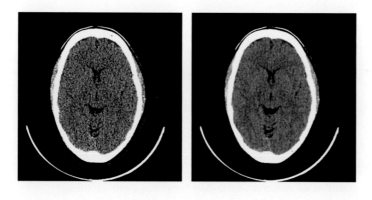

Figure 4.6 Left: Original image. Right: Salt and pepper noise suppressed using the median filter.

region (above s_{max}), the brain region is simply the largest soft tissue island in the slice. For slices in the skull base (below s_{max}), the brain region of the above slice serves as an initial guess to extract the brain region.

4.9.1.4 Noise removal

After removing the skull and background, there could be noise within the brain region. This salt and pepper noise can be reduced by using a mean or median filter. The median filter is commonly used (Shahangian and Pourghassem, 2013; Tong et al., 2011) because it is effective and preserves sharp edges as shown in Fig. 4.6. Maduskar and Acharyya (2009) have also used anisotropic diffusion for noise reduction by setting the coefficient such that intra-region smoothing was given higher weightage to the inter-region smoothing.

4.9.1.5 Composite image creation

In order to reduce the number of slices being processed, standardize them while not losing out the slice level information available, creation of composite images has been employed in our previous work (Vidya et al., 2019). Composite images aim to reduce the number of slices being processed while avoiding loss of information. In order to generate composite images, the brain-extracted region containing X slices were divided into N sub-volumes, resulting in approximately X/N slices in each sub-volume. For each sub-volume i of shape (J,K,L), where $i = \{i_1, i_2...., i_n\}$, $j = \{1,2...J\}$, $k = \{1,2...K\}$, $l = \{1,2...L\}$, multiple composite images can be generated. Three composite images namely, MIP, MinIP, and OtsuIP are generated as follows.

(A)   (B)   (C)

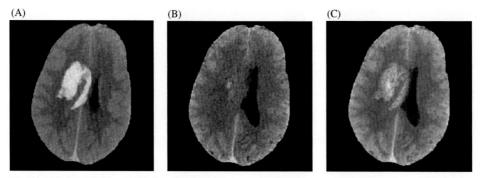

Figure 4.7 (A) MIP, (B) MinIP, and (C) OtsuIP of an axial scan containing hemorrhage with ventricular compression.

Figure 4.8 Left: Represents the original brain region extracted scan with a hemorrhage. Right: Represents the binary image obtained using Otsu's method.

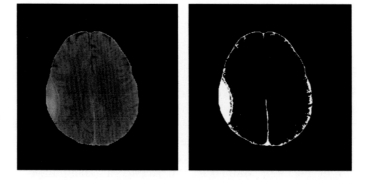

$$\text{MIP}\left(i_{jk}\right) = max\left(i\left(J=j, K=k\right)\right) \tag{4.2}$$

$$\text{MinIP}\left(i_{jk}\right) = min\left(i\left(J=j, K=k\right)\right) \tag{4.3}$$

$$\text{OtsuIP}\left(i_{jk}\right) = otsu\left(i\left(J=j, K=k\right)\right) \tag{4.4}$$

where *otsu* is the Otsu's adaptive thresholding algorithm (Otsu, 1979) where the threshold represents the maximum variance point in the reduction of a gray-level image to a binary image.

As shown in Fig. 4.7, the MIP image highlights the hyperdense regions (like acute hemorrhages). MinIP enhances the abnormalities in the ventricles, subdural region, and hypodense regions and finally OtsuIP highlights both hyper and hypodense regions.

4.9.1.6 Identification of hemorrhage region of interest

For creation and extraction of hand-crafted features, it is vital to first identify a ROI of the hemorrhages in the scan and extract parameters from this region alone to ensure that the features are truly representative and characteristic of the class.

Once the region of the brain is extracted, and the image has been enhanced, a threshold is commonly used to approximate the hemorrhage region, either determined by a defined value (Grewal et al., 2018; Phan et al., 2019) or Otsu's adaptive threshold method (Al-Ayyoub et al., 2013; Sun et al., 2015). The binary image is obtained with this thresholding process, where the pixels above the threshold are assigned the value 1 and below, 0. Hemorrhagic regions, usually being brighter than other parts of the intracranial region, are likely assigned to 1. Fig. 4.8 shows how Otsu's method can be used to obtain an initial guess of the hemorrhagic region. Morphological operations can be used to suppress the background region and retrieve a more accurate estimate of location.

In order to further localize the hemorrhagic region, Sun et al. (2015), used a template of a specific size which was convolved onto the binary image to determine the number of hemorrhagic pixels in a location. The pixel with the maximum number of 1's was set as the center of the hemorrhagic region and a square around this center pixel defined an initial candidate region. A simple linear iterative clustering super voxel segmentation was then used for an accurate region extraction.

Liu et al. (2008) employed a simple subtraction of a mean value to generate an image with the hemorrhages left and background removed. The images were decomposed twice using the Haar wavelet transforms and then reconstructed by setting the detail coefficient to 0 to generate the homogenous intensity map.

Although extraction of an ROI is not a necessity for DL based models, it could be useful to direct the model to focus on a specific region by additionally providing a thresholded image as demonstrated by Ker et al. (2019). Ker et al. (2019), similar to Liu et al. (2008), discarded the common range of intensities between normal and hemorrhagic scans. Using the histograms of the two classes, an optimal threshold that highlights the class difference was identified. This enhances the sharp edges around the ROI which aids the CNN performance.

Maduskar and Acharyya (2009) used a semiautomatic 3D segmentation technique to identify hemorrhage candidates. In order to obtain the estimation of the region of the bleed, the range of bleed intensities was dynamically computed, using an identified

Table 4.1 Overview of texture and intensity-based features used in the detection of intracranial hemorrhage (ICH).

SI. no.	Feature type	Sub-feature(s)	References
1.	First order statistics from the intensity histogram	Mean, skewness, and kurtosis	Liu et al. (2008)
		Standard deviation	Liu et al. (2008) and Maduskar and Acharyya (2009)
2.	Second order statistics from the gray-level co-occurrence matrix (GLCM)	Variance and energy	Liu et al. (2008), Maduskar and Acharyya (2009), and Shahangian and Pourghassem (2013)
		Contrast, correlation, and homogeneity	Liu et al. (2008) and Shahangian and Pourghassem (2013)
		Entropy and maximum probability	Liu et al. (2008)
3.	Local binary patterns from each hemisphere of the brain		Tong et al. (2011)

representative seed point. The binary image was then generated by computing the high and low threshold values. The binary map was refined using connected component analysis to keep only the components containing the seed point. Finally, in each slice the connected components overlapping with the bleed cluster on the reference slice were selected. Clusters that met the optimal centroid distance between itself and a reference cluster were then selected.

4.9.2 Traditional machine learning

As described earlier, extracting differentiating, complete, and useful features from the images is a critical step in traditional feature engineering. In prior work on hemorrhage detection, various shape and texture features were extracted to differentiate between hemorrhagic and non hemorrhagic slices as well as sub-categorizing the ICH regions into the respective subtypes (Tables 4.1 and 4.2).

Shape-based features are primarily intended to differentiate between various hemorrhage types. If the task at hand to detect ICH versus non-ICH, it would be equally or more important to include texture descriptors as well. Additionally, although LBP itself maybe an efficient descriptor, comparing the left and right

Table 4.2 Overview of shape/geometric based features used in the detection of intracranial hemorrhage (ICH) and its subtypes.

Sl. no.	Feature	Description	References
1.	Size of the hemorrhage	In order to determine the seriousness of the hemorrhage	Al-Ayyoub et al. (2013), Phan et al. (2019), and Shahangian and Pourghassem (2013)
2.	Perimeter of the hemorrhagic area		Al-Ayyoub et al. (2013) and Shahangian and Pourghassem (2013)
3.	Centroid/location of the hemorrhage	In order to determine the location in the cortex which is vital in treatment planning	Al-Ayyoub et al. (2013) and Phan et al. (2019)
4.	The distance between the hemorrhagic region and the skull	Vital in determining the ICH types. For example, epidural hemorrhage (EDH) and subdural hemorrhage (SDH) will have very small values of this feature when compared to intra-parenchymal hemorrhage (IPH)	Al-Ayyoub et al. (2013)
5.	Equivdiameter	Diameter of a circle with the same size as the ROI	Al-Ayyoub et al. (2013), and Shahangian and Pourghassem (2013)
6.	Solidity/convexity	Aids in differentiation of EDH and IPH that are convex from SDH which is concave	Al-Ayyoub et al. (2013) and Shahangian and Pourghassem (2013)
7.	Convex area	The size of the smallest bounding box containing the ROI	Al-Ayyoub et al. (2013) and Shahangian and Pourghassem (2013)
8.	Extent	The ratio of the pixels in the ROI to pixels in the bounding box of the ROI	Al-Ayyoub et al. (2013) and Shahangian and Pourghassem (2013)
9.	Orientation	Angle between the x axis and the major axis of the ellipse that has the same second moments as the ROI	Al-Ayyoub et al. (2013), Maduskar and Acharyya (2009), and Shahangian and Pourghassem (2013)
10.	Major axis and minor axis length	Length of major and minor axes of the ellipse that have the same second moments as the ROI	Al-Ayyoub et al. (2013) and Shahangian and Pourghassem (2013)
11.	Eccentricity	Eccentricity of the ellipse that has the same second moments as the ROI	Al-Ayyoub et al. (2013) and Maduskar and Acharyya (2009)
12.	Filled area	The number of pixels in filled image	Shahangian and Pourghassem (2013)
13.	The smallest, average and largest Hounsfield units (HU) in each hemorrhagic region	Important in determining bleed timing for treatment determination	Phan et al. (2019)

hemispheres to detect hemorrhage would fail in cases where both the hemispheres are affected equally.

Once the above-mentioned features are extracted, they are passed into a classifier for making the final decision. SVM with linear kernel (Liu et al., 2008; Tong et al., 2011), K-nearest neighbor or KNN (Phan et al., 2019; Shahangian and Pourghassem, 2013), and multilayer perceptron (MLP) neural network (Al-Ayyoub et al., 2013; Shahangian and Pourghassem, 2013) were used in prior work in the detection and sub-classification of ICH. Shahangian and Pourghassem (2013) demonstrated a significantly better performance by using an MLP (with 12 neurons in hidden layer and tansigmoid function as activation function) when compared to a KNN model. Al-Ayyoub et al. (2013) were able to achieve a slighter better but comparable performance by using a multinomial logistic regression classifier with a ridge estimator when compared to an MLP.

4.9.3   Deep learning

Usage of DL methods has several advantages, the major ones being that they learn high level features incrementally from structured data and eliminate the need for handcrafting of features and domain expertise. Since these methods also learn features incrementally, they are able to learn generic feature representations that can be re-used and transfer learned to several other tasks. However, one of the major constraints is that they need relatively large-scale datasets in order to learn the significant number of parameters when compared to their traditional counterparts. In order to increase dataset size various augmentation techniques such as rotation, flipping, clipping, etc. are commonly used.

DL methods can be broadly divided in to three classes: 3D models, 2D models, and hybrid models, which combine 2D and 3D aspects. Fig. 4.9 shows a sample architecture for each type.

2D models are popular because they require less data and computational resources for training when compared to 3D models. 3D models require more GPU memory. Down sampling of data is often necessary for training and prediction of 3D models, which causes loss of information. For example, small regions of bleeds can be easily missed as a result of consecutive pooling layers in 3D DCNNs, since pooling acts as down sampling of data in deep neural networks. This problem is further compounded when the inter-slice pixel spacing of the CT volume is significantly larger than that of the in-plane spacing. Resampling of the image volume to create an isotropic voxel,

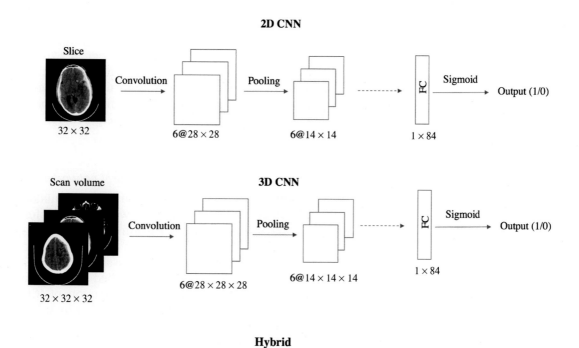

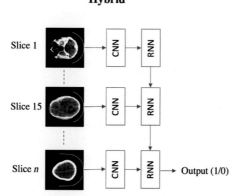

Figure 4.9 Example of a two-dimensional convolutional neural network (2D CNN), three-dimensional (3D) CNN, and a hybrid CNN-RNN model.

which is used as a solution for this, adds intensity noise. Additionally, the scale of data required to train these networks is much larger than a 2D model.

2D models overcome the need for isotropic resampling, large datasets for training, and lead to localization that is more accurate. However, there are several drawbacks to a slice level analysis. Since the inter-slice context is lost in these models, detection of some anomalies becomes challenging (e.g., differentiating between edges of calcification vs hemorrhage), unless also provided with contextual information (Chang et al., 2018; Grewal et al., 2018; Vidya et al., 2019; Ye et al., 2019). Although they perform well in the detection of minute anomalies, slice level analysis could be compute/time intensive. Additionally, it is also an extremely time consuming and expensive process for an expert to label each slice required for the training of these models.

4.9.3.1 Two-dimensional deep convolutional neural networks

With the availability of ImageNet (containing over a million images), creation of 2D DCNNs has been widely successful. Additionally, there have been a significant number of residual-based algorithms such as ResNets/DenseNets that have led to improvement in the performance of image classification tasks. These methods have also been extensively applied to the field of medical imaging. Current methods in the detection of ICH utilize 2D DCNNs for a slice level prediction of ICH, which can then be used to create a scan level prediction.

Desai et al. (2017) evaluated the effect of pretraining and augmentation for the detection of hemorrhage per slice. AlexNet and GoogLeNet were trained with/without ImageNet pre-training and with/without augmentation. Pretraining the models with ImageNet and augmenting the datasets that were used for training enhanced the performance of the models.

Chilamkurthy et al. (2018), detailed a method for the detection of ICH and its various subtypes including IPH, IVH, SAH, SDH, and EDH at a scan level. Having slice level labels, a modified 2D ResNet18 was trained on multiwindowed inputs, by using five parallel fully connected layers (for each ICH type), with the assumption that features for detecting each type of hemorrhage would be similar. The slice level confidences were then combined to a scan level prediction using a random forest.

4.9.3.2 Three-dimensional deep convolutional neural networks

When compared to a 2D DCNN, the datasets available for 3D analysis such as action recognition are relatively small. The ActivityNet/Kinetic datasets are sometimes used for the pretraining of these models, although the performance for object detection is still not as good as that of a 2D DCNN. With respect to medical imaging, 3D models consider context across slices while making predictions and hence could perform better if trained adequately and correctly with the sufficient amount of data.

Arbabshirani et al. (2018), obtained a large datasets of over ~37,000 scans for the training of their custom 3D DCNN (consisting of five convolutional layers and two fully connected layers) to detect ICH at a scan level. The method is perhaps limited due to the 3D analysis and scan level labels available. However, even though the area under ROC curve (AUC) achieved is not as high as some of the other work, the solution was implemented in clinical workflow to prioritize scans where ICH was detected which led to a reduction in median time to diagnosis of positive studies.

Ker et al. (2019) demonstrated the value of highlighting the affected hemorrhagic region by applying a thresholding to the input scan and passing the processed image to the 3D DCNN consisting of three convolutional layers followed by two fully connected layers. The processed image enhances the sharp edges around the ROI which aids the CNN to focus on the affected region and hence improves performance. In the task of classification of normal versus each hemorrhage type at a scan level, F1 scores relatively improved by an average of 13%. This shows that localization helps with object detection as well.

There are several challenges with creating a 3D DCNN model. Small regions of bleeds can be easily missed on consecutive pooling which is further compounded since the z-axis pixel spacing is much larger than the in-plane pixel spacing. When compared to the 2D models, the size of the data needed for training of 3D models is significantly larger due in increased parameters. Visualization and decoding 3D models are also an additional challenge.

4.9.3.3 Hybrid deep convolutional neural networks

Some of the recent methods have transitioned from the traditional 2D and 3D DCNNs to hybrid approaches, aiming to combine the advantages of 2D and 3D processing, and also looking at localization which improves object detection. Thus mimicking the radiologists and their pattern of movement across slices while focussing on the affected or potentially affected regions.

Grewal et al. (2018), proposed a DenseNet-40 augmented with an attention mechanism for slice level predictions/computations of hemorrhagic regions known as DenseNet-A. They proposed RADNet which additionally models the inter-slice dependencies between the slices by using a RNN (bidirectional long short-term memory) for incorporating 3D context. The analysis shows that adding the attention, that is, DenseNet-A outperforms a regular 2D DenseNet in terms of recall, precision, and F1, increasing relatively by 8%. A relative improvement of precision by 3.4% from DenseNet-A to RADNet (i.e., with 3D context) was also shown. This further reinforces that in addition to attention, 3D context aids the model in the learning process.

Chang et al. (2018), proposed a hybrid 2D/3D DCNN for the detection and quantification of IPH, EDH, SDH, and SAH on NCHCTs. With the availability of large-scale data and segmentation and classification of each hemorrhage region, a custom architecture based on mask-RCNN was proposed, which allows for parallel attention (bounding boxes), classification, and segmentation. A predetermined distribution of bounding boxes was first tested for the presence of an abnormality. Region proposals were then generated from the most confidently rated boxes, ensuring the model focuses on the box for increased accuracy of segmentation. Using nonmaximal suppression, these region proposals were pruned to determine the presence/absence of hemorrhage. A custom backbone network was created using residual bottleneck blocks. The custom network allows for a $5 \times 512 \times 512$ input, which maps to a 2D output, allowing the network to utilize contextual information from the five slices surrounding the ROI in its prediction. The ability of the network to segment as well consider that 3D context leads the solution to have a very high sensitivity/specificity of 0.951/0.973 for hemorrhage detection.

Although the accuracy of some of the previously discussed approaches is high, there is still a challenge in obtaining such high-quality data required for the training of some of these models. Ye et al. (2019), proposed a joint CNN-RNN network, that has the flexibility to train when scan level or slice level labels are available. This method, similar to the work of Grewal et al. (2018), mimics how the radiologist interprets scans, that is, across slices. The CNN focuses on extracting features from each slice and the RNN captures sequential information or context to boost classification performance. In the proposed workflow, first the presence of ICH is detected. If present, it is further classified into the subtypes. The method also allows for a coarse localization using GradCAM for easy interpretation of the model outputs by the clinicians.

In our previous work (Vidya et al., 2019), we addressed the detection of ICH at a scan level by utilizing a small number of scans for training, scan level labels, and in the absence of localization/segmentation ground truth. We proposed a hybrid

CNN-RNN architecture, consisting of a DenseNet-121 and an RNN, which was able to achieve comparable results to the prior art with the initial testing and shows promising results. Scans were processed in sub-volumes or chunks by the DenseNet-121, by creating three composite images (as discussed previously) from each sub-volume. Features from each chunk or sub-volume were then cascaded with an RNN to create a scan level prediction of ICH and consider context. The thickness of the composite images (number of slices in each composite image) can be varied from one (i.e., slice level processing like in 2D CNN) to the total number of slices in the scan (i.e., full scan analysis like in 3D CNN). By doing so, an optimal balance between 2D versus 3D analysis and time versus accuracy can be determined.

4.10 Clinical applications

Worldwide there is a challenge of trained experts in radiology despite the availability of instruments to perform the imaging procedures. Additionally, it is well understood as to how a lack of an accurate and early diagnosis in acute neurological cases is detrimental to the patient's health. Further, the radiologists can also face burnouts and reporting errors when burdened with large workloads.

The widespread availability and use of NCHCT for reporting acute neurological conditions, in relation to the above problem statement makes tools for automated interpretation of NCHCT, an ideal candidate for screening, classification, localization, and prioritization to aid clinicians.

The present work focuses on automated detection of ICH, which is one of the common pathology encountered in an acute neurological emergency. Automated solutions that detect ICH can be used as a building block to prioritize and flag critical scans. In addition, if these solutions highlight the affected region detected, this could automatically draw the attention of the clinician to the region, reducing the time to detection. Sub-classification of ICH and quantification of the bleed could aid in determining accurate treatment pathways. By understanding the treatment pathway, the solution can be used to intimate the respective departments of neurology/neurosurgery.

We believe in the near future automated detection of pathologies on CT and their characterization will run automatically as a scan is being performed and will be a critical tool aiding radiologists seated in the CT consoles to the right diagnosis.

4.11   Discussion and conclusion

In this study, we provide a comprehensive summary of all the efforts in the area of automated image analysis focusing on automated ICH detection in NCHCT. There have been numerous contributions that look at handcrafting features for the detection of ICH. The variability of the presentation of ICH limits the wide usage of traditional models in clinical practice. A majority of these traditional methods are also trained and tested on smaller datasets and hence not thoroughly validated. However, it is easy to comprehend and analyze these solutions.

In the recent years, there has been a focus on DL when compared to traditional methods, due to its wide adoption and success in other fields. DL also is more robust and generalizable to multi-site data and can uncover patterns that are not visible to the human eye. Within DL as well, there is a paradigm shift toward hybrid models, trying to combine the advantages of 2D and 3D analysis. Despite the high performance achievable by DL models, there are several challenges that need to be overcome before these solutions are widely adopted in clinical workflows. DL is essentially a black box. It is extremely challenging to comprehend what the model has learnt and why it makes a certain decision. Without having an understanding of this, the end user is unlikely to trust it. Blind trust on these back-box techniques may also lead a radiologist to fail to correct a report if the system has made an error. Additionally, in order to truly ensure these solutions work in all critical scenarios, it is vital to understand not only where they fail but also why they fail in order to improve it.

In here, we look at a tool, which is in the medical domain, errors in which could be fatal for people's lives. Hence, it is critical that these solutions are validated across multiple sites and populations, for their specific use before deployment.

Current solutions on analysis of hemorrhagic head scans primarily focus on detection of ICH and its subtypes. Although detection algorithms could help in triaging and alerting the physician, in order to be fully useful, they would also have to provide the quantification, anatomical location, and related findings in order to aid the physician to make treatment decisions.

References

Aguilar, M.I., Freeman, W.D., 2018. Spontaneous intracerebral hemorrhage. Semin. Neurol. 30, 334–342.e2. Available from: https://doi.org/10.1016/B978-0-323-43140-8.00022-6.

Al-Ayyoub, M., Alawad, D., Al-darabsah, K., Aljarrah, I., 2013. Automatic detection and classification brain hemorrhages. WSEAS Trans. Comput 12 (10), 395−405.

Arbabshirani, M.R., Fornwalt, B.K., Mongelluzzo, G.J., Suever, J.D., Geise, B.D., Patel, A.A., et al., 2018. Advanced machine learning in action: identification of intracranial hemorrhage on computed tomography scans of the head with clinical workflow integration. NPJ Digit. Med. 1 (1), 9. Available from: https://doi.org/10.1038/s41746-017-0015-z.

Carley, S., 2012. Diagnostic imaging for the emergency physician. Emerg. Med. J. 29 (5), 427−428.

Chang, P.D., Kuoy, E., Grinband, J., Weinberg, B.D., Thompson, M., Homo, R., et al., 2018. Hybrid 3D/2D convolutional neural network for hemorrhage evaluation on head CT. Am. J. Neuroradiol. 39 (9), 1609−1616. Available from: https://doi.org/10.3174/ajnr.A5742.

Chilamkurthy, S., Ghosh, R., Tanamala, S., Biviji, M., Campeau, N.G., Venugopal, V.K., et al., 2018. Deep learning algorithms for detection of critical findings in head CT scans: a retrospective study. Lancet 392 (10162), 2388−2396. Available from: https://doi.org/10.1016/S0140-6736(18)31645-3.

Desai, V., Flanders, A.E., Lakhani, P., 2017. Application of deep learning in neuroradiology: automated detection of basal ganglia hemorrhage using 2D-convolutional neural networks. ArXiv Preprint, ArXiv:1710.03823, pp. 1−7.

Grewal, M., Srivastava, M.M., Kumar, P., Varadarajan, S., 2018. RADnet: radiologist level accuracy using deep learning for hemorrhage detection in CT scans. In: Proceedings of International Symposium on Biomedical Imaging, April 2018, pp. 281−284. <https://doi.org/10.1109/ISBI.2018.8363574>.

Gupta, R., Phan, C.M., Leidecker, C., Brady, T.J., Hirsch, J.A., Nogueira, R.G., et al., 2010. Evaluation of dual-energy CT for differentiating intracerebral hemorrhage from iodinated contrast material staining. Radiology 257 (1), 205−211. Available from: https://doi.org/10.1148/radiol.10091806.

Guyon, I., Elisseeff, A., et al., 2003. An introduction to variable and feature selection. J Mach Learn Res. 1157−1182.

Ker, J., Singh, S.P., Bai, Y., Rao, J., Lim, T., Wang, L., 2019. Image thresholding improves 3-dimensional convolutional neural network diagnosis of different acute brain hemorrhages on computed tomography scans. Sensors (Basel) 19 (9), 2167. Available from: https://doi.org/10.3390/s19092167.

Khan, A., Qashqari, S., Al-Ali, A.A., 2013. Accuracy of non-contrast CT brain interpretation by emergency physicians: a cohort study. Pak. J. Med. Sci. 29 (2), 549−553. Available from: https://doi.org/10.12669/pjms.292.3220.

Khoo, N.C., Duffy, M., 2007. "Out of hours" non-contrast head CT scan interpretation by senior emergency department medical staff. Emerg. Med. Australas. (EMA) 19 (2), 122−128. Available from: https://doi.org/10.1111/j.1742-6723.2007.00914.x.

Liu, R., Tan, C.L., Leong, T.Y., Lee, C.K., Pang, B.C., Lim, C.C.T., et al., 2008. Hemorrhage slices detection in brain CT images. In: Proceedings of the International Conference on Pattern Recognition, pp. 1−4. <https://doi.org/10.1109/icpr.2008.4761745>.

Maduskar, P., Acharyya, M., 2009. Automatic identification of intracranial hemorrhage in non-contrast CT with large slice thickness for trauma cases. Med. Imaging 2009 Comput. Diagn. 7260 (October), 726011. Available from: https://doi.org/10.1117/12.812276.

Maier, A., Syben, C., Lasser, T., Riess, C., 2019. A gentle introduction to deep learning in medical image processing. Z. Med. Phys. 29, 86−101. Available from: https://doi.org/10.1016/j.zemedi.2018.12.003.

Otsu, N., 1979. Threshold selection method from gray-level histograms. IEEE Trans. Syst. Man Cybern (SMC) 9 (1), 62−66. Available from: https://doi.org/10.1109/tsmc.1979.4310076.

Phan, A.-C., Vo, V.-Q., Phan, T.-C., 2019. A Hounsfield value-based approach for automatic recognition of brain haemorrhage. J. Inf. Telecommun. 3 (2), 196−209. Available from: https://doi.org/10.1080/24751839.2018.1547951.

Saad, A.F., Chaudhari, R., Fischbein, N.J., Wintermark, M., 2018. Intracranial hemorrhage imaging. Semin. Ultrasound CT MRI 39 (5), 441−456. Available from: https://doi.org/10.1053/j.sult.2018.01.003.

Shahangian, B., Pourghassem, H., 2013. Automatic brain hemorrhage segmentation and classification in CT scan images. In: Iranian Conference on Machine Vision and Image Processing. MVIP, pp. 467−471. <https://doi.org/10.1109/IranianMVIP.2013.6780031>.

Sun, M., Hu, R., Yu, H., Zhao, B., Ren, H., 2015. Intracranial hemorrhage detection by 3D voxel segmentation on brain CT images. In: 2015 International Conference on Wireless Communications and Signal Processing. WCSP 2015, pp. 1−5. <https://doi.org/10.1109/WCSP.2015.7341238>.

Tong, H.L., Ahmad Fauzi, M.F., Haw, S.C., 2011. Automated Hemorrhage Slices Detection for CT Brain Images. Lecture Notes in Computer Science (Including Subseries Lecture Notes in Artificial Intelligence and Lecture Notes in Bioinformatics), LNCS (Part 1), vol. 7066, pp. 268−279. Springer, Singapore. <https://doi.org/10.1007/978-3-642-25191-7_26>.

van Asch, C.J., Luitse, M.J., Rinkel, G.J., van der Tweel, I., Algra, A., Klijn, C.J., 2010. Incidence, case fatality, and functional outcome of intracerebral haemorrhage over time, according to age, sex, and ethnic origin: a systematic review and meta-analysis. Lancet Neurol. 9 (2), 167−176. Available from: https://doi.org/10.1016/S1474-4422(09)70340-0.

Vasuki, P., Kanimozhi, J., Devi, M.B., 2017. A survey on image preprocessing techniques for diverse fields of medical imagery. In: Proceedings of 2017 IEEE International Conference on Electrical, Instrumentation and Communication Engineering. ICEICE 2017, December 2017, pp. 1−6. <https://doi.org/10.1109/ICEICE.2017.8192443>.

Vidya, M.S., Mallya, Y., Shastry, A., Vijayananda, J., 2019. Recurrent sub-volume analysis of head CT scans for the detection of intracranial hemorrhage. In: International Conference on Medical Image Computing and Computer-Assisted Intervention, pp. 864−872. Springer.

Ye, H., Gao, F., Yin, Y., Guo, D., Zhao, P., Lu, Y., et al., 2019. Precise diagnosis of intracranial hemorrhage and subtypes using a three-dimensional joint convolutional and recurrent neural network. Eur. Radiol. 29 (11), 6191−6201. Available from: https://doi.org/10.1007/s00330-019-06163-2.

5

Segmentation techniques for the diagnosis of intervertebral disc diseases

Bazila Hashia and Ajaz Hussain Mir

Department of Electronics and Communication Engineering, National Institute of Technology Srinagar, Srinagar, Jammu and Kashmir, India

Chapter Outline

5.1   Introduction

A lot of work has been done on the diagnosis and treatment planning of the abnormalities of the spine, especially on the segmentation of spinal anatomy, either as an end-goal in itself or as a part of a processing course. These proposed techniques are reviewed here. In segmentation of spinal anatomy there comes segmentation of vertebra, intervertebral discs, and spinal cord. As per the structure of the spine there is a boundary which vertebra and discs do share called as endplate and also there is a common vertical boundary with the spinal cord. So, the segmentation of either of the two, vertebra or the disc consists of repetition of the endplate and the segmentation of the spinal cord consists of repetition of its anterior boundary. Since magnetic resonance image (MRI) provides appreciable soft tissue contrast and is a very useful modality for disc disease

Advances in Computational Techniques for Biomedical Image Analysis. DOI: https://doi.org/10.1016/B978-0-12-820024-7.00005-0

diagnosis so disc segmentation has been mainly done on MRI (Liu et al., 2018; Dong and Zheng, 2016). Also MRI provides clear boundaries of the anterior and the posterior parts, whereas they are nearly imperceptible in computed tomography (CT). But some work has been done on disc segmentation of CT images also, for example, by Korez et al. (2015) for prosthetic disc mold design. As far as the dimensionality of the dataset is concerned, segmentation has been done on both two-dimensional (2D) and three-dimensional (3D) datasets, also both 2D and 3D algorithms have been used. In MRI, 3D and 2D methods are both used equally, whereas, in CT, almost all spinal segmentation methods work in 3D. Full vertebra are being segmented using CT rather than MRI, as the complex posterior elements lack clear boundaries with ligaments and adipose tissue in MRI. MRIs are usually used for disc segmentation for various disc disease diagnoses. For disc segmentation usually 2D methods are used because only one slice is required for the diagnosis of different diseases and also 2D methods are simple and fast. 3D methods are definitely more accurate and robust but at the cost of computational time and implementation complexity (Carballido-Gamio et al., 2004; Castro-mateos et al., 2014). Also 2D methods work in sagittal view which is most commonly used for disc herniation diagnosis, very rarely axial, coronel views are used (Alomari et al., 2010). Different computer vision methods have been applied for spine segmentation, (vertebra, disc, and spinal cord). Some methods are directly from computer vision, for example, Kelm et al. (2012) and some are made suitable to work for the spine segmentation task such as by Law et al. (2013). The methods being proposed and implemented are broadly from four different categories: Firstly, curve evolution methods, for example, snake, active contour model (ACM), level sets, applied mostly for disc segmentation in magnetic resonance (MR) images. For example, Alomari et al. (2010), Law et al. (2013), and Castro-mateos et al. (2014). Secondly graph-based methods, for example, graph cuts, Boykov and Jolly (2001), or normalized cuts, Shi and Malik (2000) have been used mostly for vertebral and sometimes for intervertebral disc segmentation, in both 2D and 3D, MRI and CT. Thirdly a number of deformable models have been applied by Ma and Lu (2013) mostly for 3D full vertebra segmentation in CT and very rarely for MRI as in Kadoury et al. (2013). Fourth: there are some low-level 2D image processing methods such as (1) watersheds by Chevrefils et al. (2007), (2) Hough transform by Shi et al. (2016), (3) tree-based classification by Ghosh et al. (2014). Segmentation is usually performed on image cues, such as region information, boundary information, and neighborhood information. For assessment of an intervertebral disc segmentation performance of a given method the following things are required, firstly a large number of scans, secondly, a range of different image protocols, thirdly good quality golden standard for assessment which can help in intervertebral disc degeneration diagnosis.

5.2 Intervertebral disc segmentation techniques

The intervertebral disc degeneration diagnosis has been mostly achieved by segmentation and executed on MR images, encouraged by the unique property of MRI for soft-tissue diagnosis. Intervertebral disc segmentation has been mostly performed on 2D slices, and in very few cases of 3D. Even though alot of work has been done on intervertebral disc segmentation it is still an unsolved issue, particularly for diseased discs. Also disc segmentation is considered to be more challenging rather than vertebra segmentation because (1) intervertebral discs are soft tissue parts of the spine and exhibit more variation of signal and shape, mostly due to diseases of the intervertebral disc compared to the vertebrae, (2) annulus fibrosus shows the same intensity as blood vessels, ligaments, and muscles in T2 weighted images, so the lateral boundaries of discs are more kind of invisible than those of the vertebrae. Also because of this there is an appreciable inter and intra observer variation in manual segmentation, that is, the golden standard. It has been found by Haq et al. (2014) that there is mean 0.265 mm intra and 0.285 inter observer variations in mean surface distance, and most of the variations where in the lateral region of the ambiguous boundaries of the disc.

Even though a lot of work has been done on disc segmentation and a number of papers published have attained almost 90% dice similarity index (DSI), good results haven't been able to be produced on proper diseased discs. In particular, herniated disc segmentation is still considered to be an irresolvable problem.

Michopoulou et al. (2008, 2009), Ayed et al. (2011), Lootus et al. (2014), Alomari et al. (2010), Chaudhary and Dhillon (2011), Yao et al. (2014), Ghosh et al. (2011a, 2011b, 2014), Castro-mateos et al. (2014), Oktay et al. (2014), Chevrefils et al. (2007, 2009), Shi et al. (2007), Wang et al. (2015), and Seifert et al. (2009) have done disc segmentation on 2D MRI slices.

Alomari et al. (2010), Chaudhary and Dhillon (2011), and Yao et al. (2014) have used contour evolution active shape mode (ASM) and snake models to segment the disc for herniation prediction, also Ghosh et al. (2011a,b) used similar methods for disc bounding box refinement, and leading to herniation prediction. Alomari et al. (2010), Ghosh et al. (2011a, b) used ASM of Cootes et al. (1995); Chaudhary and Dhillon (2011) used gradient vector flow (GVF) snake of Xu and Prince (2000); whereas Yao et al. (2014) used first ASM for the whole disc, and then GVF snake for the posterior section of the disc. The work in these papers has been done on the scans with fixed, known field of view. Oktay et al. (2014) performed segmentation on 102 subjects, 612 discs (349 normal, 263 with degenerative disc disease) in a fully automatic measurement pipeline using active appearance models, Cootes et al. (1995), preceding automated Pfirrmann grading. The segmentation performance of these 2D approaches has not been published since the segmentation has been performed as a part of the diagnosis course, not as an end product.

Ayed et al. (2011), Seifert et al. (2009), Law et al. (2013), Castro-mateos et al. (2014), Wang et al. (2015) used 2D MRI disc segmentation approaches which do provide quantified results and they all cite performance of about 90% of DSI coefficient. Even though they have been citing very good DSI coefficient percentage, they still have not been able to do proper segmentation of diseased discs, especially herniated intervertebral disc segmentation. Also high DSI coefficient is not being considered as an appropriate measure to evaluate the segmentation of diseased discs.

Law et al. (2013) have proposed a novel method of level sets that uses an anisotropic oriented flux detection for distinguishing discs and its neighboring parts, which have similar intensities, also to perceive unclear disc boundaries and supervise the shape and intensity deviation of the discs. It starts with tracking of vertebral body and gets knowledge about position and orientations of the target intervertebral discs using minimal user interaction. The disc segmentation result is described by an energy function, which is defined by the image descriptors formed by the information gathered by the position and orientations of the intervertebral discs. ACM is used for disc segmentation. Sixty-nine mid-sagittal slices are evaluated and 455 intervertebral discs are extracted to implement this proposed system. Under evaluation, they categorize discs according to their disease state into four categories: (1) 110 normal, (2) 109 degeneration, (3) 310 extrusion, herniation, protrusion, and bulging, (4) 74 both (2) and (3), with DSI coefficients (1) 0.92; (2) 0.91; (3) 0.92; (4) 0.91 however with significantly lower mean-square boundary errors for normal (0.8 mm) than for categories (2)−(4) (1.2, 1.0, and 1.0). Since their method is evaluated in the mid-sagittal slices yet the disease state may appear in other slices, the influence of disease may be masked.

Ayed et al. (2011) have worked on intervertebral disc segmentation in MR images of lumbar spine and have used novel object interaction priors for graph cut segmentation. There is a cost function which is optimized by the algorithm inhibiting the solution attained with preceding knowledge about the geometric interactions between different elements in the image. The proposed prototypes are fundamentally constant with respect to translation and rotation when global measure of similarity between distributions is taken into consideration. Scale invariance has been achieved with very few fast computations, by introducing a scale variable which helps in deriving an original fixed point equation. The need of large training sets and of costly pretension of estimation or registration is eliminated by the proposed prototypes and also tolerance for shape deformations was enhanced. Ten subjects were studied and from them 60 intervertebral discs were extracted, and their quantitative evaluation yielded a high correlation with independent manual segmentation by an expert. On 10 subjects, 60 disc cross-sections, each from a unique disc using manual initialization with three points per disc used graph cuts with elliptical shape priors and obtained a mean DSI score of 0.88.

Wang et al. (2015) proposed a novel M^3 approach in which they took multiple anatomic structures in multiple anatomic planes from multiple imaging modalities and introduced regression segmentation for the first time., of spinal images in one single unified framework. In this framework segmentation is taken as a boundary regression problem where the desired object boundaries are directly mapped from a highly nonlinear mapping function from diverse M^3 images. The concept of multidimensional support vector regressor is utilized and the advancement of sparse kernel machines is fully utilized making it possible to work in a high dimensional feature space where M^3 diversity and specificity can be systematically categorized, extracted and handled. One hundred and thirteen clinical subjects were studied and the proposed regression segmentation has been implemented on both disc and vertebral structures, in sagittal and axial planes and from both MRI and CT modalities. High DSI of 0.912 and low boundary distance of 0.928 mm were achieved. Each segmentation takes around 0.1 seconds on a laptop. They initialize the segmentation based on manually cropped images and the segmentation was still inaccurate on herniated areas.

Seifert et al. (2009) have proposed a reconstruction algorithm for cervical structures and it is completely an automatic algorithm. They used a very straightforward process of anatomical knowledge this concept can be implemented to other tissues of the human body. Discs are located via an object recognition approach as initial landmarks hence no seed points are required. There are already segmented vertebrae and by the surface analysis the spinal musculature is reconstructed and hence it can be used in biomechanical simulation. Both the discs and the spinal cord in the cervical spines of nine patients are segmented. They first use four open snakes for approximate, and then ASMs combined with fuzzy connectedness algorithm for more precise segmentations. Their ASMs for discs include a mean disc shape model along with gray-level profiles. They achieve 91% average DSI score. Their segmentation is initialized using automated disc detection.

Castro-mateos et al. (2014) used active contour models, with a new geometrical energy for initial segmentation, which is then again improvised using fuzzy C-means. They present an automatic classification method, which provided the Pfirrmann degree of degeneration from a mid-sagittal MR slice. AdaBoost is being employed on five specific features: the mean and the variance of the probability map of the nucleus using two different approaches and the eccentricity of the fitting ellipse to the contour of the intervertebral disc to attain classification. One hundred and fifty intervertebral discs were assessed by three experts, resulting in a mean specificity (93%) and sensitivity (83%) similar to the one provided by every expert with respect to the most voted value. DSI and root mean square error (RMSE) of the point-to-contour distance were used to evaluate the segmentation accuracy. The mean DSI ± 2 standard deviation was 91:7% $\pm$ 5:6%, the mean RMSE was 0:82 mm and the 95 percentile was 1:36 mm. These results were found accurate when compared to the state-of-the-art.

Shi et al. (2007) used Hough transform to locate spinal cord and introduced an intervertebral disks segmentation algorithm with which discs are located and labeled. The algorithm was run on the data of 50 patients which could not provide quantified results but they claimed that it was satisfactory on 48 out of the 50 patients, with 96%.

Chevrefils et al. (2007) proposed a Watershed segmentation approach and ran it on four patients with various levels of scoliosis but did not provided quantified results. Based on their results as shown on the figures of the examples in the paper, the method seems to suffer from over-segmentation.

Haq et al. (2014) considered herniated discs are explicitly. A shape model is used only for healthy discs, and switched off manually for deformed discs, in order to still allow for accurate segmentation. In their method, they utilized image gradient forces and accordingly deformed an ellipsoidal simplex template in a disc image boundary using landmark based registration. They studied and segmented 16 normal discs automatically, and 5 abnormal discs with minimal supervision as required, for example, placing points to guide the segmentation.

Neubert et al. (2012) segmented intervertebral discs in 3D MR images using a statistical shape model, initialized by manually placed points. Their model is learned on the training set and tested on 42 scans, achieving a DSI score of 89% on normal and degenerated discs. Uniquely in CT, Korez et al. (2015) used a 3D parametric super quadric disc shape model to segment the discs, initialized by segmentations of the vertebrae, obtained according to Stern et al. (2011). Kelm et al. (2012) segmented discs in both 3D MRI and CT using graph cuts, initialized by seeds obtained by vertebrae segmentations however they do not disclose quantified segmentation performances.

The review of the methods used to diagnose herniated intervertebral discs is given in the next section.

5.3 Herniated intervertebral disc segmentation techniques

Three principal sets of methods have been used in literature for automatic classification of herniated and normal discs in the sagittal plane of MR images, and they are:

1. Alomari et al. (2010), Chaudhary and Dhillon (2011), and Yao et al. (2014) based on the shape of the full segmented disc boundary in 2D slices;
2. Koh et al. (2010, 2012) based on the percentage of manually segmented vertebrae, disc, and sacrum voxels in a manually placed box at the posterior side of the disc, and
3. Ghosh et al. (2011a,b) based on a number of image features extracted from a rectangle covering the disc.

Alomari et al. (2010) measured herniation based on two shape features (distance between ASM points approximately corresponding to the sum of the height and width of the disc, and the height of the disc at the posterior third), and two intensity features (the mean and standard deviation values of a Gaussian fitted to the disc intensities in the segmented disc). Chaudhary and Dhillon (2011) used very similar shape features, in T2-SPIR, except they are extracted from snake segmentation which according to their figures segments the nuclear disc boundary. They do not use intensity features. The snake segmentations are initialized using a point automatically placed into the disc using the method of Corso et al. (2008). Yao et al. (2014) once again used only two shape features however those are one corresponding to disc width from the ASM segmentation, and another is the segmented herniated boundary length from the gradient vector flow snake segmentation of the posterior side of the disc.

Koh et al. (2012) performed extensive, fully manual annotation: they segment the discs, the vertebrae, and the dural sac, and place 27 landmark points per disc to define a region of interest (ROI)—a box in the posterior region of the disc. They are used as features the percentage of vertebra, disc, and spinal cord voxels in the box. They do not specify which slice is used in the analysis, or how they are selected (automatically or manually).

Ghosh et al. (2011a,b) used a probabilistic model for automatic disc localization and labeling in all sagittal slices according to Corso et al. (2008), resulting in a point inside each disc. Next, the disc orientation is found according to the angle of the corresponding axial images. Note that this approach will not work in studies where axial images do not follow the angle of the spine, or where axial images are unavailable. They then initialize an ASM segmenter based on these localizations, and place a rectangular support region by eroding the tight bounding box of the segmentations. Ghosh et al. (2011a) use the gray-level co-occurrence matrix (GLCM), Haralick (1979) features: divide the region into eight spatial bins and extract intensity (mean, min, max, etc.), and texture features (contrast, correlation, energy, homogeneity, entropy) from the bins, and in addition the height-width ratio of the box as shape feature. They find the highest classification accuracy with a majority vote classification scheme. Ghosh et al. (2011b) additionally to GLCM experimented with raw (similar to ours), local binary pattern, Gabor, and additional intensity and shape features extracted from the whole region (rather than each bin individually). All those approaches classify discs based on sagittal slice (s) into two categories: herniated versus normal, based on analysis of one slice, Yao et al. (2014) manually selected the slice where herniation is both visible or more slices, Chaudhary and Dhillon (2011) ran the classifier independently in all slices and if at least one slice is found herniated, the disc is classified as herniated independently. However, often a disc may be bulged instead of herniated, and yet be indistinguishable from herniation based on such classification. Alomari et al. (2010) does not disclose on which slice(s) the analysis is performed.

Alawneh et al. (2015) proposed a computer aided diagnosis system for lumbar disc hernia and tried to extract the ROI by adaptive thresholding and determining the ROI horizontally, which means top-down MRI scans were used instead of the sagittal view, with a fixed displacement before and after the closest point to the spine. Later ROI was enhanced by CLAHE, followed by feature extraction by skeletonization.

The limited work that has been done on the segmentation of the herniated discs is illustrated in Table 5.1. The accuracy and the level of the automaticity of the disc herniation diagnosis done previously are also mentioned in the table.

Table 5.1 Illustration of the accuracy and level of automaticity of the previous work on herniation diagnosis.

S. No.	Authors	Images	Image type	Accuracy (%)	Automaticity (slice, detection, and segmentation)
1.	Tsai et al. (2004)	16	Axial MRI or CT	Information not available	Fully manual
2.	Koh et al. (2010)	68	Sagittal T2	97	Fully manual
3.	Koh et al. (2012)	70	Sagittal T2	99	Fully manual
4.	Ghosh et al. (2011b)	35	Sagittal T2-SPIR	98.3	Mid scan, axial interaction, and automatic segmentation
5.	Ghosh et al. (2011a)	35	Sagittal T2-SPIR	94.9	Mid scan, axial interaction, and automatic segmentation
6.	Alomari et al. (2010a)	33	Sagittal T2-SPIR	91	Manual selection, information not available, and information not available
7.	Alomari et al. (2011b)	65	Sagittal T2-SPIR	92.5	All slices, information not available, and automatic segmentation
8.	Alomari et al. (2013)	65	Sagittal T1-T2	93.9	Manual selection, information not available, and automatic segmentation
9.	Alawneh et al. (2015)	32	Axial MRI	100	Information not available
10.	Al Kafri et al. (2017)	NA	Axial MRI	NA	Automatic

Al Kafri et al. (2017) used the concept of gray level and pixel locations as featured and did automatic labeling of lumbar spine disc pixels that too in axial view of MR spine images. Training and testing has been done on clinical MR images of spine. The performance of their method is indicated by the accuracy of pixel classification and the quality of the reconstructed disc images. 91.1% and 98.9% of classification accuracy has been acquired using weighted k-nearest neighbor (KNN) and Gaussian support vector machine classifiers, respectively.

5.4 Challenges in the segmentation of the vertebra and intervertebral discs

5.4.1 Challenges of spinal magnetic resonance imaging

The basic three types of challenges to spinal MRI analysis are:

1. Imaging limitations—MR images have low in-slice resolution as they tend to have meager slice spacing. And this is because of characteristic trade-off between scan acquisition time, signal-to-noise ratio, and image resolution in MRI. For example, in case of disc herniation, the displaced disc material may only be visible as a partial volume challenging both delineation and the diagnosis tasks.
2. Anatomical and pathological patient variation—The anatomical structures in the spine, such as vertebrae and discs show very wide variation, with the result their detection and delineation becomes very difficult. Also the pathological abnormalities have many deviations and therefore are tough to model and recognize across patients.
3. Inter-observer variability—It is not that easy to draw the line with which we can classify any anatomy as normal or abnormal because many conditions exist as interminable continuum of severity.

5.4.2 Challenges in the segmentation of the vertebra and intervertebral discs

The main challenges are: (1) intensity similarity—lack of visible boundary between the ligamentous annulus in discs, and the surrounding anatomy, either adjacent or connecting to the disc (particularly ligaments, vessels, muscles, and nerves);

(2) partial volumes—due to high slice thickness (median across dataset of 4 mm, vs median intra-slice pixel size of 0.7 mm), (3) Large shape and texture variation because of developmental variants and diseases such as degeneration, herniation, and endplate defects; (4) Confusion between image features manifestation reasons [e.g., a bright spot could be either a high intensity zone disc or limbus vertebra] or an imaging artefact; and (5) other image quality problems such as imaging noise, contrast variation, and other artifacts.

5.5 Conclusion and future work

In none of the above approaches bulge is considered as an option. It is not mentioned whether bulged discs are included in the studies. Unlike, Tsai et al. (2002) considered a number of axial slices (one or more per disc), segmenting the disc manually, and proposing features to describe the 3D geometry of the disc, to distinguish normal, herniated, and bulged discs. They fitted a B-spline model to approximate the normal disc curvature, and measured the local deviation from the normal curvature to detect herniation. However, they did not learn the model parameters nor report classification performances in comparison to a radiologist, and note that the method as is does not apply to discs that are not roughly round, or belong to aged patients.

Disc pathology, especially herniation, generally varies widely across patients and thus cannot be represented well only by strong shape prior models, and hence its detection remains an unsolved and somewhat ill-defined problem. Most of the methods only work in a single 2D slice and involve manual initialization. Since the disc boundaries smoothly morph into their surrounding ligaments which are often indistinguishable from the annulus of the disc, the task remains very challenging.

A step towards the objective of the detection of herniated intervertebral discs can be achieved in the future work by making an attempt to make use of texture features for classification of herniated intervertebral discs. In addition to the disc analysis, segmentation review could be extended to the other parts of the spine, such as vertebrae, spinal cord, ligaments, and muscles. Detection and segmentation could be performed on all these parts of the spine for diagnosis of a broader range of conditions.

References

Al Kafri, A.S., et al., 2017. Intelligent computing methodologies,10363, 107–116.

Alawneh, K., Al-dwiekat, M., Alsmirat, M., Al-Ayyoub, M., 2015. Computer-aided diagnosis of lumbar disc herniation. In: 2015 6th International Conference on Information and Communication Systems (ICICS), pp. 286–291. Available from: https://doi.org/10.1109/IACS.2015.7103190.

Alomari, R.S., Corso, J.J., Chaudhary, V., Dhillon, G., 2010. Automatic diagnosis of lumbar disc herniation with shape and appearance features from MRI. Prog. Biomed. Opt. Imaging 11, 76241A. Available from: https://doi.org/10.1117/12.842199.

Alomari, R.S., Corso, J.J., Chaudhary, V., Dhillon, G., , 2010a. Automatic diagnosis of lumbar disc herniation with shape and appearance features from MRI. *Prog. Biomed. Opt. imaging.* 11, 76241A–76241A.

Alomari, R.S., Chaudhary, V., Dhillon, G., 2011b. Toward a clinical lumbar CAD: herniation diagnosis, 119–126.

Ayed, I.B., Punithakumar, K., Garvin, G., 2011. Graph cuts with invariant object-interaction priors: application to intervertebral disc segmentation. Inf. Process. Med. Imaging 22, 221–232.

Boykov, Y.Y., Jolly, M-P., 2001. Interactive graph cuts for optimal boundary and region segmentation of objects in N-D images. In: Proceedings Eighth IEEE International Conference on Computer Vision. ICCV 2001, July, IEEE, pp. 105–112.

Carballido-Gamio, J., Belongie, S.J., Majumdar, S., 2004. Normalized cuts in 3-D for spinal MRI segmentation. IEEE Trans. Med. Imaging 23 (1), 36–44. Available from: https://doi.org/10.1109/TMI.2003.819929.

Castro-mateos, I., Pozo, J.M., Lazary, A., Frangi, A.F., 2014. 2D segmentation of intervertebral discs and its degree of degeneration from T2-weighted magnetic resonance images In: Proceedings of SPIE, vol. 9035 (figure 1), pp. 1–11. Available from: https://doi.org/10.1117/12.2043755.

Chaudhary, V., Dhillon, G., 2011. Toward a clinical lumbar CAD: herniation diagnosis. Int. J. Comput. Assist. Radiol. Surg. 6 (1), 119–126. Available from: https://doi.org/10.1007/s11548-010-0487-7.

Chevrefils, C., Chériet, F., Grimard, G., Aubin, C.-E., 2007. Watershed segmentation of intervertebral disk and spinal canal from MRI images. Image Anal. Recognit. 4633 (3), 1017–1027. Available from: https://doi.org/10.1007/978-3-540-74260-9.

Chevrefils, C., Cheriet, F., Aubin, C.-E., Grimard, G., 2009. Texture analysis for automatic segmentation of intervertebral\ndisks of scoliotic spines from MR images. IEEE Trans. Inf. Technol. Biomed. 13 (4), 608–620.

Corso, J.J., Alomari, R.S., Chaudhary, V., 2008. Lumbar disc localization and labeling with a probabilistic model on both pixel and object features. In: Medical Image Computing and Computer-Assisted Intervention – MICCAI 2008. Lecture Notes in Computer Science (Including Subseries Lecture Notes in Artificial Intelligence and Lecture Notes in Bioinformatics), vol. 5241 LNCS (PART 1). Springer, Berlin, pp. 202–210. Available from: https://doi.org/10.1007/978-3-540-85988-8_25

Dong, X., Zheng, G., 2016. Automated 3D lumbar intervertebral disc segmentation from MRI data sets. In: Computational Radiology for Orthopaedic Interventions. Lecture Notes in Computational Vision and Biomechanics, vol. 23. Springer, Cham, pp. 25–41. Available from: https://doi.org/10.1007/978-3-319-23482-3.

Ghosh, S., Alomari, R.S., Chaudhary, V., Dhillon, G., 2011a. Composite features for automatic diagnosis of intervertebral disc herniation from lumbar MRI. In: Proceedings of the Annual International Conference of the IEEE

Engineering in Medicine and Biology Society, EMBS (MD), pp. 5068−5071. Available from: https://doi.org/10.1109/IEMBS.2011.6091255.

Ghosh, S., Alomari, R.S., Chaudhary, V., Dhillon, G., 2011b. Computer-aided diagnosis for lumbar mri using heterogeneous classifiers. In: Proceedings of International Symposium on Biomedical Imaging, pp. 1179−1182. Available from: https://doi.org/10.1109/ISBI.2011.5872612.

Ghosh, S., Malgireddy, M.R., Chaudhary, V., Dhillon, G., 2014. Segmentation of clinical MRI for automatic lumbar diagnosis. In: Proceedings of the Workshop held at the 16th International Conference on Medical Image Computing and Computer Assisted Intervention, pp. 185−195. Available from: https://doi.org/10.1007/978-3-319-07269-2.

Haq, R., Aras, R., Besachio, D.A., Borgie, R.C., Audette, M.A., 2014. 3D lumbar spine intervertebral disc segmentation and compression simulation from MRI using shape-aware models. Int. J. Comput. Assist. Radiol. Surg. 10, 45−54. Available from: https://doi.org/10.1007/s11548-014-1094-9..

Haralick, R.M., 1979. Statistical and structural approach to texture. Proc. IEEE 67 (5), 786−804. Available from: https://doi.org/10.1109/PROC.1979.11328.

Kadoury, S., Labelle, H., Paragios, N., 2013. Spine segmentation in medical images using manifold embeddings and higher-order MRFs. IEEE Trans. Med. Imaging 32 (7), 1227−1238.

Kelm, B.M., Wels, M., Zhou, S.K., Seifert, S., Suehling, M., Zheng, Y., 2012. Spine detection in CT and MR using iterated marginal space learning. Med. Image Anal. 17 (8), 1283−1292. Available from: https://doi.org/10.1016/j.media.2012.09.007.

Koh, J., Chaudhary, V., Dhillon, G., 2010. Diagnosis of disc herniation based on classifiers and features generated from spine MR images. SPIE Med. Imaging Comput. Aided Diagn. 7624, 762430-1−762430-8. Available from: https://doi.org/10.1117/12.844386.

Koh, J., Chaudhary, V., Dhillon, G., 2012. Disc herniation diagnosis in MRI using a CAD framework and a two-level classifier. Int. J. Comput. Assist. Radiol. Surg. 7 (6), 861−869. Available from: https://doi.org/10.1007/s11548-012-0674-9.

Korez, R., Ibragimov, B., Likar, B., Pernus, F., Vrtovec, T., 2015. A framework for automated spine and vertebrae segmentation. IEEE Trans. Med. Imaging 34 (8), 1649−1666. Available from: https://doi.org/10.1109/TMI.2015.2389334.

Law, M.W.K., Tay, K.Y., Leung, A., Garvin, G.J., Li, S., 2013. Intervertebral disc segmentation in MR images using anisotropic oriented flux. Med. Image Anal. 17 (1), 43−61. Available from: https://doi.org/10.1016/j.media.2012.06.006.

Liu, J., Pan, Y., Li, M., Chen, Z., Tang, L., Lu, C., et al., 2018. Applications of deep learning to MRI images: a survey. Big Data Min. Anal. 1 (1), 1−18. Available from: https://doi.org/10.26599/BDMA.2018.9020001.

Lootus, M., Kadir, T., Zisserman, A., 2014. Automated radiological grading of spinal MRI. In: Recent Advances in Computational Methods and Clinical Applications for Spine Imaging. Lecture Notes in Computational Vision and Biomechanics, vol. 20. Springer, Cham, pp. 1−12.

Ma, J., Lu, L., 2013. Hierarchical segmentation and identification of thoracic vertebra using learning-based edge detection and coarse-to-fine deformable model. Comput. Vis. Image Und. 117 (9), 1072−1083. Available from: https://doi.org/10.1016/j.cviu.2012.11.016.

Michopoulou, S., Costaridou, L., Panagiotopoulos, E., Speller, R., Todd-pokropek, A., 2008. Segmenting degenerated lumbar intervertebral discs from MR images In: Proceedings of IEEE Nuclear Science Symposium and Medical Imaging Conference, pp. 4536–4539.

Michopoulou, S.K., Costaridou, L., Panagiotopoulos, E., Speller, R., Panayiotakis, G., Todd-Pokropek, A., 2009. Atlas-based segmentation of degenerated lumbar intervertebral discs from MR images of the spine. IEEE Trans. Biomed. Eng. 56 (9), 2225–2231. Available from: https://doi.org/10.1109/ TBME.2009.2019765.

Neubert, A., Fripp, J., Engstrom, C., Schwarz, R., Lauer, L., Salvado, O., et al., 2012. Automated detection, 3D segmentation and analysis of high resolution spine MR images using statistical shape models. Phys. Med. Biol. 57 (24), 8357–8376.

Oktay, A.B., Albayrak, N.B., Akgul, Y.S., 2014. Computer aided diagnosis of degenerative intervertebral disc diseases from lumbar MR images. Comput. Med. Imaging Graph. 38 (7), 613–619. Available from: https://doi.org/ 10.1016/j.compmedimag.2014.04.006.

Ootes, T.F.C., Aylor, C.J.T., Ooper, D.H.C., Graham, J., 1995. Active shape models— their training and application. Comput. Vis. Image Underst. 61 (1), 38–59.

Seifert, S., Wächter, I., Schmelzle, G., Dillmann, R., 2009. A knowledge-based approach to soft tissue reconstruction of the cervical spine. IEEE Trans. Med. Imaging 28 (4), 494–507.

Shi, J., Malik, J., 2000. Normalized cuts and image segmentation. IEEE Trans. Pattern Anal. Mach. Intell. 22 (8), 888–905.

Shi, R., Sun, D., Qiu, Z., Weiss, K.L., 2007. An efficient method for segmentation of MRI spine images. In: 2007 IEEE/ICME International Conference on Complex Medical Engineering, CME 2007, May, pp. 713–717. Available from: https://doi.org/10.1109/ICCME.2007.4381830.

Shi, R., Sun, D., Qiu, Z., Weiss, K.L., 2016. An efficient method for segmentation of MRI spine images. In: 2007 IEEE/ICME International Conference on Complex Medical Engineering, June 2007. Available from: https://doi.org/ 10.1109/ICCME.2007.4381830.

Stern, D., Likar, B., Pernus, F., Vrtovec, T., 2011. Parametric modelling and segmentation of vertebral bodies in 3D CT and MR spine images. Phys. Med. Biol. 56 (23), 7505–7522. Available from: https://doi.org/10.1088/0031-9155/ 56/23/011.

Tsai, M.D., Der Yeh, Y., Hsieh, M.S., Tsai, C.H., 2004. Automatic spinal disease diagnoses assisted by 3D unaligned transverse CT slices. Comput. Med. Imaging Graph, 28 (6), 307–319.

Tsai, M.D., Jou, S.B., Hsieh, M.S., 2002. A new method for lumbar herniated inter-vertebral disc diagnosis based on image analysis of transverse sections. Comput. Med. Imaging Graph. 26 (6), 369–380. Available from: https://doi. org/10.1016/S0895-6111(02)00033-2.

Wang, Z., Zhen, X., Tay, K.Y., Osman, S., Romano, W., Li, S., 2015. Regression segmentation for M3 spinal images. IEEE Tran. Med. Imaging 34 (8), 1640–1648.

Xu, C., Prince, J.L., 2000. Gradient vector flow deformable models In: Handbook of Medical Imaging. Academic Press, New York, p. 159.

Yao, J., Klinder, T., Li, S., 2014. Computational methods and clinical applications for spine imaging. In: Proceedings of the Workshop held at the 16th International Conference on Medical Image Computing and Computer Assisted Intervention, September 22–26, 2013, Nagoya, Japan. *Lect. Notes Comput. Vis. Biomech*, vol. 17. Available from: https://doi.org/10.1007/978-3-319-07269-2.

Medical Image Classification and Analysis

Heartbeat sound classification using Mel-frequency cepstral coefficients and deep convolutional neural network

Shamik Tiwari, Varun Sapra and Anurag Jain

School of Computer Science, University of Petroleum & Energy Studies (UPES), Dehradun, India

6.1   Introduction

Audio recording of heartbeat sounds using a stethoscope during a cardiac cycle is generally called a phonocardiogram (PCG) signal. Phonocardiography is a suitable investigative mechanism for heartbeat analysis (Adithya et al., 2017). PCG assists cardiologists to envision the acoustic energies which are generated through the electromechanical aspect of cardiac activity. Cardiovascular auscultation is the primary and modest

Advances in Computational Techniques for Biomedical Image Analysis. DOI: https://doi.org/10.1016/B978-0-12-820024-7.00006-2

diagnosing mechanism performed to monitor the action and working of the heart. The prime cause of heart sound is owing to blood turbulence. Phonocardiography delivers the utmost appreciated qualitative and quantitative evidence of abnormal heart sounds, that is, heart murmurs. An enormous variance in the sound pattern can be established among a normal heart sound signal and murmur heart sound PCG signal as their signals differ from each other pertaining to amplitude, intensity, time, spectral content, homogeneity, etc. (Gharehbaghi et al., 2015).

The Mel-frequency cepstral coefficients (MFCC) as a feature extraction scheme are a prominent scheme for audio signals. A discrete cosine transform (DCT) plays an important role in calculation of MFCC features (Dahake et al., 2016). It states a finite series of data points as a sum of cosine functions fluctuating at diverse frequencies. MFCC coefficients are given by a set of DCT decorrelated parameters that are computed from the transformed logarithmically compressed filter-output energies which are resulting from a perceptually spaced triangular filter bank, which processes the discrete Fourier transformed (DFT) audio signal. DCT works as a compression step. Usually with MFCCs, first DCT is applied on the input signal and only the first few coefficients are retained. This is principally the same intention that the DCT is used in Joint Photographic Experts Group compression. The other reason due to which DCT is preferred over DFT is that their boundary conditions work better on these types of signals. When you take the DCT and discard the higher coefficients, the signal can withstand relatively more coefficient truncation but still keep the desired shape due to the continuous periodic structure. It is corresponding to a DFT of approximately double the length, functioning on real data with uniform proportion (Bhalke et al., 2016). However, in a few alternatives the either or both input and output data are shifted by half a sample. Eight typical alternates of DCT basis function are available. Out of these eight variants, three are commonly used. The most common variant of DCT is the type-II DCT, which is regularly called basically DCT, the type-I DCT and the type-III DCT. In this work, three variants of DCT are considered for MFCC feature extraction and their impact is studied for heartbeat sound classification. The rest of the chapter is distributed into six sections. Section 6.2 offers literature review. Sections 6.3 and 6.4 discuss MFCC features and convolution neural network (CNN) respectively. The description of the heartbeat sound database is given in Section 6.5. Section 6.5 provides experiment details and results. The conclusion is provided in Section 6.7.

6.2 Literature review

Redlarski et al. (2014) have proposed an artificial intelligence-based heart sound classification method. The proposed model is able to categorize the input heart sound into eight different pathological and four normal heart sounds. By combining linear predictive coding coefficient with support vector machine classifier and modified cuckoo search algorithm, the authors have framed the model for heart sound classification. Further, they have compared it with four major classification methods and results have shown 93% accuracy. Kumar and Saha (2015) et al. have discussed PCG (digitized version of heart sound) signal usage to detect the heart condition. Authors have developed an integrated framework, which works in two stages. In the first stage framework fetches the artifact-free PCG signal. To achieve this authors have used discrete wavelet packet transform. In the second stage it forms the heart sound cycle segments which are later used for analysis purpose. Authors have also tested the framework on three different databases and framework has shown an accuracy around 90%.

Rubin et al. (2016) have used deep learning to detect abnormalities in heart sound. By combining the deep convolutional network with MFCC heat map, authors have devised heartbeat sound classification algorithm in normal and abnormal sound. Authors have used modified loss function for the training of the architecture. By submitting to 2016 PhysioNet computing, authors have evaluated their algorithm. Potes et al. (2016) have proposed a heart sound classifier by combining deep convolutional neural network (DCNN) and time frequency features. Proposed classifier categorizes heart sound into normal and abnormal sound. Rubin et al. (2017) have developed an algorithm for classifying heart sound into three classes: normal, abnormal, and uncertain respectively. First, authors have done the segmentation of heart sound. Second, using MFCC, one-dimensional (1D) waveform was transformed into two-dimensional (2D) time frequency heat map. In the third step, using deep CNN, MFCC heat map was classified. Rahmandani et al. (2018) have used heart sound to diagnose heart disease symptoms. It requires lots of concentration and expertise to diagnose abnormality in heart sound. Prior to their research, accuracy of model in diagnosis of heart disease through heart sound was 92%. To prepare their model, authors have used the data of heart sound from Michigan Sound Heart Database. To extract features and also for result classification from heart sound, authors have used artificial neural network (ANN) along with MFCCs. Authors have mentioned to achieve accuracy around 100%. To maximize accuracy, authors have used thirteen types of heart sound classification, which was two more than prior research work.

Noman et al. (2019) have proposed a framework for classification of heart sound through small segments of heartbeats. Authors have used DCNN for designing of the framework. First, authors have designed a 1D CNN model to learn features from heart sound signal. Second, authors have designed 2D CNN model, which takes input of 2D time frequency feature based on MFCCs. Finally, authors have combined the 1D and 2D CNN model. Authors have compared the accuracy of the proposed model with traditional classifier models based on hidden Markov model and support vector machine. Through simulation, authors have shown that their hybrid model outperforms the models based on the traditional classifier models.

6.3   Mel-frequency cepstral coefficients

MFCC feature extraction emphasizes on the perceptually significant characteristics of the audio spectrum. The MFCC feature extraction process depends on the following six major steps (Zheng et al., 2001):

1. Preemphasis: this step is used to amplify the high frequencies by passing the audio signal through high pass filter.
2. Framing: in this step, audio signals are divided into overlapped frames. This framing is performed to capture local spectral properties.
3. Windowing: to minimize discontinuities at edges, windowing is performed on frames. Hamming windowing is widely acceptable method.
4. DFT: after windowing, fast Fourier transform is applied to the audio signal to transform time domain signal to frequency domain signal.
5. Mel-frequency warping: this step is used to estimate, amount of energy occurs in numerous areas of the frequency domain. The *mel* scale is a measure of pitches recognized by human auditory system to be identical in space from each other. The reference point between normal frequency and this *mel* scale is given by associating 1000 Hz tone, 40 dB above the auditor's threshold, using a pitch of 1000 mels. This nonlinear outcome to frequencies is computed by the mel-scale.

6. Log compression and discrete cosine transforming: After getting the filter bank energies, the logarithmic function is used. It uses inverse fast Fourier transform in the final stage. The MFCC feature extraction applies the DCT on the calculated logarithm of the energies. So, MFCC(n) is calculated as:

$$M(f) = 1125 log\left(1 + \frac{f}{700}\right) \qquad (6.1)$$

where f is the frequency term, and $M(f)$ is the corresponding mel-scale frequency. The energy is then assessed over a set of overlapped mel-filter banks by calculating the power spectrum of the audio signal and then adding up the energies in respectively filter bank area.

$$\text{MFCC}(n) = \frac{1}{T}\sum_{r=1}^{R} log[\text{MF}(t)] cos\left[\frac{2\pi}{T}\left(r + \frac{1}{2}\right)n\right] \qquad (6.2)$$

where MFCC(n) is the nth MFCC coefficient computed from a specific audio section via T triangular filters and MF(t) is the mel-spectrum of the tth filter.

6.4 Convolution neural network

CNN is a kind of deep artificial neural network that is generally used for image processing jobs, for example, object detection and classification. CNN has a lot in common with other types of ANNs, including feed forward architecture and learning by back propagation. In feed forward network, the information passes only in a forward direction, from the input neurons, through the hidden nodes and to the output nodes. Back propagation is a proficient way of calculating the gradients of the loss function pertaining to the neural network parameters. CNNs are generally composed by a set of multiple layers that can be brought together by their specific roles (Tiwari, 2018a,b). A CNN mainly consists of three layers, namely convolution layer, pooling layer, and dense layer (fully connected layer).

Convolutional layers are the most important building blocks used in CNN. The convolution mathematical operation is performed in this layer. In continuous case, convolution of two functions f and g is given by:

$$(f \times g)(t) = \int_{-\infty}^{\infty} f(\tau)g(t - \tau)d\tau = \int_{-\infty}^{\infty} f(t - \tau)g(\tau)d\tau \qquad (6.3)$$

In discrete case the equivalent convolution operation is given by:

$$(f \times g)(n) = \sum_{m=-\infty}^{\infty} f(m)g(n-m) = \sum_{m=-\infty}^{\infty} f(n-m)g(m) \quad (6.4)$$

This 1D convolution can be extended to 2-D convolution for digital image as:

$$(f \times g)(x,y) = \sum_{m=-M}^{M} \sum_{n=-N}^{N} f(x-n, y-m)g(n,m) \quad (6.5)$$

In this case the function g is referred as filter or kernel applied to input image f.

The principle of 2D convolution is to move a convolution filter on the input image. The filter (kernel) moves by a number of pixels that is termed as stride. At each position, the convolution between the filter and the part of the image is achieved. The result is a two-dimensional array referred as feature map. After getting the feature map, it is passed through a nonlinear activation layer, such as Softmax, rectified linear unit (ReLU), randomized leaky ReLU, leaky ReLU, parameterized ReLU, and exponential linear units, etc. (Xu et al., 2015)

A pooling layer (subsampling layer) is another structural block of a CNN. The job of any pooling layer is to gradually decrease the spatial size of the activation map to lessen the number of parameters used for further computation. It works on each feature map independently. There are a various methods to implement pooling, but the most effective is max pooling.

Finally, a fully connected layer receives the results of the last pooling layer and uses them to categorize the image into a label. It is the actual component of CNN that performs the discriminative learning. It acts like a simple multi-layer perceptron that can learn weights and recognize an image class.

6.5 Heartbeat sound database

Heartbeat sound dataset consists of 176 sound recordings collected by PhysioNet (Goldberger et al., 2003) from a range of surroundings and patients. There are a total of three classes considered in the database namely artifact, normal, and murmur. The heartbeat sound database is separated into training and testing database with a ratio of 80:20 respectively. In the normal heartbeat sound class there are normal and healthy heart sounds. Heart murmurs generally result from an abnormal blood flow through the heart. An abnormal heart valve usually causes the murmur sound. In the artifact class there are an extensive range of dissimilar sounds, containing feedback squeals speech, music, echoes, and noise. There are typically no discernible heart sounds, and thus slight or no temporal periodicity at frequencies less than 195 Hz. This class is highly dissimilar from the other classes. It is significant to be competent enough to discriminate this class from the other three classes.

6.6   Experiments

Three separate heartbeat sound classification models using CNN are designed in this study. The three standard type of DCT basis are used to calculate MFCC features for each experiment. The CNN architecture consists of three convolutional layers followed by ReLu activation layer. The first layer has $64 - 3 \times 3$ convolution filters, the second layer has $128 - 3 \times 3$ convolution filters, and the last layer has $512 - 3 \times 3$ convolution filters. All these convolution layers are followed by max-pooling layers. All three max-pooling layers have a size of 2×2. The last layer is a fully connected layer, which consists of Softmax activation function with three units in the output layer, which are necessary for this multiclassification problem of three classes.

Overfitting is the most commonly encountered problem in the area of machine and deep learning. Various methods for regularization are used to get rid of overfitting such as data augmentation, batch normalization, early stopping, and dropout, etc. (Wan et al., 2013). The CNN model used in this study has utilized data augmentation and Gaussian dropout to design a regularized model.

Data augmentation is also applied over the MFCC images due to the low number of sample data. Five main types of data augmentation techniques are utilized which consist of shifting in both horizontal and vertical directions of 1 pixel, horizontal vertical flipping, rotations with 10 degrees, brightening, and zooming. The model is compiled with the learning parameters as in Table 6.1. Table 6.2 provides the learning hyper-parameters used in this model.

6.6.1   Experiment 1: Heartbeat sound classification with discrete cosine transform basis type-1

This experiment is conducted with DCT basis type-1. The MFCC features are calculated with type-1 DCT basis and passed

Table 6.1 Learning parameters.

Learning parameter	Value
Metric	Accuracy
Loss function	Categorical cross entropy
Optimizer	Adam

Table 6.2 Training hyper-parameters.

Training hyperparameter	Value
Learning rate	0.001
Epochs	50
Batch size	32
Gaussian dropout ratio	0.2

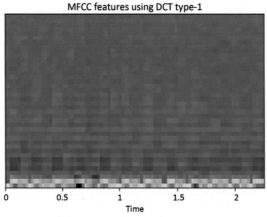

Figure 6.1 Mel-frequency cepstral coefficient (MFCC) spectrum with discrete cosine transform (DCT) type-1.

to CNN for learning and testing. Fig. 6.1 presents the plot of DCT basis type-1. The DCT basis function for type-1 is defined as (Milner and Vaseghi, 1995):

$$cos\,jk\frac{\pi}{N-1} \quad \left(\text{divide by } \sqrt{2} \text{ when } j \text{ or } k \text{ is } 0 \text{ or } N-1\right) \qquad (6.6)$$

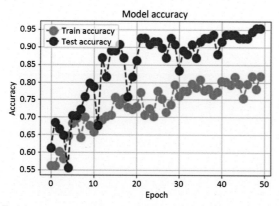

Figure 6.2 Training accuracy curve for heartbeat sound classification with discrete cosine transform (DCT) basis type-1.

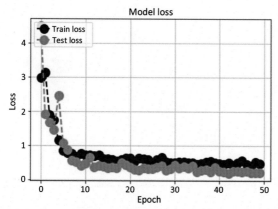

Figure 6.3 Training loss curve for heartbeat sound classification with discrete cosine transform (DCT) basis type-1.

The model is trained for 50 epochs. Fig. 6.2 shows training accuracy curve and Fig. 6.3 presents training loss curves for training and testing heartbeat sound database. Table 6.1 shows the confusion matrix. The precision, sensitivity, and $f1$-score performance metrics are calculated from the confusion matrix and presented in Table 6.2. The precision values are 0.91, 1.0, and 0.91 respectively for artifact, normal, and murmur heartbeat sound classes. The sensitivity values are 1.0, 0.87, and 1.0 respectively for artifact, normal, and murmur heartbeat sound classes. The $f1$-scores are 0.96, 0.93, and 0.95 respectively for artifact, normal, and murmur heartbeat sound classes. Test loss and test accuracy values are 0.21 and 0.95 respectively.

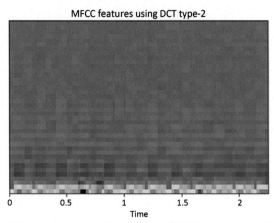

Figure 6.4 Mel-frequency cepstral coefficient (MFCC) spectrum with discrete cosine transform (DCT) type-2.

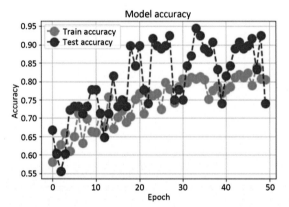

Figure 6.5 Training accuracy curve for heartbeat sound classification with discrete cosine transform (DCT) basis type-2.

6.6.2   Experiment 2: Heartbeat sound classification with discrete cosine transform basis type-2

This experiment is conducted with DCT basis type-2. The MFCC features are calculated with type-2 DCT basis and delivered to CNN for learning and testing. Fig. 6.4 presents the plot of DCT basis type-2. The DCT basis for type-2 is defined as:

$$cos\left(j + \frac{1}{2}\right)k\frac{\pi}{N} \quad \left(\text{divide by } \sqrt{2} \text{ when } k = 0\right) \qquad (6.7)$$

The model is trained for 50 epochs. Fig. 6.5 shows training accuracy curve and Fig. 6.6 presents training loss curves for

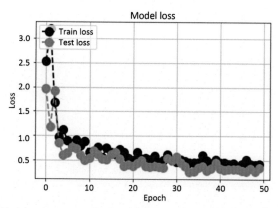

Figure 6.6 Training loss curve for heartbeat sound classification with discrete cosine transform (DCT) basis type-2.

training and testing heartbeat sound database. Table 6.1 shows the confusion matrix. The precision, sensitivity, and $f1$-score performance metrics are calculated from the confusion matrix and presented in Table 6.2. The precision values are 1.0, 0.71, and 0.39 respectively for artifact, normal, and murmur heartbeat sound classes. The sensitivity values are 0.92, 0.33, and 0.78 respectively for artifact, normal, and murmur heartbeat sound classes. The $f1$-scores are 0.96, 0.45, and 0.52 respectively for artifact, normal, and murmur heartbeat sound classes. Test loss and test accuracy values are 0.34 and 0.74 respectively.

6.6.3 Experiment 3: Heartbeat sound classification with discrete cosine transform basis type-3

The third experiment is conducted with DCT basis type-3. The MFCC features are calculated with type-3 DCT basis and supplied to CNN for learning and testing. Fig. 6.7 presents the plot of DCT basis type-3. The DCT basis for type-3 is defined as:

$$cos\, j\left(k + \frac{1}{2}\right)\frac{\pi}{N} \quad \left(\text{divide by } \sqrt{2} \text{ when } j = 0\right) \qquad (6.8)$$

The model is trained for 50 epochs. Fig. 6.8 shows training accuracy curve and Fig. 6.9 presents training loss curves for training and testing heartbeat sound database. Table 6.3 shows the confusion matrix. The precision, sensitivity (recall) and $f1$-score performance metrics are calculated from the confusion matrix and presented in Table 6.4. The precision values are 0.55, 0.1, and 0.83 respectively for artifact, normal, and murmur

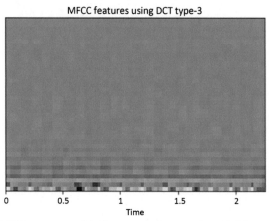

Figure 6.7 MFCC spectrum with discrete cosine transform (DCT) type-3.

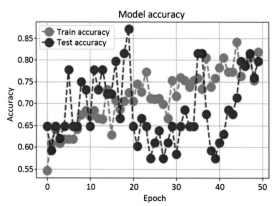

Figure 6.8 Training accuracy curve for heartbeat sound classification with discrete cosine transform (DCT) basis type-3.

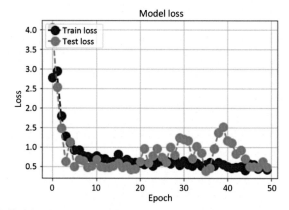

Figure 6.9 Training loss curve for heartbeat sound classification with discrete cosine transform (DCT) basis type-3.

Table 6.3 Confusion matrix for heartbeat sound classification with different discrete cosine transform (DCT) basis.

Class	Experiment with DCT basis type-1			Experiment with DCT basis type-2			Experiment with DCT basis type-3		
	Artifact	Normal	Murmur	Artifact	Normal	Murmur	Artifact	Normal	Murmur
Artifact	11	0	0	11	0	1	12	0	0
Normal	1	13	1	0	5	10	8	8	1
Murmur	0	0	10	0	2	7	2	0	5

Table 6.4 Performance metrics for heartbeat sound classification with different discrete cosine transform (DCT) basis.

Class/ metric	Experiment with DCT basis type-1			Experiment with DCT basis type-2			Experiment with DCT basis type-3		
	Precision	Sensitivity	f1-score	Precision	Sensitivity	f1-score	Precision	Sensitivity	f1-score
Artifact	0.92	1	0.96	1	0.92	0.96	0.55	1	0.71
Normal	1	0.87	0.93	0.71	0.33	0.45	1	0.47	0.64
Murmur	0.91	1	0.95	0.39	0.78	0.52	0.83	0.71	0.77
Average	0.95	0.94	0.94	0.73	0.64	0.64	0.82	0.69	0.69
Test loss		0.21			0.34			0.47	
Test accuracy		0.95			0.74			0.79	

heartbeat sound classes. The sensitivity values are 1.0, 0.47, and 0.71 respectively for artifact, normal, and murmur heartbeat sound classes. The $f1$-scores are 0.71, 0.64, and 0.77 respectively for artifact, normal, and murmur heartbeat sound classes. Test loss and test accuracy values are 0.47 and 0.79 respectively. From these results it is evident that the DCT basis Type-1 has the superior performance in terms of all metrics.

To further confirm the results, receiver operating characteristic curve (ROC) is also plotted for each experiment. The ROC curve is one of the prominent approaches for envisioning the classification accuracy. It displays the dependency between true positive rate and false positive rate. The performance of the classifier is considered better with more convex curve (Tiwari, 2018a,b). The accuracy of classification model can be assessed with the ROC curve by computing the area under ROC curve.

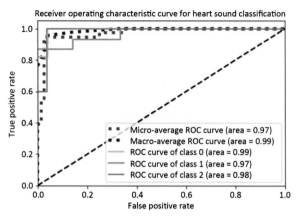

Figure 6.10 Receiver operating characteristic curve (ROC) curve for heartbeat sound classification with discrete cosine transform (DCT) basis type-1.

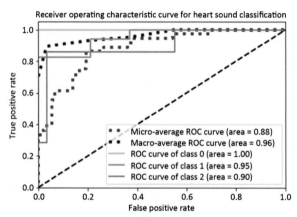

Figure 6.11 Receiver operating characteristic curve (ROC) curve for heartbeat sound classification with discrete cosine transform (DCT) basis type-2.

In the case of binary classification, the ROC curve is a single function of two classes. On the other hand, ROC curve is calculated class-wise and an average of the number of classes is considered as a final decision point. Micro-average and macro-average are the two types of averages that are calculated for multiclass ROC curve. In the case of macro-average ROC curve calculation, all the classes are provided the same weight while in the case of micro-average ROC calculation weights are dependent on the number of samples in each class. These ROC plots are presented in Figs. 6.10, 6.11, and 6.12 separately for each experiment.

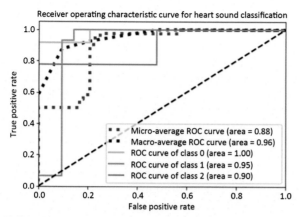

Figure 6.12 Receiver operating characteristic curve (ROC) curve for heartbeat sound classification with discrete cosine transform (DCT) basis type-3.

Table 6.5 Receiver operating characteristic curve (ROC) based performance metrics for heartbeat sound classification.

Experiment/ROC area	Micro-average curve area	Macro-average curve area	ROC curve area for artifact class	ROC curve area for normal class	ROC curve area for murmur class
Experiment with DCT basis type-1	0.97	0.99	0.99	0.97	0.98
Experiment with DCT basis type-2	0.88	0.96	1	0.95	0.90
Experiment with DCT basis type-3	0.89	0.95	0.98	0.91	0.89

DCT, Discrete cosine transform.

Table 6.5 provides these metrics, that is, micro-average, micro-average, ROC curve area of each experiment. The micro-average, macro-average, and ROC curve areas of each class are 0.97, 0.99, 0.99, 0.97, and 0.98 respectively for experiment with DCT basis type-1 which are the highest in all experiments. This also confirms that the DCT basis type-1 has superiority over the other two basis function in heartbeat sound classification.

6.7 Conclusion

In this chapter an effort to find a CNN classification model for proficient heartbeat sound classification has been offered. The designed CNN model performs well and provides satisfying results using MFCC features. The designed model acceptably recognized and classified three different heartbeat sounds namely artifact, murmur, and normal. The most important part of this study is to identify the role DCT basis function in feature calculation and its impact on classification accuracy. It has been demonstrated that by using the DCT basis type-1, it is possible to increase the amount of distinguishable features from heartbeat sounds.

It can be projected that potential research regarding heartbeat classification will need a large number of samples to get more regularized classification model. Furthermore, a large number of heartbeat classes can be presented to additionally increase the model capabilities. Future research can present such a system that can provide the foundation for developing a smart heart health observing systems.

References

Adithya, P.C., Sankar, R., Moreno, W.A., Hart, S., 2017. Trends in fetal monitoring through phonocardiography: challenges and future directions. Biomed. Signal Process. Control 33, 289–305.

Bhalke, D.G., Rao, C.R., Bormane, D.S., 2016. Automatic musical instrument classification using fractional Fourier transform based-MFCC features and counter propagation neural network. J. Intell. Inf. Syst. 46 (3), 425–446.

Dahake, P.P., Shaw, K., Malathi, P., 2016. Speaker dependent speech emotion recognition using MFCC and Support Vector Machine. In: 2016 International Conference on Automatic Control and Dynamic Optimization Techniques (ICACDOT). IEEE, pp. 1080–1084.

Gharehbaghi, A., Ekman, I., Ask, P., Nylander, E., Janerot-Sjoberg, B., 2015. Assessment of aortic valve stenosis severity using intelligent phonocardiography. Int. J. Cardiol. 198, 58–60.

Goldberger, A.L., Amaral, L.A.N., Glass, L., Hausdorff, J.M., Ivanov, P.Ch, Mark, R.G., et al., 2003. PhysioBank, PhysioToolkit, and PhysioNet: components of a new research resource for complex physiologic signals. Circulation 101 (23), E215–E220.

Kumar, A., Saha, G., 2015. Interpretation of heart sound signal through automated artifact-free segmentation. Heart Res. Open J. 2 (1), 25–34.

Milner, B.P., Vaseghi, S.V., 1995. An analysis of cepstral-time matrices for noise and channel robust speech recognition. In: Fourth European Conference on Speech Communication and Technology.

Noman, F., Ting, C.M., Salleh, S.H., Ombao, H., 2019. Short-segment heart sound classification using an ensemble of deep convolutional neural networks. In: ICASSP 2019—2019 IEEE International Conference on Acoustics, Speech and Signal Processing (ICASSP). IEEE, pp. 1318–1322.

Potes, C., Parvaneh, S., Rahman, A., Conroy, B., 2016. Ensemble of feature-based and deep learning-based classifiers for detection of abnormal heart sounds. In: 2016 Computing in Cardiology Conference (CinC). IEEE, pp. 621–624.

Rahmandani, M., Nugroho, H.A., Setiawan, N.A., 2018. Cardiac sound classification using Mel-frequency cepstral coefficients (MFCC) and artificial neural network (ANN). In: 2018 3rd International Conference on Information Technology, Information System and Electrical Engineering (ICITISEE). IEEE, pp. 22–26.

Redlarski, G., Gradolewski, D., Palkowski, A., 2014. A system for heart sounds classification. PLoS One 9 (11), e112673.

Rubin, J., Abreu, R., Ganguli, A., Nelaturi, S., Matei, I., Sricharan, K., 2016. Classifying heart sound recordings using deep convolutional neural networks and mel-frequency cepstral coefficients. In: 2016 Computing in Cardiology Conference (CinC). IEEE, pp. 813–816.

Rubin, J., Abreu, R., Ganguli, A., Nelaturi, S., Matei, I., Sricharan, K., 2017. Recognizing abnormal heart sounds using deep learning. arXiv preprint arXiv:1707.04642.

Tiwari, S., 2018a. An analysis in tissue classification for colorectal cancer histology using convolution neural network and colour models. Int. J.Inf. Syst. Model. Des. (IJISMD) 9 (4), 1–19.

Tiwari, S., 2018b. Blur classification using segmentation based fractal texture analysis. Indones. J. Electr. Eng. Inform. (IJEEI) 6 (4), 373–384.

Wan, L., Zeiler, M., Zhang, S., Le Cun, Y., Fergus, R., 2013. Regularization of neural networks using dropconnect. In: International Conference on Machine Learning, pp. 1058–1066.

Xu, B., Wang, N., Chen, T., Li, M., 2015. Empirical evaluation of rectified activations in convolutional network. arXiv preprint arXiv:1505.00853.

Zheng, F., Zhang, G., Song, Z., 2001. Comparison of different implementations of MFCC. J. Comput. Sci. Technol. 16 (6), 582–589.

7

Comparative analysis of classification techniques for brain magnetic resonance imaging images

D. Bhargava, S. Vyas and Ayushi Bansal
University of Petroleum and Energy Studies, Dehradun, India

Chapter Outline

7.1 Introduction

Brain-related problems are the most common problems found nowadays. Brain cancer, brain tumor, or clots are some of them. They are deadly problems that cannot be cured easily. A brain tumor is a collection of unwanted cells present inside the brain. These abnormal cells form clots inside the brain. Clots lead to brain cancer. These abnormal cells are increasing exponentially if not cured timely. So, for curing brain-related problems, doctors prescribe an X-ray as the first step. An X-ray highlights the tumor part or clots with the rest of the brain gray matter mass. But a few cases have been recorded where doctors

Advances in Computational Techniques for Biomedical Image Analysis. DOI: https://doi.org/10.1016/B978-0-12-820024-7.00007-4

are also not able to find the tumor inside the X-ray images. As they check the preferred area inside the brain, some areas are left unseen. Keeping this issue in mind, different authors used different approaches for classifying the tumor. This literature contains various techniques for classifying the brain tumor. Probabilistic neural network (PNN) (Ibrahim et al., 2013) procedure aimed to calculate the parent probability distribution, used for classifying the tumor. The probability value is calculated for all the features when the classifier is classifying the tumor, and it takes the highest amount of distribution. It is based on the Bayes classifier approach. Fuzzy c-means clustering (Khurana and Lambha, 2013) is the method of classifying the features common for both classes. Generally, fuzzy c-means clustering is using the fuzzy logic concept. The features, which are in common, are passed into both classes, then the mean of all the clusters is taken. After calculating the mean, classes are defined. Convolution neural network (CNN) (Deepa and Devi, 2012) concept is also discussed in this literature where convolution layers, subsampling layers are used for extracting the features of the image. Multiple convolution layers are used for calculating the features. Complex features require more layers.

At last sigmoid activation, function is used for classification as it is the binary classifier. For multilayer classification softmax layer is used. Support vector machine (SVM) concept is also used for dividing the features into two different planes. The same features came in one plane. Like, the same features are clustered in a single plane. SVM is used when data is not that complex. Complex data are classified using CNNs. Gray-level co-occurrence matrix (GLCM) (Jain, 2013) distinguishes between the two textures present inside the image. The tumor area has a different texture or homogeneity value as compared to the gray matter homogeneity value. After calculating the homogeneity value, a matrix is created. If there is a sharp change in the matrix values, then those denote the edges of the tumor. Here discrete cosine transform [13] is also used.

7.2 Literature review

For brain tumor classification, various methods are discussed in this section. PNN (Ibrahim et al., 2013) for brain tumor classification uses two methods for classification of brain tumor. Probability density distribution is calculated for all the classes, and accordingly, classification is performed. Secondly, the principle component analysis (PCA) method is used for the classification of the tumor. In John (2012), Joshi et al. (2010), and Kharat et al. (2012), classification of brain cancer using ANN, in this approach, had some preprocessing performed on the dataset. Preprocessing of the dataset includes creating the bar graphs, enhancing the images by converting them into gray-scaled images, then applying the morphological operations and segmentation techniques for creating the mask of the tumor. After doing all these preprocessing, texture classification is performed using the GLCM value. At last, the fuzzy classifier is used for classifying the tumor value. In preprocessing for brain tumor classification [13] using discrete cosine transform and PNN, the discrete cosine transform values are used for reducing the features of an image. If the number of features are more, then the complex classifier is required. After preprocessing the author used the PNN approach for classification. In Badran et al. (2010) brain tumor classification u wavelet and texture-based neural network are used. Texture values or homogeneity values are calculated for every pixel value after that values are plotted on the graph. If there is a sharp change in the value, then that change determines the edges of the tumor. In Badran et al. (2010) an algorithm for detecting brain tumors in MRI images, this algorithm incorporates the preprocessing, feature extraction, classification, segmentation, and neural network techniques. In the preprocessing conversion of an image into gray-scaled images, resizing of images, performing the thresholding operations on the images for distinguishing between the background and the foreground area. After doing the preprocessing, features are extracted from the images, that feature is passed for the training purpose, and then classification is performed. In Kharat et al. (2012) deep learning neural networks (Deepa and Devi, 2012) were used for classifying brain tumors, here in this approach the author is using a very deep convolution neural network (DCNN) for classifying the tumor. Complex features are difficult to gather, as initial layers collect the points, edges of an image. Secondary features are color and the shape is formed by further layers. At last, a fully connected layer is used. Sigmoid activation function is used for classification (Vyas and Vaishnav, 2017; Manivannan et al., 2012).

7.3 Methodology

7.3.1 Gray level co-occurrence matrix

A GLCM uses the texture classification concept. The texture classification concept is classified using the homogeneity value.

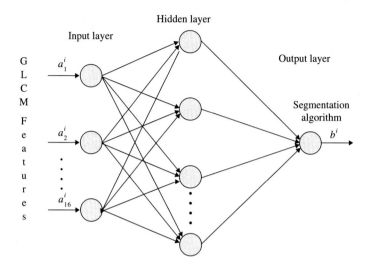

Figure 7.1 Gray-level co-occurrence matrix (GLCM)-based artificial neural network (ANN) model using multilayer perceptron (MLP) network. *Source*: From Manivannan, K., Aggarwal, P., Devabhaktuni, V., Kumar, A., Nims, D., Bhattacharya, P., 2012. Particulate matter characterization by gray level co-occurrence matrix based support vector machines. J. Hazard. Mater. 223, 94—103.

The homogeneity value is calculated for every pixel to present inside the image. After calculating the homogeneity values, a matrix of values is created. If there is a change in the homogeneity value of the particular pixel, then the GLCM value is calculated. In the brain, the X-ray tumor part is different from the rest of the gray mass. The gray mass has a different texture in comparison to the tumor texture. At that point, GLCM is the best approach. If there is a sharp change in the matrix value, there is the highest chance of getting the tumor. GLCM is the best approach for classifying the pixel by pixel values. Gray level co-occurrence value is mostly used in X-ray analysis. X-ray is a black and white film, and it contains different shades of the gray (Fig. 7.1).

7.3.2 Support vector machine

SVM is the algorithm of machine learning. The SVM follows the concept of separating the features from one another. The classifier separates features from one another. The same types of features come on one plane, and another feature comes on another plane. The classifier is using the concept of the aircraft, lines, and hyperplanes to separate the features. The classifier line for one-dimensional, plane for two-dimensional, and hyperplanes for three-dimensional data. The human does not describe higher aspects, but the computer can reach there. SVM is best when all the elements are tightly bounded. If the features are not together then this concept does not work correctly. SVM classifier does not give good accuracy in comparison with CNN.

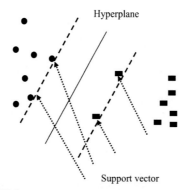

Figure 7.2 Support vector machine (SVM). *Source*: From Ramakrishnan, T., Sankaragomathi, B., 2017. A professional estimate on the computed tomography brain tumor images using SVM-SMO for classification and MRG-GWO for segmentation. Pattern Recognit. Lett. 94, 163–171.

The SVM classifier is used when the dataset is less. SVM is not well suited to bigger datasets. For image classifications, CNN is the best approach to be used in place of the SVM (Fig. 7.2).

7.3.3 Self-organizing maps

Some papers highlighted self-organizing maps (SOM), which were used to view the high dimensional image into the low dimensional view. The self-organizing neural networks used organizing maps. SOMs are different from the other neural networks, as other neural networks use the concept of the neighborhood pixels for calculating the values of the features. It is used as a morphological operation in classifying the brain tumor (Khurana and Lambha, 2013). Lower dimensional datasets (Shree and Kumar, 2018; Saritha et al., 2013) reduce the computation cost of the network. Self-organized neural network uses these small dimensional images and training the model for classification. SOM required a smaller number of computing power, and training in SOM becomes fast. The brain tumor dataset initially converted into very low dimensional values, and then were passed for self-organizing networks (Fig. 7.3).

7.3.4 Fuzzy c-means clustering

Fuzzy c-means clustering is used to cluster the same types of features together. Some features follow the property of both features, and then the fuzzy comes. Fuzzy is used where there are overlapping conditions (Bernal et al., 2019).

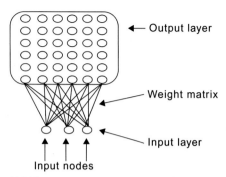

Figure 7.3 The self-organizing map (SOM) architecture. *Source:* From Ismail, S., Shabri, A., Samsudin, R., 2011. A hybrid model of self-organizing maps (SOM) and least square support vector machine (LSSVM) for time-series forecasting. Expert Syst. Appl. 38 (8), 10574–10578.

Algorithm of fuzzy C-means
1. Assign the number of clusters.
2. Assign various points in the clusters.
3. Calculate the centroid of the clusters.
4. Then again, follow steps 3 and 4.
5. Loop until the algorithm converges.

7.3.5 Probabilistic neural network

PNN concept is the concept of the feed-forward neural. PNN is used in classification and recognition. In PNN, the parent probability distribution is calculated using the parser window and nonparametric concepts. If the parent PNN value is greater than the other value, then according to that value classification is performed. PNN is used for segmentation purposes. Heatmap is using the concepts of PNN. If the feature probability is higher than the other feature, then the higher value is the output of the classification. In brain tumor X-ray images, if the probability of the tumor is higher than the probability of the gray mass, then accordingly, it is classified.

In calculating the heat-map, the value of the weight of the features multiplied with the last layer weight. Further, average weights are calculated. If the value is higher than the value, then that feature is classified into that particular classifier.

PNN approach is faster than the multiple perceptron approach but seems to be slower when new cases added. PNN follows the Bayes optimal search, but it requires a lot of memory (Fig. 7.4).

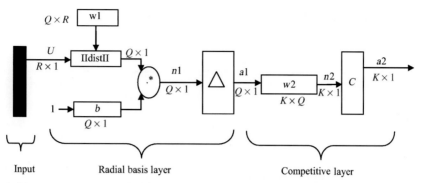

Figure 7.4 Probabilistic neural network (PNN) structure. *Source*: From Saritha, M., Joseph, K.P., Mathew, A.T., 2013. Classification of MRI brain images using combined wavelet entropy based spider web plots and probabilistic neural network. Pattern Recognit. Lett. 34 (16), 2151−2156.

7.3.6   Convolution neural network

CNN is another method for the classification of brain tumors. For performing the classification, initial preprocessing of the data is performed using thresholding concept, morphological operations. Initially, the author converts the images into the gray-scaled images, and then performs the thresholding concept. Thresholding is used to convert the value into either black value or in the white value. If the value is less than the thresholding value, then it will be black; rest, it will be white after performing the morphological thresholding operations, re-performed. Morphological is for separating the background and the foreground techniques (Purohit and Bhargava, 2017; Sridhar and Krishna, 2013).

After performing all the preprocessing, convolution network, architecture is defined. The architecture is consisting of the layers. Convolution and subsampling layers used for classification, for example, pooling layers, fully connected layers, and batch normalization (BN) layers. Convolution layers are convolving the filter value with the image pixel value for extracting the features of an image. Image values contain the values of the pixels. Filters can be according to the need. Here in brain tumor classification, sobel filter values are used. Sobel filter is used for calculating the horizontal and vertical edges of the tumor portion. Image pixel values are convolved with the filter values. After the convolution operation size of the image is decreased by using the formula $\{[(n - f + 2p)/s] + 1\}$, where "n" is the input size, "f" is the size of the filter used, "p" is the padding value, and "s" is the stride value (Vyas and Vaishnav, 2017; Vyas et al., 2015).

Further, the pooling layer is applied for getting the maximum or average value of the features. Pooling layers are

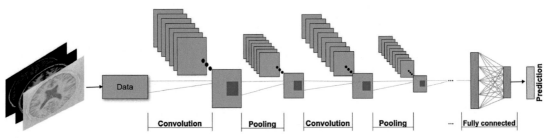

Figure 7.5 Generic architecture of convolutional neural networks (CNNs). *Source*: From Bernal, J., Kushibar, K., Asfaw, D.S., Valverde, S., Oliver, A., Martí, R., et al., 2019. Deep convolutional neural networks for brain image analysis on magnetic resonance imaging: a review. Artif. Intell. Med. 95, 64–81.

generally used for taking out the essential features of an image. Pooling layers reduce the size of an image to the half. Further, the BN layer is used for the weight values. After some values of training, the weight is becoming zero. To handle this issue, BN and activation function ADAM is used. At last, dense layer or fully connected layer is used. For classification, sigmoid is used, as it is a binary classifier (Fig. 7.5).

7.4 Comparative analysis of various approaches

	Probabilistic neural network (PNN)	Support vector machine (SVM)	Fuzzy C-means	Gray-level co-occurrence matrix (GLCM)	Convolution neural network (CNN)
Description	PNN is used for calculating the probability distribution of the features, and based on the probability density, defines the classes for classification (Othman and Basri, 2011)	Support vector machines (SVMs) are an algorithm of machine learning. It uses the concept of creating the perfect boundary between the two outputs. (Shen et al., 2005)	Fuzzy C-means clustering is used when some images contain the features, which occur in multiple categories, in that fuzzy clusters are used (Khurana and Lambha, 2013)	GLCM is used to distinguish between the different textures present in the image. It uses the pixel values for classification (John, 2012)	CNN is a special type of neural network, which uses various convolution layers, pooling layers, subsampling layers, dense layers for classification. CNN uses the concept of deep learning (Shen et al., 2005)

(Continued)

(Continued)

	Probabilistic neural network (PNN)	Support vector machine (SVM)	Fuzzy C-means	Gray-level co-occurrence matrix (GLCM)	Convolution neural network (CNN)
Performance	PNN is very fast, when there is a distribution based on probability, but fails when the probability density function is similar for different classes (Sridhar and Krishna, 2013)	SVM works at a very high speed, when there is a clear gap between the classes. And there is a proper distinguisher present between the classes. But it fails when classes are merged and with high dimensional features (Joshi et al., 2010)	Fuzzy C-means clustering has outstanding outputs on the overlapping classes, when a class has the multiple outputs classes, and it tends to be there in two or more than two classes (Khurana and Lambha, 2013)	GLCM technique has good output, when there is texture classification, as some gray matter mass looks like a tumor. In that scenario, GLCM is the best classifier (Jain, 2013)	CNN is the best technique, which can classify on any of the bases. But, in CNN, the data requirement is on huge demand (Ibrahim et al., 2013)
Dataset used for training	PNN is tested on open source dataset, that is, kaggle. It contains around 500 – 600 images (Sridhar and Krishna, 2013)	SVM is also tested on open source dataset kaggle, same as PNN (Shen et al., 2005)	Fuzzy c-means clustering works on the augmented dataset, containing multiple diseases (Khurana and Lambha, 2013)	GLCM is trained on the brain tumor segmentation (BRATS) dataset. BRATS is the dataset, which is released in the completion of tumor segmentation (Jain, 2013)	CNN is initially trained on the ImageNet dataset, which uses the weights of ImageNet dataset, that is, transfer learning. After that it is trained on BRATS dataset (Deepa and Devi, 2012)
Minimum dataset required	500 images (Sridhar and Krishna, 2013)	500 images (Shen et al., 2005)	1000 images	5000 images (John, 2012)	5000 images (Ibrahim et al., 2013)
Parameters (Sridhar and Krishna, 2013)	Probability density function	Planes and hyperplanes	Cluster distance	Gray level pixel value	Features

(Continued)

(Continued)

	Probabilistic neural network (PNN)	Support vector machine (SVM)	Fuzzy C-means	Gray-level co-occurrence matrix (GLCM)	Convolution neural network (CNN)
Working (Othman and Basri, 2011; Sridhar and Krishna, 2013)	In PNN parent probability distribution is calculated using the parzen window. After that on the basis of PDF classes are defined. For new data Bayes theorem is used for classification	SVM works when there are clear margins between the features. It works well with high dimensional data. It is not good, if there are a large number of images, and noise is present, that is, overlapping in features	It is using the concept of distance calculation between the points and the cluster center, the smaller the distance, the more prone to that class	In GLCM, gray level pixel value is calculated for every pixel, based on that pixel value homogeneity value is calculated, which is used for classification	It is the best suited approach used for classification. Different convolution networks like U-Net, are basically used for only biomedical purposes as they give good results on small datasets
Pertinent	Signals	Signals, 2D and 3D images	Signals	Images	Images
Limitations	In PNN, all learning rules work for calculating the probability, which makes the PNN a greedy approach (Othman and Basri, 2011)	It does not work well for bigger datasets, and final model interpretations cannot be gathered or difficult to analyze (Khurana and Lambha, 2013)	It does not work with high dimensional datasets, and contains the rule base for classification, which is a greedy approach (Khurana and Lambha, 2013)	It only works on gray-scaled images. It fails on colored images	It requires a huge amount of dataset, training of deep models requires a lot of time and a huge memory (Shen et al., 2005)
Size	Variable (MB's)	Variable (KB's)	Variable (MB's)	16 bits matrix	Variable generally in MB's
Output accuracy	~94%	~94%	~95.8%	~96%	~98%

7.5   Conclusion

In this chapter, various approaches are discussed for classifying the brain tumor. Different authors use different strategies to classify the brain tumor. Most of the authors preferred the CNN technique for classification of the tumor. If the number of data images is very large, then CNN is the best tool. For smaller datasets, SVM is preferred for classification. Different probabilistic approaches are used for classification, and it is used for the parent probability distribution for classifying the tumor. Characteristic features are also handled in this literature using the C-means clustering technique; it is also used for the fuzzy approach for classification.

References

Badran, E.F., Mahmoud, E.G., Hamdy, N., 2010. An algorithm for detecting brain tumors in MRI images. In: The 2010 International Conference on Computer Engineering & Systems. IEEE, pp. 368–373.

Bernal, J., Kushibar, K., Asfaw, D.S., Valverde, S., Oliver, A., Martí, R., et al., 2019. Deep convolutional neural networks for brain image analysis on magnetic resonance imaging: a review. Artif. Intell. Med. 95, 64–81.

Deepa, S.N., Devi, B.A., 2012. Artificial neural networks design for classification of brain tumour. In: 2012 International Conference on Computer Communication and Informatics. IEEE, pp. 1–6.

Ibrahim, W.H., Osman, A.A.A., Mohamed, Y.I., 2013. MRI brain image classification using neural networks. In: 2013 international conference on computing, electrical and electronic engineering (ICCEEE). IEEE, pp. 253–258.

Ismail, S., Shabri, A., Samsudin, R., 2011. A hybrid model of self-organizing maps (SOM) and least square support vector machine (LSSVM) for time-series forecasting. Expert Syst. Appl. 38 (8), 10574–10578.

Jain, S., 2013. Brain cancer classification using GLCM based feature extraction in artificial neural network. Int. J. Comput. Sci. Eng. Technol. 4 (7), 966–970.

John, P., 2012. Brain tumor classification using wavelet and texture based neural network. Int. J. Sci. Eng. Res. 3 (10), 1–7.

Joshi, D.M., Rana, N.K., Misra, V., 2010. Classification of brain cancer using artificial neural network. In: 2010 2nd International Conference on Electronic Computer Technology. IEEE, pp. 112–116.

Kharat, K.D., Kulkarni, P.P., Nagori, M.B., 2012. Brain tumor classification using neural network based methods. Int. J. Comput. Sci. Inform. 1 (4), 2231–5292.

Khurana, K., Lambha, C.S., 2013. An efficient brain tumor detection system using fuzzy clustering & neural network. Int. J. Digit. Appl. Contemp. Res. 1 (7).

Manivannan, K., Aggarwal, P., Devabhaktuni, V., Kumar, A., Nims, D., Bhattacharya, P., 2012. Particulate matter characterization by gray level co-occurrence matrix based support vector machines. J. Hazard. Mater. 223, 94–103.

Othman, M.F., Basri, M.A.M., 2011. Probabilistic neural network for brain tumor classification. In: 2011 Second International Conference on Intelligent Systems, Modelling and Simulation. IEEE, pp. 136–138.

Purohit, R., Bhargava, D., 2017. An illustration to secured way of data mining using privacy preserving data mining. J. Stat. Manag. Syst. 20 (4), 637–645.

Ramakrishnan, T., Sankaragomathi, B., 2017. A professional estimate on the computed tomography brain tumor images using SVM-SMO for classification and MRG-GWO for segmentation. Pattern Recognit. Lett. 94, 163–171.

Saritha, M., Joseph, K.P., Mathew, A.T., 2013. Classification of MRI brain images using combined wavelet entropy based spider web plots and probabilistic neural network. Pattern Recognit. Lett. 34 (16), 2151–2156.

Shen, S., Sandham, W., Granat, M., Sterr, A., 2005. MRI fuzzy segmentation of brain tissue using neighborhood attraction with neural-network optimization. IEEE Trans. Inf. Technol. Biomed. 9 (3), 459–467.

Shree, N.V., Kumar, T.N.R., 2018. Identification and classification of brain tumor MRI images with feature extraction using DWT and probabilistic neural network. Brain Inform. 5 (1), 23–30.

Sridhar, D., Krishna, I.M., 2013. Brain tumor classification using discrete cosine transform and probabilistic neural network. In: 2013 International Conference on Signal Processing, Image Processing & Pattern Recognition. IEEE, pp. 92–96.

Vyas, S., Vaishnav, P., 2017. A comparative study of various ETL process and their testing techniques in data warehouse. J. Stat. Manag. Syst. 20 (4), 753–763.

Vyas, V., Saxena, S., Bhargava, D., 2015. Mind reading by face recognition using security enhancement model. Proceedings of Fourth International Conference on Soft Computing for Problem Solving. Springer, New Delhi, pp. 173–180.

8

Hybrid feature selection-based feature fusion for liver disease classification on ultrasound images

Puja Bharti and Deepti Mittal

Department of Electrical and Instrumental Engineering, Thapar Institute of Engineering and Technology, Patiala, India

8.1   Introduction

Chronic liver disease is progressive damage and regeneration of liver parenchyma, leading to formation and progression of cirrhosis, common malignant liver cancer [i.e., heptocellular carcinomas (HCC)], and liver failure (Bharti et al., 2018). The frequently used noninvasive modality for initial identification of liver diseases is ultrasound imaging (Allan et al., 2010). The variations in ultrasound images can assist in detecting various liver abnormalities. The abnormalities can be quantitatively analyzed

Advances in Computational Techniques for Biomedical Image Analysis. DOI: https://doi.org/10.1016/B978-0-12-820024-7.00008-6

by evaluating texture of the ultrasound images. Commonly extracted texture features include gray-level co-occurrence matrices (GLCM), Fourier power spectrum, gray-level difference matrix (GLDM), Laws' texture energy measures, gray-level run length statistics, Gabor filter, texture edge co-occurrence matrix, first-order statistics, and multiresolution fractal features (Bharti et al., 2017; Wu et al., 1992, 2012; Pavlopoulos et al., 2000; Horng, 2007; Andrade et al., 2012; Virmani et al., 2013; Singh et al., 2013). In this paper, for characterizing liver diseases texture features are extracted from multiresolution ranklet transformed images and by using GLDM and GLCM methods. However, using all features may increase computation complexity as well as time. The feature space may contain features with less discriminating abilities, which can be regarded as redundant or irrelevant features. Moreover, which feature is relevant or will become relevant when merged with another feature is not known in advance. Thus, selection of features is essential to reduce computational complexity and improve performance. Feature selection methods include filter, wrapper, and embedded (Bolón-Canedo et al., 2013). The filter methods are based on the general characteristics of the training data, that is, distance, information gain (or uncertainty), and dependence (or correlation) to select features independent of any classifier. These methods are usually computationally less expensive than wrapper and embedded methods. Wrapper methods use classifiers as a black box and its prediction performance to assess the relative effectiveness of feature subsets. Embedded methods perform feature selection in the process of training and are usually specific to a given classifier (Sheikhpour et al., 2017).

Mitrea et al. (2012) used correlation feature selection (CFS) to find relevant texture feature set for differentiating HCC and HCC evolved over cirrhotic liver images. CFS is a simple multivariate filter method that ranks feature subset according to a correlation-based heuristic evaluation function (Sheikhpour et al., 2017). However, as each feature is treated individually, CFS is not capable of identifying strong interactions. Chi-square and information gain are univariate filter methods that consider each feature independently of another feature (Tang et al., 2014). These methods are computationally efficient however they do not show good results with nonlinear database (Tang et al., 2014). Zhang et al. (2008) presented a two-stage feature selection method by combining ReliefF and minimum redundancy maximum relevance, to improve the effectiveness of gene selection and provide discrimination for biological subtypes (Zhang et al., 2008). The ReliefF, multivariate filter method can handle multiclass problems and is capable of dealing with incomplete and noisy data (Bolón-Canedo et al., 2015). The ReliefF method includes interactions among features and can capture local dependencies, making it a robust filter method. Wu et al. also reported increase in accuracy after using ReliefF as feature selection method (Wu et al., 2016).

Santos et al. (2014) used classifiers namely support vector machine (SVM), artificial neural network (ANN), and k-nearest neighbor (k-NN) for normal and fatty liver classification; and results showed that after applying sequential forward selection (SFS), the classification accuracy improved by 12.81%, 14.38%, and 0.25% for ANN, SVM, and k-NN respectively. Pudil et al. (1994) suggested a floating search methods sequential forward/ backward floating search (SFFS, SFBS) that performed a greedy search with backtracking. However, recent study demonstrated that SFFS is not superior to SFS and SFBS is not feasible for feature sets of more than about 100 features (Bensch et al., 2005). The stochastic algorithm such as genetic algorithms (GA) and particle swarm optimization were used by Kalyan and Virmani to select an optimal feature set (Virmani et al., 2013; Kalyan et al., 2014). Although these methods efficiently capture feature redundancy and interaction, they are computationally expensive (Stoean and Stoean, 2013). Table 8.1 shows advantages and disadvantages of generally used feature selection methods. Some authors have proposed hybrid methods taking advantage of both filter and wrapper methods (Solorio-Fernández et al., 2016). The examples include CFS and GA, mutual information and GA, Chi-square method, and a multiobjective optimization method (Osei-Bryson et al., 2003; Huang et al., 2006; Shazzad and Park, 2005).

In general, the choice of feature selection method depends on data characteristics, that is, data type, size, and noise. In this work, liver ultrasound dataset is considered, which does not show linear characteristics, overlapping of disease characteristic leading to noise; and there are four liver classes. All these characteristics can be best handled by ReliefF filter method, that is, data with multiple classes, noise, and nonlinear. ReliefF method gives ranking to features. So, in order to find out the subset of the best features, SFS can be used. Thus, in this research work, a hybrid method using ReliefF and SFS is proposed. Where, preselection is done by considering features that have weights (given by ReliefF method) above the threshold, and from these preselected features a subset is selected by SFS.

In recent works, it is also observed that features extracted from the same pattern by different feature extraction methods

Table 8.1 Advantages and disadvantages of feature selection methods applied on ultrasound images data.

Feature selection method	Type	Advantage	Disadvantage
Correlation (Mitrea et al., 2012)	Filter	Multivariate filter method that ranks feature subset according to a correlation-based heuristic evaluation function	Not capable of identifying strong interactions
Chi-square (Tang et al., 2014)	Filter	Computationally efficient	Does not show good results with nonlinear database
ReliefF (Bolón-Canedo et al., 2015)	Filter	Multivariate filter method that can handle multiclass problems and is capable of dealing with incomplete and noisy data	May fail to remove redundant Features
Sequential forward selection (Pudil et al., 1994)	Wrapper	Simple, avoid overfitting	Selected subset will be specific to the classifier under consideration
Particle swarm optimization (Kalyan et al., 2014)	Wrapper	Efficiently captures feature redundancy and interaction	long time to converge
Genetic algorithm (Virmani et al., 2013)	Wrapper	Efficiently captures feature redundancy and interaction	Complexity increases, more CPU time, and memory to run

may lead to complementary information. The combination of multiple feature sets, which probably has more useful distinguishing information, is termed as feature fusion (Yang et al., 2003). The commonly used feature fusion schemes are serial feature combination (SFC) and serial feature fusion. The SFC is integration of multiple feature sets (Mangai et al., 2010). The serial feature fusion is a process of feature selection based on SFC (Yang et al., 2003). Wu et al. (2013) presented evolutionary-based hierarchical feature fusion to classify normal, cirrhosis, and HCC liver images and obtained 96.62% accuracy (Wu et al., 2013). Singh et al. (2013) fused the best features from different feature sets along with their weights and weighted z-score. A survey of feature fusion schemes for pattern classification can be found in Mangai et al. (2010). It is evident from literature that the performance of classifier largely depends on the dimension of feature space. The increase in size of search space makes generalization harder and it also impacts training time of classifier and higher risk of overfitting (Sun et al., 2010). The instance-based classifiers, such as k-NN, are very susceptible to irrelevant features. SVM can also suffer in high-dimensional spaces where many features are irrelevant (Sun et al., 2010; Mittal et al., 2011; Rani et al., 2016). Hence, efficient feature selection and fusion schemes can enhance the performance of classifiers.

The primary objective of this paper is to present a hybrid feature selection (HFS)-based feature fusion system that selects the best features among multiple feature sets to classify liver ultrasound images into four classes: normal, chronic, cirrhosis, and HCC evolved over cirrhosis. HFS method is proposed by combining ReliefF algorithm and SFS method. In the first stage, ReliefF is applied to rank features so that irrelevant features are discarded and computational complexity is reduced. In the second stage, SFS method is applied to find the best set with the minimum number of features and maximum accuracy. Thereafter, feature fusion schemes are implemented, aiming to further improve the resulting classification performance.

The rest of the paper is organized as follows: in Section 8.2 a brief description of features extracted, feature selection, and classification methods is given. In Sections 8.3 and 8.4 experiments and results, and their discussions are detailed. Finally, the conclusion is presented in Section 8.5.

8.2 Method

Fig. 8.1 shows the framework of the proposed system which consists of three main steps: (1) feature extraction, (2) feature selection, and (3) classification.

8.2.1 Feature extraction

Feature extraction is a key step in classifying liver classes. The analysis of spatial variations in pixel intensities can provide information about the roughness of liver surface and regularity of echotexture. In this work, a total 148 features comprising of 112 features from GLDM and GLCM using the original image, and 36 features from multiresolution ranklet images are extracted. These features are shown in Table 8.2. The details of these features can be found in references mentioned (Wu et al., 1992; Yang et al., 2013; Gomez et al., 2012).

8.2.1.1 Feature normalization

The features extracted from various methods are normalized before classification. Normalization of textural features is achieved by $\hat{f}_n = (f_n - \bar{f})/\sigma$, $n = 1, 2,\ldots, 754$. Let $\bar{f}$ and σ be the

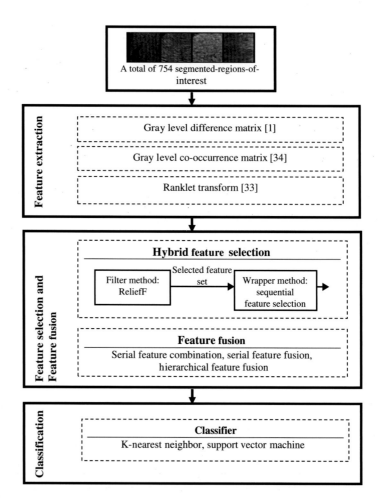

Figure 8.1 Framework of proposed system.

respective mean and standard deviation values, computed using the values of specific feature, f, from all liver classes, and $\hat{f}_n$ represent the normalized feature. The value of n represents the total number of images.

8.2.2   Feature selection

The feature selection method is used to choose the optimal subset from the original feature space, while retaining capability of features to distinguish among classes. The HFS method formed by combining filter method (ReliefF algorithm) and wrapper method (SFS) leverages the benefits of both. These methods have their respective weaknesses and are complementary to each other. The filter methods have low computational

Table 8.2 The extracted texture features.

Method	Texture features	Parameters	No. of features
Gray-level difference matrix (Bharti et al., 2018)	Contrast, angular second moment, entropy, mean	• $\theta = \{0, 45, 90, 135 \text{ degrees}\}$ • $GLDM_{2p}, GLDM_{3p}, GLDM_{5p}, GLDM_{7p}$	64
Gray-level co-occurrence matrix (Gomez et al., 2012)	Contrast, correlation, energy, homogeneity, dissimilarity, entropy, cluster prominence, cluster shade, variance, max probability, autocorrelation, inverse difference moment normalized	• $\theta = \{0, 45, 90, 135 \text{ degrees}\}$ • $d = 1$	48
Ranklet transform (Yang et al., 2013)	Mean, entropy, standard deviation	• Resolutions: 4,6,8,10 • Orientations: vertical, horizontal, diagonal	36

cost but are insufficiently reliable for classification, whereas wrapper methods tend to have superior classification accuracy but require great computational power. Fig. 8.2 shows the flow diagram of proposed feature selection method.

8.2.2.1 ReliefF

The ReliefF is a multiclass extension of Relief method that uses a statistical method to select the relevant features (Cui et al., 2016). ReliefF method is multivariate, robust and noise tolerant filter method. It is a feature weight-based algorithm. Initially, the weights of features are initialized to zero. An instance, x, is randomly selected from a set of training instances that determines *near hit* and *near miss* instances based on Euclidean distance. *Near hit* is the instance having minimum Euclidean distance among all instances of the same liver class as that of the selected instance. *Near miss* is the instance of having minimum Euclidean distance among all instances of a different liver class. The weights of features are updated based on an intuitive idea that a feature is more relevant if it distinguishes between an instance and its *near miss*, and less relevant if it distinguishes between an instance and its *near hit*. After selecting all instances in the training set, a final ranking is performed.

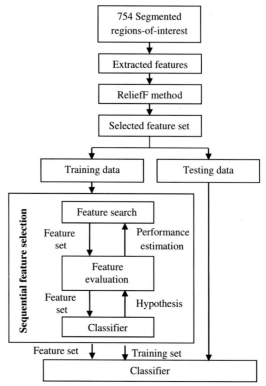

Figure 8.2 Flow diagram of proposed hybrid feature selection method.

8.2.2.2   Sequential forward selection

SFS is a wrapper-based method (Panthong and Srivihok, 2015). It is simple and an efficient greedy search method wherein features are sequentially added to an empty candidate set. Every time one feature is added that minimizes the error the most, till any further addition does not significantly minimize the error. The performance of each added feature is estimated using cross-validation measures. SFS, being a wrapper method, interacts with classifiers. In this work, SFS is combined with classifiers namely, SVM and k-NN.

8.2.2.3   Hybrid feature selection

In HFS, ReliefF method is used to rank features according to the assigned weights. Thereafter, a subset of features is selected having weights greater than or equal to user defined threshold. The value of threshold varies with classifier. The selected high ranked features aid in reducing complexity of the resulting model and computation time for feature selection. Then, SFS is applied to extract the optimal feature set. Finally, the subset with highest accuracy, is considered the best (if two or more subsets obtain the same accuracy, the one using the smallest number of features is selected). In this paper, two sets $HFS_{k\text{-NN}}$ (set obtained after HFS using ReliefF, and SFS with k-NN as classifier) and HFS_{SVM} (set obtained after HFS using ReliefF, and SFS with SVM as classifier) are formed.

8.2.2.4 Feature fusion

The multiple feature sets contain complementary information which when combined increases the quality of classification process. To take the advantage of this information, feature fusion schemes (1) serial feature combination, (2) serial feature fusion, and (3) hierarchical feature fusion are implemented (Bharti et al., 2018; Yang et al., 2003; Wu et al., 2013).

1. Serial feature combination: It is a process of serial combination of feature sets, and the resulting feature set is called serial feature combination (SFC) set. Suppose α and β are two feature sets where α is k-dimensional and β is l-dimensional. Then, the serial combined feature set is defined by $\gamma = (\alpha/\beta)$, where γ is a $(k + l)$-dimensional feature vector.

2. Serial feature fusion: It is a process of selection of relevant features from SFC set, and resulting feature set is called serial-fused feature (SFF) set. In this paper, two sets $SFF_{k\text{-NN}}$ ($HFS_{k\text{-NN}}$ applied on SFC set) and SFF_{SVM} (HFS_{SVM} applied on SFC set) are formed.

3. Hierarchical feature fusion: It is a two-stage process: (1) HFS is performed on individual feature sets to obtain the best reduced individual feature subsets (2) then, derived subsets are integrated to form a fused feature set, and again HFS is applied on the fused feature space to obtain the optimal feature subset (Wu et al., 2012). In this paper, two sets $HFF_{k\text{-NN}}$ and HFF_{SVM} are formed.

8.2.3 Classification methods

In this work, two classifiers are used for performance evaluation, that is, k-NN and SVM. The k-NN method is frequently used as a benchmark method, due to its simplicity and relatively high performance. In contrast, the SVM method is a powerful and relatively complex method with higher learning capability.

The k-NN classifier algorithm computes the nearest neighboring occurrences and assigns the liver class to the test data by taking majority vote of the class of neighboring occurrences (Lee, 2013). The similarity in Euclidean distances between the stored training data and test data is used as the basis for the majority (Kuncheva, 2014). In this work, for k-NN classifier $k = 1$, the closest neighbor was considered and its class-value was assigned to the test data.

The idea behind SVM classifier is to transform a nonlinear separable data into a linear separable data by projecting data into a higher dimensional feature space and then find the optimal separable hyper-plane by using a different kernel function (Winters-Hilt et al., 2006). Although SVM is primarily a binary classifier, to handle multiclass cases, one may use *one*-versus-*one* (1-1) or *one*-versus-*rest* (1-*r*) approaches. In this work, SVM (1-1) approach is used to classify four liver classes, and radial basis function kernel was used. The tradeoff parameter C was taken as 1 and the gamma parameter that sets the spread of the kernel function, γ was set at 0.5.

8.3 Experiments and results

In this work, a database of 189 liver ultrasound images was clinically acquired from 94 subjects. These 189 images of database consist of 48 normal, 50 chronic, 50 cirrhosis, and 41 HCC evolved on cirrhosis. The images were collected during routine liver diagnostic procedures at the Manipal Hospital of Bangalore, India from March 2013 to August 2014. Images were acquired by GE LOGIQ E9 (General Electric Medical System, Milwaukee, WI, United States), using a 3−5 MHz curvilinear array probe with an extended width beam. The ethical clearance was granted by the hospital to the authors in order to carry out this research work. The visual decision concerning diagnostic quality and representativeness of each image class was made by a domain expert (also the co-author of this paper), having more than 20 years of experience in abdominal ultrasound imaging. In addition to visual interpretation of ultrasound image, clinical history of patients and confirmation of disease by CT/MRI/biopsy were also used as assessment criteria.

Further, the segmented-regions-of-interest (SROIs) in each image were marked by the expert radiologist. In this work, an interactive segmentation approach was used to segment the regions-of-interest for classification, where only initial seed points have to be entered. The marked SROIs are regions with the most diagnostic information in textural form of the specific liver tissue class. These SROIs are nonoverlapping regions and the artifacts such as costal shadows and spikes, and blood vessels were kept out of the segmented regions. Here, an image contributed more than one SROI to the dataset. Consequently, the resulting dataset of 754 SROIs includes 192 normal liver, 200 chronic liver, 200 cirrhosis, and 162 HCC evolved over cirrhosis was formed.

The experimental parameters are as follows:

1. The number of features in the preselection subset, R_p: $|R_p| =$ 40% of total features. This means 40% of total features are selected for the consideration of wrapper method; different values of $|R_p|$ would influence the feature selection. If $|R_p|$ is equal to the number of features, it becomes the traditional SFS approach. If $|R_p|$ is too small, then preselection would limit the SFS. In this work, range varies from 40% to 90% of total features used for preselection.

2. In wrapper approach, cross-validation is used to evaluate the performance of selected features. The number of folds for cross-validation is set to $k = 10$.

3. The performance of classifiers is evaluated in terms of accuracy. The repeated holdout method, that is, 15 times 10-hold out method is employed. This improves the reliability of the holdout estimate by repeating the process with different subsamples. In each iteration, 90% of data is randomly selected for training and 10% for testing. The error rates on different iterations are averaged to yield an overall error rate.

8.3.1 Experiment 1: Effectiveness of texture features and feature dimensionality reduction

In this work, texture features are extracted to characterize different classes of liver. Texture features generated by using GLDMs are 64 (i.e., 4 texture codes × 4 directions × 4 neighboring pixel stencils), GLCMs are 48 (i.e., 12 texture codes × 4 directions × 1 distance), and ranklets are 36 (i.e., 4 resolutions × 3 orientations × 3 texture codes). In this experiment, the efficiency of individual feature sets and reduced feature sets by HFS (HFS$_{k-NN}$ and HFS$_{SVM}$) are studied, and classification is performed using k-NN and SVM classifiers.

Result: Table 8.3 shows classification accuracy of different texture features. The classification accuracies obtained from GLDM, GLCM and features extracted from ranklets were 92.2%, 89.8%, and 91.2% with k-NN, and 91.1%, 88.7%, and 89.2% with SVM.

Table 8.3 The classification accuracy of the different texture features.

Texture features methods	Accuracy (%)	
	k-NN	SVM
GLDM	92.2	91.1
GLCM	89.8	88.7
Ranklet	91.2	89.2

Table 8.4 The classification accuracy of the different texture features after feature selection.

	Total no. of features	Selected no. of features by HFS$_{k-NN}$	Accuracy (%) k-NN	Selected no. of features by HFS$_{SVM}$	Accuracy (%) SVM
GLDM	64	12	93.2	21	91.2
GLCM	48	09	90.5	20	89.4
Ranklet	36	13	92.1	19	91.2

Table 8.4 shows classification accuracy of the different texture features after HFS. The classification accuracies obtained for GLDM, GLCM and features extracted from *ranklets* with k-NN were 93.2%, 90.5%, and 92.1% and with SVM were 91.2%, 89.4%, and 91.2%. The selected number of features for GLDM, GLCM, and features extracted from *ranklets* with HFS$_{k-NN}$ were 12, 9, and 13 respectively, and with HFS$_{SVM}$ were 21, 20, and 19 respectively. It is observed that feature dimensional space got reduced with the application of HFS, thereby, discarding the redundant and irrelevant features.

8.3.2 Experiment 2: Effectiveness of feature fusion

The second set of experiments is designed to obtain the best feature set. Here, feature fusion schemes are implemented in order to exploit the complementary information that is extracted from different texture features. The flow diagram of the experiment is shown in Fig. 8.3. The investigations conducted for designing the experiment are as follows:

i. SFC scheme is implemented in order to observe the impact of all the features, taken together, on characterization of liver classes. A set of 148 features is created by combining

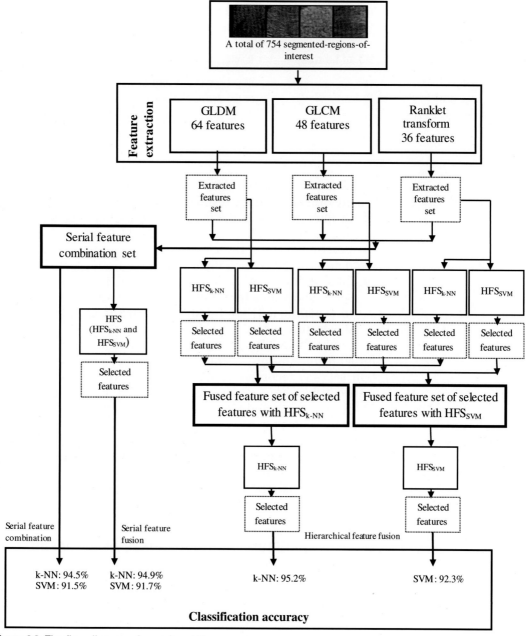

Figure 8.3 The flow diagram of experiment 2.

Table 8.5 The classification accuracy result for classifiers namely, k-NN and SVM, after feature fusion.

Feature fusion	No. of features	k-NN	No. of features	SVM
Serial combination	148	94.5 ± 0.5	148	91.5 ± 1.0
Serial fusion	13	94.9 ± 0.8	21	91.7 ± 0.3
Hierarchical fusion	11	95.2 ± 0.4	16	92.3 ± 0.7

all feature sets. The classification performances of classifiers are evaluated on the test data.

ii. In the next step, serial feature fusion scheme is implemented. HFS is applied to the set of 148 features (formed in experiment 2(i)). The classification performances of classifiers are evaluated on the test data.

iii. Finally, hierarchical feature fusion is implemented. The selected features from individual the feature sets (extracted in experiment 1) are fused. Then, HFS is again applied on this feature set.

Result: Table 8.5 provides the classification accuracy results for all feature fusion schemes. The accuracy of serial combination set was recorded 94.5% and 91.5% with k-NN and SVM respectively. The accuracy of serial fusion set was 94.9% and 91.7% with k-NN and SVM respectively. Finally, the accuracy of hierarchical fusion set was 95.2% and 92.3% with k-NN and SVM respectively.

It can be inferred from Table 8.5 that all feature fusion results improved the classification accuracy relative to individual feature sets. The hierarchical feature fusion set is the best reduced feature set with maximum accuracy.

8.3.3 Experiment 3: Effectiveness of proposed feature selection strategy

The proposed feature selection consists of two components: feature selection by ReliefF and feature selection by SFS. To demonstrate the effectiveness of the proposed selection strategy, the proposed method is compared with mostly used feature selection methods: ReliefF, SFS, and sequential backward search (SBS). Figs. 8.4−8.6 present the comparison based on accuracy, computation time, and number of selected features. Here, feature selection is carried out on 148 features, that is, on SFC set.

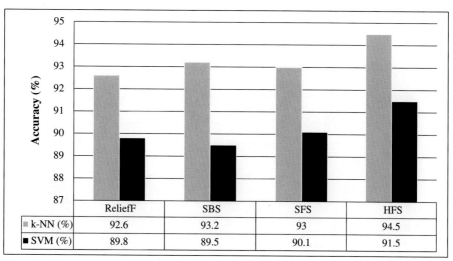

	ReliefF	SBS	SFS	HFS
k-NN (%)	92.6	93.2	93	94.5
SVM (%)	89.8	89.5	90.1	91.5

Figure 8.4 The classification accuracy obtained when ReliefF, SBS, SFS and proposed method (HFS) were used as feature selection methods with classifiers, k-NN and SVM.

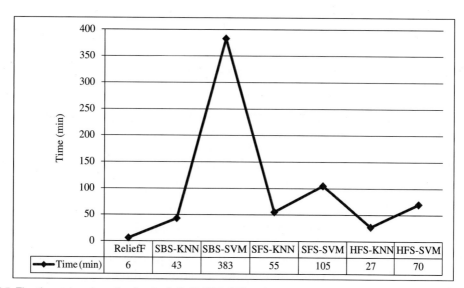

	ReliefF	SBS-KNN	SBS-SVM	SFS-KNN	SFS-SVM	HFS-KNN	HFS-SVM
Time (min)	6	43	383	55	105	27	70

Figure 8.5 The time taken for selection by ReliefF, SBS, SFS and proposed method (HFS) with classifiers, k-NN and SVM.
Notes: SBS-kNN, Sequential backward selection with classifier k-NN; SBS-SVM, sequential backward selection with classifier SVM; SFS-kNN, sequential forward selection with classifier k-NN; SFS-SVM, sequential forward selection with classifier SVM; HFS-kNN, hybrid feature selection with classifier k-NN; HFS-SVM, hybrid feature selection with classifier SVM.

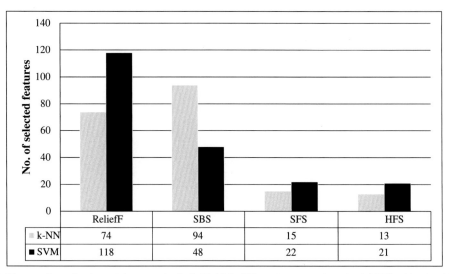

Figure 8.6 The number of selected features by ReliefF, SBS, SFS and proposed method (HFS) with classifiers, k-NN and SVM.

Result: It was observed from Fig. 8.5 that ReliefF method took minimum computation time for ranking features. The best threshold value selected for input of SFS_{k-NN} and SFS_{SVM} (after ReliefF ranking) was 50% and 80% of features respectively, were fixed (after several experiments) as this percentage of selected features gave maximum accuracy. These thresholds resulted in a large number of selected features, that is, 74 and 118 features for SFS_{k-NN} and SFS_{SVM} respectively (Fig. 8.6). Next, the number of features selected were 15 and 22 by using SFS_{k-NN} and SFS_{SVM}, whereas with proposed HFS method was 13 and 21 features for HFS_{k-NN} and HFS_{SVM}, respectively. The selected features were almost the same but computation time for selecting features with SFS_{k-NN} and SFS_{SVM} was nearly double than the proposed feature selection method (Fig. 8.5). Hence, with the best balance between accuracy, the number of selected features and computational time, the proposed method outperformed the compared feature selection methods.

8.4 Discussions

In this paper, the HFS-based feature fusion system is proposed to obtain the optimal feature set for characterizing four liver classes as normal, chronic, cirrhosis, and HCC evolved over cirrhosis. Regarding the proposed system, the following deductions can be made:

1. It can be noticed that feature dimensional space got reduced with the application of HFS method. For instance, the reduction in the number of features of GLDM, GLCM and *ranklets* with SFS_{kNN} were recorded as 84%, 81%, and 63%, and SFS_{SVM} were recorded as 67%, 58%, and 47%, respectively. This reduction in dimensionality of features increases the speed and reduces the complexity for the next set of experiments.

2. The results shown in Table 8.4 indicate that fusion of features improves classification accuracy considerably. For instance, the individual feature sets GLDM, GLCM, and *ranklets* have classification accuracy less than 92.2% whereas with fusion schemes classification accuracy was more than 91.5%. It is also observed that the classification accuracy of the serial-fused feature set was not significantly higher than that of the serial combined feature set. However, there was a significant reduction in the number of selected features; nearly 90% and 85% of serial combined features were discarded while using $HFS_{k\text{-}NN}$ and HFS_{SVM}, respectively. Next, as compared to serial feature fusion, hierarchical feature fusion set had more discriminating ability. The feature reduction rate of hierarchical feature fusion was also higher in comparison to serial feature fusion set; 90% for serial feature fusion and 92% for hierarchical feature fusion with respect to 148 features. Hence, hierarchical feature fusion selected features had more discrimination ability for classification and classifiers k-NN and SVM gave the highest accuracy of 95.2% and 92.3%, respectively. Hence, all the components of proposed feature selection method proved to complement each other and helped to generate the optimal feature set for classifying ultrasound images of liver into four classes.

8.5 Conclusion

In this paper, proposed HFS-based feature fusion system generated an optimal feature set for classifying liver ultrasound images into four classes, that is, normal, chronic, cirrhosis, and HCC evolved over cirrhosis. The set of 148 descriptive features were extracted, including 64 GLDM, 48 GLCM, and 36 from ranklet transformed images. HFS eliminated irrelevant or duplicate features, thereby improving the classification performance. The experimental results exhibit that the classification accuracy of the fused feature subset is superior to that derived by using individual feature subsets. We can also conclude from the experiments that proposed HFS method- based on hierarchical feature fusion gave the best results compared to SFC and serial fusion schemes. In particular, the accuracy was more by using proposed method as compared to ReliefF, SFS_{SVM}, SFS_{kNN}, SBS_{SVM}, and SBS_{kNN} feature selection methods. With the best balance between accuracy, the number of selected features and computational time, the proposed HFS method proved to be beneficial for differentiating ultrasound images of liver. In the future, we will do more tests on different datasets for robust algorithm.

References

Allan, R., Thoirs, K., Phillips, M., 2010. Accuracy of ultrasound to identify chronic liver disease. World J. Gastroenterol. 16 (28), 3510–3520.

Andrade, A., Silva, J.S., Santos, J., Belo-Soares, P., 2012. Classifier approaches for liver steatosis using ultrasound images. Proc. Technol. 5, 763–770.

Bensch, M., Schröder, M., Bogdan, M., Rosenstiel, W., 2005. Feature selection for high-dimensional industrial data. In: ESANN, D-Side Publishing, pp. 375–380.

Bharti, P., Mittal, D., Ananthasivan, R., 2017. Computer-aided characterization and diagnosis of diffuse liver diseases based on ultrasound imaging. Ultrason. Imaging 39 (1), 33–61.

Bharti, P., Mittal, D., Ananthasivan, R., 2018. Preliminary study of chronic liver classification on ultrasound images using an ensemble model. Ultrason. Imaging 40 (6), 357–379.

Bolón-Canedo, V., Sánchez-Maroño, N., Alonso-Betanzos, A., 2013. A review of feature selection methods on synthetic data. Knowl. Inf. Syst. 34 (3), 483–519.

Bolón-Canedo, V., Sánchez-Maroño, N., Alonso-Betanzos, A., 2015. Feature Selection for High-Dimensional Data. Springer International Publishing.

Cui, C., Hu, M., Weir, J.D., Wu, T., 2016. A recommendation system for meta-modeling: a meta-learning based approach. Expert. Syst. Appl. 46, 33–44.

Gomez, W., Pereira, W.C.A., Infantosi, A.F.C., 2012. Analysis of co-occurrence texture statistics as a function of gray-level quantization for classifying breast ultrasound. IEEE Trans. Med. Imaging 31 (10), 1889–1899.

Horng, M.H., 2007. An ultrasonic image evaluation system for assessing the severity of chronic liver disease. Comput. Med. Imaging Graph. 31 (7), 485–491.

Huang, J., Cai, Y., Xu, X., 2006. A wrapper for feature selection based on mutual information. 18th International Conference on Pattern Recognition (ICPR'06). IEEE, pp. 618–621.

Kalyan, K., Jakhia, B., Lele, R.D., Joshi, M., Chowdhary, A., 2014. Artificial neural network application in the diagnosis of disease conditions with liver ultrasound images, *Adv. Bioinformatics*, 2014, 14 p.

Kuncheva, L.I., 2014. Combining Pattern Classifiers: Methods and Algorithms. John Wiley & Sons, Inc.

Lee, W.-L., 2013. An ensemble-based data fusion approach for characterizing ultrasonic liver tissue. Appl. Soft Comput. 13 (8), 3683–3692.

Mangai, U., Samanta, S., Das, S., Chowdhury, P., 2010. A survey of decision fusion and feature fusion strategies for pattern classification. IETE Tech. Rev. 27 (4), 293.

Mitrea, D., Nedevschi, S., Socaciu, M., Badea, R., 2012. The role of the superior order GLCM in the characterization and recognition of the liver tumors from ultrasound images. Radioengineering 21 (1), 79–85.

Mittal, D., Kumar, V., Saxena, S.C., Khandelwal, N., Kalra, N., 2011. Neural network based focal liver lesion diagnosis using ultrasound images. Comput. Med. Imaging Graph. 35 (4), 315–323.

Osei-Bryson, K.-M., Giles, K., Kositanurit, B., 2003. Exploration of a hybrid feature selection algorithm. J. Oper. Res. Soc. 54 (7), 790–797.

Panthong, R., Srivihok, A., 2015. Wrapper feature subset selection for dimension reduction based on ensemble learning algorithm. Proc. Comput. Sci. 72, 162–169.

Pavlopoulos, S., Kyriacou, E., Koutsouris, D., Blekas, K., Stafylopatis, A., et al., 2000. Fuzzy neural network-based texture analysis of ultrasonic images. IEEE Eng. Med. Biol. Mag. 19 (1).

Pudil, P., Novovičová, J., Kittler, J., 1994. Floating search methods in feature selection. Pattern Recognit. Lett. 15 (11), 1119–1125.

Rani, A., Mittal, D., Ritambhara, 2016. Detection and classification of focal liver lesions using support vector machine classifiers. J. Biomed. Eng. Med. Imaging 3 (1), 21.

Santos, J., Silva, J.S., Santos, A.A., Belo-Soares, P., 2014. Detection of pathologic liver using ultrasound images. Biomed. Signal. Process. Control. 14, 248–255.

Shazzad, K.M., Park, J.S., 2005. Optimization of intrusion detection through fast hybrid feature selection. Sixth International Conference on Parallel and Distributed Computing Applications and Technologies (PDCAT'05). IEEE, pp. 264–267.

Sheikhpour, R., Sarram, M.A., Gharaghani, S., Chahooki, M.A.Z., 2017. A survey on semi-supervised feature selection methods. Pattern Recognit. 64 (November 2016), 141–158.

Singh, M., Singh, S., Gupta, S., 2013. An information fusion based method for liver classification using texture analysis of ultrasound images. Inf. Fusion 19, 91–96.

Solorio-Fernández, S., Carrasco-Ochoa, J.A., Martínez-Trinidad, J.F., 2016. A new hybrid filter–wrapper feature selection method for clustering based on ranking. Neurocomputing 214, 866–880.

Stoean, R., Stoean, C., 2013. Modeling medical decision making by support vector machines, explaining by rules of evolutionary algorithms with feature selection. Expert. Syst. Appl. 40 (7), 2677–2686.

Sun, Y., Todorovic, S., Goodison, S., 2010. Local-learning-based feature selection for high-dimensional data analysis. IEEE Trans. Pattern Anal. Mach. Intell. 32 (9), 1610–1626.

Tang, J., Alelyani, S., Liu, H., 2014. Feature selection for classification: a review. Data Classif. Algorithms Appl. 37–64.

Virmani, J., Kumar, V., Kalra, N., Khandelwal, N., 2013. SVM-based characterization of liver ultrasound images using wavelet packet texture descriptors. J. Digit. Imaging 26 (3), 530–543.

Winters-Hilt, S., Yelundur, A., McChesney, C., Landry, M., 2006. Support vector machine implementations for classification & amp; clustering. BMC Bioinforma. 7 (Suppl. 2), S4.

Wu, C.M., Chen, Y.C., Hsieh, K.S., 1992. Texture features for classification of ultrasonic liver images. IEEE Trans. Med. Imaging 11 (2), 141–152.

Wu, C.-C., Lee, W.-L., Chen, Y.-C., Lai, C.-H., Hsieh, K.-S., 2012. Ultrasonic liver tissue characterization by feature fusion. Expert. Syst. Appl. 39 (10), 9389–9397.

Wu, C., Lee, W., Chen, Y., Hsieh, K., 2013. Evolution-based hierarchical feature fusion for ultrasonic liver tissue characterization. IEEE J. Biomed. Health 17 (5), 967–976.

Wu, W., Parmar, C., Grossmann, P., et al., 2016. Exploratory study to identify radiomics classifiers for lung cancer histology. Front. Oncol. 6, 71.

Yang, J., Yang, J., Zhang, D., Lu, J., 2003. Feature fusion: parallel strategy vs. serial strategy. Pattern Recognit. 36 (6), 1369–1381.

Yang, M.-C., Moon, W.K., Wang, Y.-C.F., et al., 2013. Robust texture analysis using multi-resolution gray-scale invariant features for breast sonographic tumor diagnosis. IEEE Trans. Med. Imaging 32 (12), 2262–2273.

Zhang, Y., Ding, C., Li, T., 2008. Gene selection algorithm by combining reliefF and mRMR. BMC Genom. 9 (Suppl 2), S27.

Biomedical Image Compression and Transmission

Discrete cosine transform—based compressive sensing recovery strategies in medical imaging

Amira S. Ashour[1], Yanhui Guo[2], Eman Elsaid Alaa[1] and Hossam M. Kasem[1]

[1]*Department of Electronics and Electrical Communications Engineering, Faculty of Engineering, Tanta University, Tanta, Egypt* [2]*Department of Computer Science, University of Illinois, Springfield, IL, United States*

9.1   Introduction

Medical images from different modalities are characterized by their outsized dimensions. From the other side, telemedicine systems for consultation with a dramatic increase in the medical information raise the need for efficient use of the transmission channel bandwidth, which depends on the size of the

Advances in Computational Techniques for Biomedical Image Analysis. DOI: https://doi.org/10.1016/B978-0-12-820024-7.00009-8

transmitted information. Subsequently, there is an urgent need for developing efficient compression approaches, which keep the significant details in the medical images. The main concept of the compression methods is to minimize the required number of bits by manipulating the perceptual and spatial redundancy in the image. This procedure represents the image information while preserving adequate visual image quality.

Commonly, lossy- and lossless-compression methods are the main categories for image compassion. Lossy methods, including fractal compression, and transform coding, provide high compression ratios (CRs). Nevertheless, it is difficult to restore the original image from the compressed image due to the loss of information from the original image during the compression procedure. Conversely, the lossless methods, including predictive coding, arithmetic encoding, and Huffman encoding, tolerate the original image retrieval deprived of any information loss in the compressed image.

One of the efficient lossy techniques, which preserve the image's details, is the compressive sensing (CS). Hence, it can be used in medical image compression and telemedicine systems as it reconstructs the compressed images using a few measurements. The key of the CS is using the sparsity of the image to compress the image with a rate less than the Nyquist rate of sampling. In CS approaches, incoherence and sparsity are the main required conditions. Generally, the sparsity can be fulfilled in the time-domain, frequency-domain, such as wavelet transform (WT) and discrete cosine transform (DCT), or time-frequency domain. Unlike the conventional compression approaches, the CS has the capability to decrease the sampling rate of the sparse image with its robustness against noise.

Typically, for image compression, the CS directly acquires the compressed image by avoiding compression after image acquisition with the ability to reconstruct the total information subsequently. The missing information in the image appears as a series of omitted samples which are recovered using CS recovery algorithms. The recovery phase is a challenging task owing to the required prior knowledge of the image. It is modeled as an optimization problem searching for the appropriate minimum number of coefficients to the sampled information of the image.

The recovery algorithms can be classified into three main categories, namely (1) convex optimization-based algorithms, such as basis pursuit (BP) and BP denoising, and adaptive gradient-based algorithm, (2) greedy algorithms, such as matching pursuit (MP), orthogonal matching pursuit (OMP), compressive sampling matching pursuit (CoSaMP), and (3) threshold-based algorithms, such as iterative hard and soft thresholding, and automated threshold-based iterative solution.

Since the sparsity of an image at a specific time-instant is closely correlated to the sparsity of the preceding time-instance, weighted-CS methods can be used to improve the performance of the traditional CS. For image compression, the weighted-CS can be used with the images that have smooth sparsity changes with time. It uses the previous time-instance to estimate a model for the image for further use in the reconstruction process.

This chapter conducted a comparative study between the well-known CS approaches, from the greedy algorithms and convex optimization methods, with and without using the weighting procedure. The proposed weighted-CS employed the DCT of medical images using a threshold weighting matrix.

The structure of the further coming sections is as follows. Section 9.2 reports the preceding studies related to the traditional CS as well as the weighted-CS. In Section 9.3, the proposed weighted-CS with a detailed explanation of the CS techniques are introduced. Then, Section 9.4 discusses the results including comparative studies between the different CS techniques as well as the weighted-CS techniques. Finally, the conclusion is considered in Section 9.5.

9.2 Literature review

Numerous studies carried out the compression process using the CS due to its advantages by the transmission of a few measurements in several applications. For sampling rate reduction for further data detection, Pan et al. (2014) employed CoSaMP and L1 minimization to achieve minimum mean square error after the reconstruction process. Wang et al. (2014) offered a novel CS scheme based on Bregman split technique to optimize the CS function for compressing remote sensing images. Rouabah et al. (2018) proposed CS-based fast Fourier transform by using OMP in the compression phase and CoSaMP procedure in the recovery phase. The simulation results reported high-quality reconstruction process from only 30% of data with reduced processing time.

For medical image compression, Sevak et al. (2012) applied WT with the CS on computed tomography (CT) images. The results showed that the maximum value of the peak signal-to-noise ratio (PSNR) was 25 dB using 60% CR. Bhatt and Bamniya (2015) designed a hybrid medical image reconstruction method with less computational time compared to using greedy algorithm, and L1 method. The results established the superiority of the hybrid greedy algorithm with L1 method technique which provided improved reconstructed image quality compared to each of them separately. Furthermore, Graff and Sidky (2015) discussed the impact of the CS in compressing magnetic resonance imaging (MRI), CT, and X-ray images. Kher and Patel (2017) implemented a CS-framework using DWT and DCT to find the sparsity in the image. The results proved the superiority of the DWT-based CS compared to the DCT-based CS in terms of the PSNR for compressing MRI and CT images.

Other studies were employed weighted-CS to improve the performance of the conventional CS. A weighting scheme was implemented for image compression by Yang et al. (2009) using the frequency components of the image in the sampling matrix. The image was divided firstly into 8×8 and 16×16 blocks before applying two-dimensional DCT. This procedure enhanced CS performance with few complexities.

For fast recovery, Wan et al. (2011) designed a weighted-CS with the standard L1-based minimization procedure. For updated weights, an iterative procedure was applied for signal proportional to weights using the total variation and BP methods for a test. Li et al. (2012) developed a weighted block CS method for image recovery to diminish the aliasing. Initially, the image was segmented and divided into blocks, and various measurements were calculated for each block. Afterward, Lee et al. (2012) recommended a visual weight-based CS framework from the WT on Phantom and Baboon images. Wang and Lee (2015) designed a weighted DCT and iterative singular value decomposition (DCT-SVD) for CS recovery. The key of this method was the training procedure of the singular value decomposition from the preceding reconstruction leading to perfect recovery of the original image. Xu et al. (2016) implemented a perceptual distortion optimized rate based on dividing the image into blocks. Each block was then considered an optimization problem, which was solved by the relaxation Lagrangian scheme.

9.3 Methodology

9.3.1 Compressive sensing

The main concept of the CS starts from the Shannon/Nyquist sampling theory, which stated the sampling limit to avoid information loss. The limit of sampling rate to preserve the information is to perform the sampling at least two times faster than the signal bandwidth. In digital image processing and medical applications, the Nyquist rate may be high ending up with a huge number of samples. Hence, for efficient transmission and storage requirements, the compression becomes a must. At the same time, the concept of the Nyquist rate is applied in the CS to reduce the required number of measurements for a complete description of a signal/image by exploiting its compressibility using a linear expression of the signal to perform the CS as follows:

$$x = \Psi\theta \qquad (9.1)$$

where Ψ is an $N \times N$ basis matrix of the original image x, and θ is a self-possessed column vector of the coefficients of x, where x includes K nonzero elements on basis Ψ which is a sparse origin of x. The compressed image m_{cs} is given by:

$$\begin{aligned} m_{cs} &= \phi \cdot x \\ &= \phi \cdot \psi \cdot \theta \\ &= Ax \end{aligned} \qquad (9.2)$$

where m is a measurement vector of dimensions $M \times 1$, A is the measurement matrix of dimensions, $x \in R^N$ and $m \in R^M$. The design of the A matrix guarantees that the sparsity of the information in the image. Afterward, a recovery method is used to reconstruct x from m. For CS, a restricted isometry property (RIP) condition must be satisfied, which is given as follows:

$$(1 - \partial_k)||x_i||_2^2 \leq ||A_i x_i||_2^2 \leq (1 + \partial_k)||x_i||_2^2 \qquad (9.3)$$

To reconstruct the sparse image x correctly, ∂_k should be $\ll 1$ (i.e., $\partial_k \ll 1$) to ensure stable sensing matrix. In addition, A should be incoherent with the sparsifying basis Φ. Also, different transform domains, such as DCT, WT, and discrete sine transform (DST), can be used to achieve the sparsity in an image.

The basis of the DCT has concentrated energy in some coefficients in comparison with the energy distribution in the image. The DCT was applied in this chapter before applying the CS to guarantee the sparsity of the image. The DCT coefficients are then used in the proposed weighted CS method, and the recovery procedure. Then, to reconstruct the original image from the CS compressed version, optimization recovery methods are applied.

9.3.2 CS recovery algorithms

Different optimization-based recovery schemes were applied in this chapter for image recovery after the CS. These methods are L1-magic, OMP, CoSaMP, and CVX.

9.3.2.1 L1-magic

To solve the linear equation of CS, minimizing ℓ_o norm can be used such that $m = Ax$. For a sparse image, it is possible to relax ℓ_o norm to ℓ_1 norm, where

$$\min_x \|x\|_1 \quad \text{s.t. } m = Ax \tag{9.4}$$

where ℓ_1 norm for x is defined as follows:

$$\|x\|_1 = \sum_i |x_i| \tag{9.5}$$

The L1-magic is type of interior point algorithms for image recovery, which is expressed as follows:

$$\min_x \langle k_0, x \rangle \quad \text{s.t. } m = Axz_i(x) \leq 0 \tag{9.6}$$

where $m = R^M$, $x = R^N$, $i = 1, \ldots, k$, and $z_i(x)$ is a linear function, which is given by:

$$z_i(x) = \langle k_i, x \rangle + q_i \tag{9.7}$$

where $k_i, d_i \in R^M$. The L1-magic determines the optimal solution $\check{x}$ using dual vectors, namely and $\lambda^* \in R^M$, which represent the Karush-Kuhn-tucker conditions (Vujović et al., 2014). It is an iterative method for solving the convex optimization problems in the CS.

9.3.2.2 Orthogonal matching pursuit

The OMP is a type of greedy algorithm, which selects the columns of A by defining the greatest correlation among the residual of A and m. The highest correlation between A and m is then subtracted from the residual, where the image can be approximated after K iterations. The main principle for the MP was implied by Mallat and Zhang (1993), which was applied by Tropp and Gilbert (2007) for signals recovery using the OMP method.

9.3.2.3 Compressive sampling matching pursuit

The CoSaMP is another type of greedy algorithm which discovers the majority of useful basis. It constructs the image approximation by preserving only the biggest accesses in the least-squares estimated image x. Unlike the OMP, the CoSaMP is fast and powerful in solving the CS problems to approximate the image. The CoSaMP identifies the sparse pixels using a matched filter in an iterative process (Needell and Tropp, 2009). It decreases the reconstruction error of the sparse image and takes less computational compared to the OMP. The sensing matrix of CoSaMP has to fulfill the RIP condition.

9.3.2.4 CVX

CVX is a modeling tool based on Matlab for convex optimization, which relaxes the minimization problems from ℓ_o norm to ℓ_1 norm and solves this linear equation for the CS to find the optimal solution of the image. It is an iterative procedure that depends on the number of pixels in the image to solve the convex problem (Baraniuk, 2007).

9.3.3 Proposed weighted compressive sensing

In CS, the weighting conception is used to improve the CS performance through the recovery process using any recovery procedure, including the L1-magic, OMP, CoSaMP, and CVX. In this chapter, a proposed weight matrix W was generated from the original image's DCT coefficients. This weight is multiplied by the selected DCT coefficients using a proposed threshold. This threshold was determined by scanning the DCT matrix. The generated weight, which has values higher than the threshold, was then used to create a weighted image, where the weighting matrix can be given by:

$$W = \text{diag}(w) \tag{9.8}$$

Then, to find the weighted image x_w, W is multiplied by the DCT coefficients matrix of the original image as follows:

$$x_w = W\Psi\theta \tag{9.9}$$

Afterward, the compressed image m_{cs} can be stated as follows:

$$\begin{aligned} m_{cs} &= \Phi W\Psi\theta \\ &= AWx \\ &= Ax_w \end{aligned} \tag{9.10}$$

After transmitting the compressed image to the receiver through a transmission channel, the image is reconstructed using a recovery procedure. The general proposed algorithm of the proposed weighted-based CS and recovery is as follows.

Algorithm: Proposed weighted CS with recovery procedures

Start

    Transform the colored image to grayscale images

At the transmitter:

    Generate a random measurement matrix for further use in the CS process

    Transform the image to DCT domain to increase the image sparsity

    Extract the DCT coefficients from the image to create the DCT matrix

    Find the threshold by scanning the DCT coefficients to determine the best value that achieves the best peak-signal-to-noise ratio (PSNR)

    Determine the weight value using the threshold value, where the weighting process is performed on the DCT matrix

    Construct the weighted image by multiplying the weight matrix by the DCT coefficients

    Compress the weighted image using the CS

At the receiver:

    Recover the compressed image using the different recovery algorithms, namely L1-magic, OMP, CoSaMP, and CVX or OMP

End

9.3.4 Performance metrics

Different evaluation metrics can be calculated for evaluating the compression procedure, including the structural similarity index measure (SSIM), CR, and the PSNR. Generally, the SSIM measures the matching between two compressed and recovered images in terms of the image structure, contrast, and luminance, which is expressed as follows:

$$\text{SSIM}(g, h) = \frac{\left(2\alpha_g \alpha_h + j_1\right)\left(2S_{gh} + j_2\right)}{\left(\alpha_g^2 + \alpha_h^2 + j_1\right)\left(S_g^2 + S_h^2 + j_2\right)} \tag{9.11}$$

where α_g, α_h, S_{gh}, S_g, and S_h are the local means, cross-covariance, and standard deviations, respectively, of the images g and h. Moreover, the CR is the ratio of the pixels' number of the compressed image N_2 to those in the original image N_1, which is defined as follows:

$$\text{CR} = \frac{N_2}{N_1} \tag{9.12}$$

The PSNR measures the peak error to the peak value of the image, which is given by:

$$\text{PSNR} = 10\log_{10}\frac{(255)^2}{\text{MSE}} \tag{9.13}$$

where MSE is the mean square error.

9.4 Results and discussion

To evaluate the different recovery methods of the CS framework using the weight procedure, diabetic retinopathy images were used. MATLAB R2018b software was used during the experiments on Intel-Core i5−2410M 2.3 GHz processor with 4 GB of RAM.

Generally, the DCT has energy compaction property, which means that the energy is more concentrated in some elements compared to the energy distribution in the original image (Rao and Yip, 2014). Thus in this chapter, the proposed threshold and weight values were determined from DCT basis matrix of the original image. These values were used to form the weighted image matrix. In the present work, the threshold was chosen as a boundary between the relevant and irrelevant DCT coefficients of the image. Thus from the DCT basis matrix ranging from −2 to 2, the best threshold value was selected which achieved the best PSNR −1.3122. Then, based on this threshold, the determined weight value was 0.98 which was used to raise the effect of the relevant DCT coefficients and generated the weight image using the image characteristics. Fig. 9.1 demonstrated sample diabetic retinopathy images from the used dataset using 35 images, where 20 images were used for training and 15 images for the test to assess the proposed weighted-based CS recovery procedure.

The weighted image is then compressed using the CS procedure. Afterward, at the receiver, different optimization recovery procedures were tested and compared to recover the original image from the compressed one. In the present chapter, comparative studies were conducted between the different traditional recovery methods with and without using the weight-based CS methods.

9.4.1 Comparative study using traditional recovery schemes

In this section, the different traditional recovery schemes, namely L1-magic, OMP, CoSaMP, and CVX were evaluated and compared for reconstructing the compressed images using the

Figure 9.1 Sample of the diabetic retinopathy images.

CS without applying the proposed weighting process. Fig. 9.2 illustrated the visual comparison between the different recovery methods for the previously compressed images using 70% CR for five images as samples.

Fig. 9.2 depicted that the recovered images using the traditional CVX recovery method provided the best recovery results compared visually to the other methods. The numerical results were reported using the measured PSNR and the SSIM metrics for the recovered images from the corresponding compressed ones at 70% CR as reported in Table 9.1.

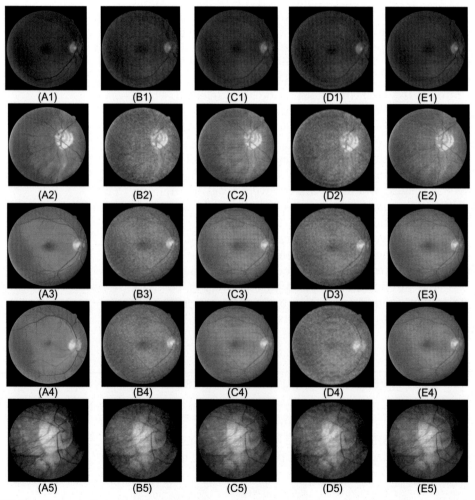

Figure 9.2 Sample images from the used dataset after recovery from 70% CR, where (A1—A5) original images, (B1—B5) recovered images using the traditional OMP, (C1—C5) recovered images using traditional L1-magic, (D1—D5) recovered images using traditional CoSaMP, and (E1—E5) recovered images using traditional CVX.

Table 9.1 Comparison for PSNR between traditional recovery techniques for compressed sensing at 70% compression ratio for five images.

Image ID	Traditional L1-magic	Traditional OMP	Traditional CoSaMP	Traditional CVX
ID30	24.56	21.62	34.73	37.33
ID31	24.81	21.85	30.34	33.00
ID32	25.60	23.36	31.75	34.58
ID33	23.18	21.97	30.28	33.21
ID34	25.95	23.56	33.01	35.47

Table 9.2 Comparison for SSIM between traditional recovery techniques for compressed sensing at 70% compression ratio for five images.

Image ID	Traditional L1-magic	Traditional OMP	Traditional CoSaMP	Traditional CVX
ID30	0.39	0.26	0.82	0.89
ID31	0.38	0.26	0.67	0.79
ID32	0.36	0.26	0.72	0.83
ID33	0.29	0.23	0.66	0.79
ID34	0.54	0.41	0.79	0.88

Table 9.1 established that the traditional CVX achieved superior performance compared to the other traditional recovery methods in terms of the PSNR and SSIM for the recovered images from the corresponding compressed ones using CS at 70% CR. Additionally, Table 9.2 included the SSIM values using the same traditional recovery procedures at 70% CR.

Table 9.2 also proved the superiority of the traditional CVX compared to the other traditional recovery algorithms in terms of the SSIM values. Moreover, Table 9.3 reported the PSNR values using the traditional recovery approaches at 30% CR.

Table 9.3 depicted that the traditional CVX has an outstanding result compared to the other recovery methods even at low CR of 30% in terms of the PSNR. In addition, the SSIM values were reported in Table 9.4 at the same 30% CR using different traditional recovery methods.

Fig. 9.3 illustrated the comparison between the traditional recovery methods at 70% CR in terms of the average PSNR and SSIM over the used dataset images.

Table 9.3 Comparison for PSNR between traditional recovery techniques for compressed sensing at 30% compression ratio for five images.

Image ID	Traditional L1-magic	Traditional OMP	Traditional CoSaMP	Traditional CVX
ID30	18.62	17.13	27.34	27.71
ID31	18.34	17.24	22.93	23.28
ID32	18.45	17.01	24.67	24.48
ID33	18.10	17.17	22.81	21.77
ID34	18.66	17.12	26.19	26.55

Table 9.4 Comparison for SSIM between traditional recovery techniques for compressed sensing at 30% compression ratio for five images.

Image ID	Traditional L1-magic	Traditional OMP	Traditional CoSaMP	Traditional CVX
ID30	0.194124	0.13064	0.5316	0.5810
ID31	0.19086	0.13513	0.3325	0.4086
ID32	0.195654	0.134294	0.4270	0.4594
ID33	0.184031	0.128234	0.3296	0.344
ID34	0.192187	0.133573	0.4974	0.5656

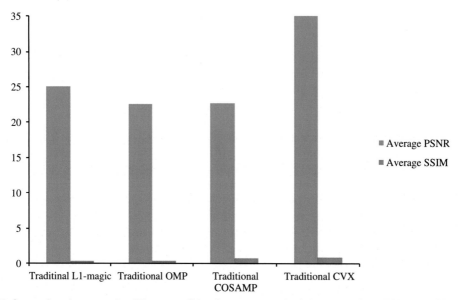

Figure 9.3 Comparison between the different traditional recovery methods in terms of the PSNR and SSIM for compressed images at 70% CR.

The preceding results proved the superiority of the traditional CVX compared to the other recovery methods even at small CR values.

9.4.2 Comparative study using proposed weighting-based recovery methods

In this section, the proposed weighted-based recovery methods of the different recovery procedures were compared. Fig. 9.4 illustrated the subjective comparison of these methods after the recovery of the compressed images at 70% CR.

Fig. 9.4 revealed that the recovered images using the weighted-CS improved the quality of recovered images, also the weighted-based CVX provided the best subjective results compared to the other weighted recovery methods. In addition, the PSNR and SSIM were measured for comparing the weighted recovery methods. Table 9.5 reported the PSNR for weighted-based recovery procedures of the compressed images at 70% CR.

Table 9.5 depicted that the weighted-based CVX achieved superior performance compared to the other recovery methods in terms of the PSNR, while the weighted-based OMP has the least performance. Furthermore, Table 9.6 included the SSIM values for the same experiment under the same conditions.

Table 9.6 confirmed the superiority of the weighted-based CVX in terms of the SSIM values for the recovery of compressed images at 70% CR for five images. The same experiments were conducted for compressed images at 30%, which provided the results in Tables 9.7 and 9.8 of the PSNR and SSIM, respectively.

Tables 9.7 and 9.8 concluded the superiority of the proposed weighted-based CVX to the other proposed weighted-based recovery algorithms in terms of the PSNR and SSIM, respectively. In addition, Figs. 9.5 and 9.6 demonstrated a comparative study of the different traditional and weighted-based recovery algorithms in terms of the average PSNR and the average SSIM values, respectively, at different CRs.

The preceding overall results concluded the superiority of the proposed weight-based CS compared to all the studied traditional recovery methods. Moreover, in the comparison between the recovery algorithms, the CVX method proved its outstanding performance compared to the L1-magic, OMP, and CoSaMP, while the OMP provided the worst performance results.

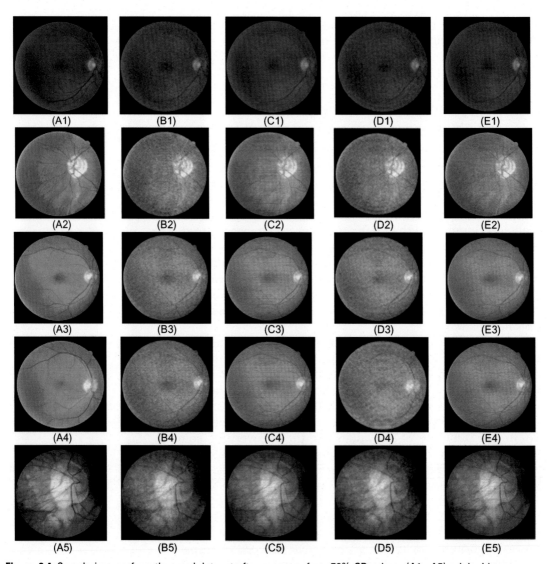

Figure 9.4 Sample images from the used dataset after recovery from 70% CR, where (A1—A5) original images, (B1—B5) recovered images using the proposed weighted-based OMP, (C1—C5) recovered images using the proposed weighted-based L1-magic, (D1—D5) recovered images using the proposed weighted-based CoSaMP, and (E1—E5) recovered images using the proposed weighted-based CVX.

9.5 Conclusions

One of the serious eye diseases that may require consultation is diabetic retinopathy. For transmitting and storing the captured images of this disease, medical image compression

Table 9.5 Comparison of PSNR between weighted-based recovery methods for the compressed images at 70% CR for five images.

Image ID	Weighted L1-magic	Weighted OMP	Weighted CoSaMP	Weighted CVX
ID30	24.57	21.63	34.74	37.34
ID31	24.82	21.86	30.35	33.01
ID32	25.61	23.37	31.76	34.60
ID33	23.19	21.98	30.29	33.22
ID34	25.97	23.57	33.02	35.48

Table 9.6 Comparison of SSIM between weighted-based recovery methods for the compressed images at 70% CR for five images.

Image ID	Weighted L1-magic	Weighted OMP	Weighted CoSaMP	Weighted CVX
ID30	0.40	0.27	0.83	0.90
ID31	0.39	0.27	0.68	0.80
ID32	0.37	0.27	0.74	0.84
ID33	0.30	0.24	0.67	0.80
ID34	0.55	0.42	0.80	0.89

Table 9.7 Comparison of PSNR between weighted-based recovery methods for the compressed images at 30% CR for five images.

Image ID	Weighted L1-magic	Weighted OMP	Weighted CoSaMP	Weighted CVX
ID30	18.63	17.14	27.35	27.72
ID31	18.35	17.26	22.95	23.29
ID32	18.46	17.03	24.68	24.49
ID33	18.11	17.18	22.82	21.78
ID34	18.67	17.14	26.20	26.57

becomes an essential task. In this chapter, well-known compressive sensing methods were introduced and compared in terms of the traditional recovery algorithms.

Table 9.8 Comparison of SSIM between weighted-based recovery methods for the compressed images at 30% CR for five images.

Image ID	Weighted L1-magic	Weighted OMP	Weighted CoSaMP	Weighted CVX
ID30	0.20	0.14	0.54	0.59
ID31	0.20	0.14	0.34	0.41
ID32	0.20	0.14	0.43	0.46
ID33	0.19	0.13	0.33	0.35
ID34	0.20	0.14	0.40	0.57

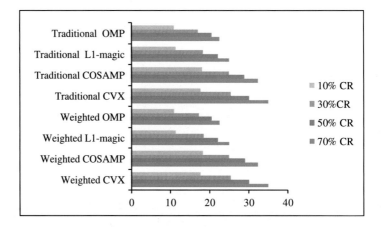

Figure 9.5 Comparison between the average PSNR of the traditional and weighted-based recovery methods at different CRs, where the x-axis represents the PSNR average values.

In addition, to improve the performance of the traditional recovery methods, a proposed weighted- CS methods were carried out in the CS framework. Accordingly, a weighting value was selected based on a threshold value. Then, a weighted matrix was generated by multiplying the weight by the DCT coefficients of the original image.

To evaluate and conduct the comparative studies between the recovery algorithms with each other as well as with and without the weighted-CS proposed framework, the PSNR and the SSIM were measured at different CRs. The results established the superiority of the weighted-based CVX compared to all the traditional recovery methods as well as the other weighted-based recovery methods.

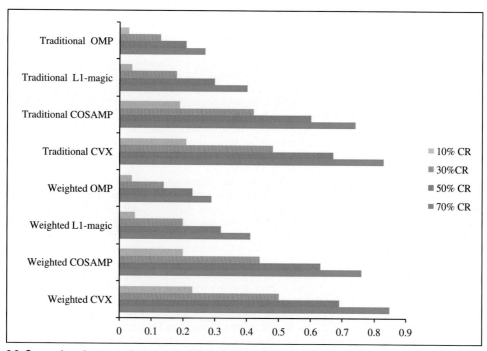

Figure 9.6 Comparison between the average SSIM of the traditional and weighted-based recovery methods at different CRs, where the x-axis represents the SSIM average values.

References

Baraniuk, R.G., 2007. Compressive sensing. IEEE Signal. Process. Mag. 24 (4).

Bhatt, M.U., Bamniya, K., 2015. Medical image compression and reconstruction using compressive sensing. J. Emerg. Technol. Innovat. Res. 2 (5).

Graff, C.G., Sidky, E.Y., 2015. Compressive sensing in medical imaging. Appl. Opt. 54 (8), C23–C44.

Kher, R., Patel, Y., 2017. Medical image compression framework based on compressive sensing, DCT and DWT. Biol. Enf. Med. 2 (2), 1–4.

Lee, H., Oh, H., Lee, S., Bovik, A.C., 2012. Visually weighted compressive sensing: measurement and reconstruction. IEEE Trans. image Process. 22 (4), 1444–1455.

Li, Y., Sha, X., Wang, K., Fang, X., 2012. The weight-block compressed sensing and its application to image reconstruction. 2012 Second International Conference on Instrumentation, Measurement, Computer, Communication and Control. IEEE, pp. 723–727.

Mallat, S.G., Zhang, Z., 1993. Matching pursuits with time-frequency dictionaries. IEEE Trans. Signal. Process. 41 (12), 3397–3415.

Needell, D., Tropp, J.A., 2009. CoSaMP: iterative signal recovery from incomplete and inaccurate samples. Appl. Comput. Harmonic Anal. 26 (3), 301–321.

Pan, K.J.L., Haque, T., DiFazio, R., Zeira, A., 2014. Enhanced data detection employing compressed sensing in wireless communications. 2014 International Conference and Workshop on the Network of the Future (NOF). IEEE, pp. 1—2.

Rao, K.R., Yip, P., 2014. Discrete Cosine Transform: Algorithms, Advantages, Applications. Academic Press.

Rouabah, S., Ouarzeddine, M., Souissi, B., 2018. SAR images compressed sensing based on recovery algorithms. IGARSS 2018-2018 IEEE International Geoscience and Remote Sensing Symposium. IEEE, pp. 8897—8900.

Sevak, M.M., Thakkar, F.N., Kher, R.K., Modi, C.K., 2012. CT image compression using compressive sensing and wavelet transform. 2012 International Conference on Communication Systems and Network Technologies. IEEE, pp. 138—142.

Tropp, J.A., Gilbert, A.C., 2007. Signal recovery from random measurements via orthogonal matching pursuit. IEEE Trans. Inf. Theory 53 (12), 4655—4666.

Vujović, S., Daković, M., Stanković, L., 2014. Comparison of the L1-magic and the gradient algorithm for sparse signals reconstruction. 2014 22nd Telecommunications Forum Telfor (TELFOR). IEEE, pp. 577—580.

Wan, X., Bai, H., Yu, L., 2011. An improved weighted total variation algorithm for compressive sensing. 2011 International Conference on Electronics, Communications and Control (ICECC). IEEE, pp. 145—148.

Wang, Z., Lee, I., 2015. Iterative weighted DCT-SVD for compressive imaging. 2015 International Conference on Intelligent Information Hiding and Multimedia Signal Processing (IIH-MSP). IEEE, pp. 405—408.

Wang, L., Lu, K., Liu, P., 2014. Compressed sensing of a remote sensing image based on the priors of the reference image. IEEE Geosci. Remote. Sens. Lett. 12 (4), 736—740.

Xu, J., Qiao, Y., Wen, Q., Fu, Z., 2016. Perceptual rate-distortion optimized image compression based on block compressive sensing. J. Electron. Imaging 25 (5), 053004.

Yang, Y., Au, O.C., Fang, L., Wen, X., Tang, W., 2009. Perceptual compressive sensing for image signals. 2009 IEEE International Conference on Multimedia and Expo. IEEE, pp. 89—92.

10

Segmentation-based compression techniques for medical images

Paramveer Kaur Sran[1], Savita Gupta[2] and Sukhwinder Singh[1]

[1]*Department of Computer Science and Engineering, University Institute of Engineering and Technology, Panjab University, Chandigarh, India*
[2]*Director, University Institute of Engineering and Technology, Panjab University, Chandigarh, India*

10.1 Introduction

The advancement in transmission and storage of data are not in position to grapple with the colossal increase of digital imaging. This requires the design and development of new compression methods in all domains but particularly in medical imaging, as a high quality of the diagnostically important is required (Shukla, 2010). To meet this challenge, a number of compression techniques and standards have been developed. All these compression approaches are broadly classified into two categories: lossy and lossless Compression (Bhavani, 2010). Lossy compression can achieve high compression ratios at the cost of a slight loss in data, which may lose the clinically critical

Advances in Computational Techniques for Biomedical Image Analysis. DOI: https://doi.org/10.1016/B978-0-12-820024-7.00010-4

information and affect the diagnosis process. On the contrary, lossless compression preserves the original information in the image, but at an unacceptable compression ratio. To address this twofold problem of high compression ratio and good image quality, segmentation-based compression techniques have been proposed in the literature. The idea is to compress the medical image in such a manner that the region of interest (ROI) (diagnostically important region) preserves the better quality than the non-ROI (unimportant region). In progressive transmission, the part of the ROI area is transmitted and decoded before the background part. As a result, segmentation-based coding is efficient in providing high quality over selected ROI in a limited time in comparison with the coding of the whole image. The general framework for the design of an ROI-based compression technique is shown in Fig. 10.1.

Several general surveys (Bhavani, 2010; Jangbari, 2016; Revathi et al., 2018; Shukla, 2010; Wong et al., 1995) on medical image compression have already been published in the literature. All the surveys are focused on lossy and lossless image compression. To the best of our knowledge, there is no article available that reviews the state-of-the-art in the field of ROI-based medical image compression based on segmentation approaches. For extracting the ROI accurately, various segmentation methods are being used. The choice of segmentation method is important because it highly affects the overall performance of the ROI coding algorithm. For medical image segmentation, different techniques have been used for different modalities. In this chapter, we have analyzed the working of various ROI-based medical image compression techniques available to date and have tried to classify them on the basis of underlying segmentation methods (supervised and unsupervised).

The key role of this analysis is to present an insight into the novices to start the study in the area of ROI-based compression for medical images. Various studies have been reviewed and their

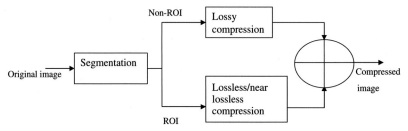

Figure 10.1 Framework for ROI-based image compression.

summary is provided by pinpointing their merits and limitations. Some challenges which need to be addressed for improving the quality of research in this field are also acknowledged.

The organization of this chapter is as follows: Section 10.2 examines the research and developments in the area of ROI coding. Section 10.3 presents ROI coding techniques and their classification on the basis of underlying segmentation methods. Section 10.4 provides a comparative analysis of some segmentation techniques used for ROI extraction in medical images. Some new techniques applied in medical image segmentation are discussed in Section 10.5. Finally, the challenges and future scope are presented in Section 10.6.

10.2 Research and developments in region of interest coding

In the early 1990s, researchers attempted to focus on compressing the ROI with higher priority, but those techniques were not recognized as ROI-based coding techniques, however, the general theme was to preserve the diagnostically important regions at a high quality, whereas the rest image at a lower quality. Several such region-based coding methods have been investigated in (Chen et al., 1994; Chant et al., 1858; Cosman, 1996; Kim et al., 1995; Ohiaki, 1993; Perlmutter et al., 1992; Pham et al., 2000; Poggi and Olshen, 1995). Perlmutter et al. (1992) segmented the MR brain images with regression tree method and then vector quantizer was used to encode different segments at different rates for improving the visual quality of compressed images. Some limitations of using different codebooks and small training data are reported. The test images resulted in brain part displaced with respect to the average brain portion of the training set. The boundaries of regions got distorted as only 10 training images were used and classified into 7 different training datasets. This problem was fixed in Cosman (1996) and recursive segmentation was used for segmentation of the CT chest scan into three parts; chest wall, chest organs, and the background region. As background region has no importance in ROI-based coding, zero bits were assigned to it. The chest wall area and chest organs area were encoded at a low bit-rate and high bit-rate respectively to achieve good visual quality.

Ohiaki (1993) used automatic segmentation to decompose left ventricular cineangiograms into three regions. The difference operation and smooth function were applied to calculate the differences within each region and their residuals were approximated to get the compressed image. Poggi and Olshen (1995) proposed a region-based method using a prediction scheme. Segmentation of CT chest images was performed by using thresholding, connectivity, and shape smoothing to get the foreground and background parts. Chen et al. (1858, 1994) developed an adaptive quantization-based method for quantizing wavelet coefficients capable of preserving strong edges. Wavelet decomposition was used to explore the characteristics of image features present in the medical image. The clustering-based method with spatial constraints was then applied to the high-frequency subbands to preserve the image features at different scales. These preserved features enabled the compression algorithm to compress the diagnostically important structures with high visually quality, even at a low bit rate. In 1995, the term ROI was first used by Vlaicu et al. (1995) for the diagnostically important region. They proposed ROI-discrete cosine transform (DCT) algorithm in which DCT was performed on a medical image where a smaller number of DCT coefficients were retained for blocks outside the important region and more coefficients were preserved inside the ROI to achieve the high quality of ROI part in the output image.

10.3 Classification of segmentation-based coding techniques

A great variety of methods with confusing names can be found in literature from 1995 to date. No specific name was given to these compression methods used for medical imagery. Some researchers named ROI-based techniques as region-based techniques (Bartrina-Rapesta and Serra-sagrist, 2009; Cosman, 1996; Perlmutter et al., 1992) and others call these object-based techniques (Vlaicu et al., 1995). The name content-based compression was used by some authors (Grinstead et al., 2000; Chan et al., 2014; Du et al., 2001). In some studies (Hannachi and Ahmed, 2017; Krishnamoorthy, 2012; Thangavelu and Krishnan, 2013), adaptive image compression also refers to ROI-based coding. Therefore the terms region-based, object-based, content-based, and adaptive image compression are the names interchangeably used in the ROI image coding literature. Until now no attempt has been made to analyze the difference among all these techniques. In this chapter, we have tried to classify all these techniques into various categories based on underlying segmentation methods used for ROI-based coding.

10.3.1 Unsupervised/region-based image compression

In medical imagery, all regions are not of equal importance. So only a few regions of the image required special consideration. Therefore ROI coding provides high reconstruction quality over the selected salient regions as compared to the compression of the full image. Moreover, a good trade-off between compression ratio and image quality is provided by region-based coding.

Yang et al. (2005) presented an ROI-based image compression method named embedded block coding with optimized truncation (EBCOT). A rectangular-shaped ROI was selected and it covered 25% of the area of the full image. The implicit ROI encoding method was modified to achieve the ROI coding. The background coefficients and ROI coefficients were assigned less priority and high priority respectively without increasing the complexity of the algorithm. Thus, in the decoding phase, ROI with good image quality appeared before the background part. The algorithm was tested on ultrasound, computed tomography, and computed radiology chest images.

The set partitioning in hierarchical trees (SPIHT) method was modified to achieve the ROI coding by generating the separate bitstreams for chromosome ROIs and the background part of the image (Liu et al., 2002). The chromosome spread and karyotype images were segmented using automatic segmentation techniques and then manual user interaction was conducted to check that the salient region was properly segmented and extracted. The ROI's shape information was coded with chain code-based shape coding scheme. To compress the digital mammograms, two ROI-based coding methods named as object-based extension of the SPIHT (OB-SPIHT) and object-based extension of the set partitioned embedded block (OB-SPECK) were proposed (Penedo et al., (2003)). The breast region was segmented with thresholding and binary masks created with segmentation were applied to provide the shape information of ROI. To preserve the exact number of wavelet coefficients, an arbitrary-shaped ROI was decomposed with region-based discrete wavelet transform (RBDWT). As compared to the existing methods like SPIHT and JPEG2000, OB-SPIHT and OB-SPECK performed better in providing higher quality in the breast regions. However, association with region-based wavelet transform made these methods computationally expensive.

The modified SPIHT algorithm was integrated with integer wavelet transform to implement the region-based coding for compression of different modalities (MRI, angiogram, and mammogram) (Tasdoken and Cuhadar, 2003). Integer wavelet decomposition with alternative feeding mechanism was applied to obtain arbitrary-shaped ROI of the partitioned image signal, which helps to map the partitioned planes of an image into a wavelet coefficient planes. Then modified SPIHT algorithm was used to encode these sparse representations. The concept of unbalanced spatial orientation tree structure was introduced to address the problem of region size sensitivity. The experimental result showed that the algorithm performed better than SPIHT-based ROI coding.

An ROI coding through component priority (ROITCOP) method based on the joint photographic experts group (JPEG) 2000 was introduced in Bartrina-Rapesta et al. (2011). In this method, a multicomponent image was generated by allocating different components to each ROI and the remaining area of that component was set to zero. The optimization stage of rate-distortion was modified to update the estimation of distortion for different components and code blocks according to Eq. (10.1). It helped to assign the desired priority to each component of ROIs.

$$D'_{c,i}n_j = \begin{cases} u'_c * D_{c,i}^{n_j} & \text{if } c \in \text{ROI} \\ D_{c,i}^{n_j} & \text{otherwise} \end{cases} \qquad (10.1)$$

where $D_{c,i}^{n_j}$ represents the distortion in component c for I (code block) at n_j (truncation point), and u'_c indicates the priority for ROI. Contextual set partitioning in hierarchical trees algorithm (CSPIHT) was formulated for abdomen ultrasound images (Ansari and Anand, 2009). To rectify the noise, preprocessing and filtering were performed. Images were segmented by using region growing method interactively. The used ROI was of arbitrary shape and the size of the ROI was very large, approximately 50%−60% of the full image. The separated parts of ROI and non-ROI were encoded at different bit rates. Various metrics like CR, MSE, PSNR, and coefficient of correlation were calculated to evaluate the results. It has been analyzed that CSPIHT performed better than JPEG, JPEG2000, and SPIHT at low bit rates. The performance of algorithm degrades at high bit rates.

A hybrid method which integrated adaptive arithmetic coding and lifting wavelet transform was proposed for compression of brain MRI images (Thomas et al., 2014). K-means clustering was applied for separating the tumor region from images. The tumor region was compressed with adaptive arithmetic coding which used fast discrete curvelet transform and background was compressed with lifting wavelet transform. The ROI-based coding algorithm for compression of brain MRI digital imaging and communications in medicine (DICOM) images was proposed (Bairagi and Sapkal, 2013). The ROI was selected by expert radiologists. Then thresholding was applied to create a mask for the selected area. ROI part was compressed with IWT and non-ROI part was compressed with SPIHT to retain the image quality of the important region and to improve the compression ratio. Brain MRI DICOM images were compressed with modified SPHIT (Rupa et al., 2014; Mohan and Venkataramani, 2014). The ROI was extracted with spatial fuzzy *c*-means clustering and discrete curvelet transform was exploited in modified SPIHT to encode this region. The SPIHT method based on biorthogonal wavelet transform was applied to the background. This method performed better in comparison to JPEG, haar SPIHT, and bi-orthogonal SPIHT.

Diagnostically lossless coding based on background suppression for compression of X-ray angiography images was proposed (Xu et al., 2016). The automatic ROI extraction was carried out with ray-casting and α-shapes. Then a logical AND operator was applied to suppress the background. The segmented images were encoded with different lossless and progressive lossy-to lossless methods, including H.264, JPEG2000, JPEG-LS, and HEVC. It was found that HEVC with background suppression was the best performer method and H.264 was the worst performer among all. The ROI-based coding method named improved medical image compression (IMIC) was presented in Zuo et al. (2015). The ROI region of MRI images was segmented with an active contour method and then the background region was blurred with a blur kernel. The selected region of ROI was encoded with JPEG-LS and the non-ROI area was encoded with wavelet-based lossy compression method. The results of IMIC method were compared with the lossless coding methods JPEG-LS, CALIC, JPEG2000, and the lossy image coding. It was observed that the method achieved good fine details and resulted in high compression ratio.

An ROI-based algorithm was proposed for teleradiological applications (Vilas et al., 2016). The preprocessing was performed with Wiener filter to remove the noise, and the skull was removed by using the morphological operations. For background removal, images were initially thresholded based on high-intensity pixels. A mask was generated and masked with the original image to provide input for the next stage. Then the lower threshold was selected to create the second mask and the tumor was segmented from the background. Finally, enhanced DPCM and Huffman coding were applied to compress the images. The algorithm was tested on a database of 25 tumorous brain MR images and obtained better results.

A wavelet transformation-based coding approach for medical images using normalization and prediction was presented (Sophia et al., 2017). The ROI was extracted with an interactive method. Initially, the approximate and the detailed coefficients were obtained by applying the wavelet transform on the image and normalization was performed for each subband separately, followed by the prediction to generate a mask of the normalized coefficients. Finally, the arithmetic coding technique was used to encode the prediction error coefficients. The prediction and transformation were combined to achieve high compression ratio along with good visual quality. The results of the proposed method were compared with such as WDR, SPIHT, EZW, EBCOT, Maxshift, JPEG2000, and CSPIHT on MRI DICOM images and ultrasound images. Fuzzy level set segmentation was combined with ROI-SPIHT for compression of CT images (Sran et al., 2013). This method performed better as compared to JPEG, JPEG2K, and SPIHT in terms of compression ratio and image quality. MRI image and CT chest data were coded with segmentation-based multilayer scheme where ROI was extracted with automatic region growing and compressed with Burrows-Wheeler transform coding method. JPEG2000 was then used for encoding the multilayer residual image (Bai et al., 2003). Table 10.1 summarizes the unsupervised techniques for ROI-based coding.

10.3.2 Supervised/content-based image compression

The content-based compression techniques use the classifier instead of a quantizer (Du et al., 2001). In medical images, salient information may lie in various shapes, contours, edges, etc. and these are known as the ROIs in the image (Namuduri and Ramaswamy, 2003). This is the case in which diagnostically important information can be preserved even at low bit rates in order to design a robust medical image analysis system. Content-based image compression (CBIC) algorithms can be developed by using different techniques like neural networks and feature preserving. CBIC is a novel idea in which segmentation is done before applying the lossy and lossless compression techniques separately at the same image parts. The diagnostically

Table 10.1 Overview of unsupervised medical image compression techniques.

Name of the method used	Image modality (size)	Segmentation technique	Findings	Reference (database used)
Modified implicit ROI coding with EBCOT (background priority adjustment)	Ultrasound image (512 × 512)	Manual	Rectangular ROI (25% of the whole image)	Yang et al. (2005) Not mentioned
Modified SPIHT (5/3 and 9/7 wavelet filters)	Chromosome spread and karyotype images (764 × 560)	Automatic	Arbitrary shape	Liu et al. (2002)
OB-SPIHT and OB-SPECK	Mammograms (5) (4096 × 5120)	Automatic	Pyramidal shape region	Penedo et al. (2003); Images collected from different hospitals
RB-IWT	Mammograms, MRI, angiogram	ROIs were taken from the center of the image	Rectangular, circular and arbitrary-shape regions	Tasdoken and Cuhadar (2003) Not mentioned
JPEG2000 compliant (ROI priority allocated)	Mammograms 2560 × 3328	ROIs defined by CAD	Rectangular and arbitrary ROIs, multiple ROIs (0.002%–4.5% area of the image size).	Bartrina-Rapesta et al. (2011) Collected from medical imaging center
CSPIHT	Abdomen ultrasound image (667 × 505)	Interactive region growing method	Arbitrary shape (50%–60%)	Ansari and Anand (2009)
ROI-SPIHT	CT liver tissue	Automatic (fuzzy level set)	Arbitrary shape	Sran et al, (2013)
BWC for ROI part and wavelet-based JPEG2000 for non-ROI part	MRI brain images (256 × 256) CT chest images (512 × 512)	Automatic (unseeded region growing)	5% area of the full image	Bai et al., (2003)

BWC, Barrows-Wheeler coding; *EBCOT*, embedded block coding with optimized truncation; *ROI*, rate of interest.

important structures like a tumor, masses, etc. are extracted with the segmentation process from the images and are further compressed losslessly to achieve high fidelity. The non-ROI parts are compressed lossily to achieve the high compression ratio. CBIC techniques apply image understanding techniques to improve object-based compression. Neural network algorithms aim to learn features for clustering and classify the images into contextual regions to perform segmentation. The techniques reported in Grinstead et al. (2000) and Chan et al. (2014) were tailored for content-based compression of mammograms. The authors have used fractal encoding for segmentation and modified JPEG 2000 for compression. In these papers, the ROI was named as the focus of attention region.

Artificial neural network and introduced difference fuzzy model (IDFM) were used for automatic segmentation of ROI (Abdou and Tayel, 2008). The non-ROI region was coded with fast and reduced bit embedded zerotree wavelet algorithm (FEZW) and ROI was coded with the same algorithm but with a higher refinement level. This algorithm reduced complexity, storage space, saved time, and it was fully automatic. A medical image compression algorithm for multi-ROIs was proposed in Hu et al. (2008). Useful edge information was extracted using a canny operator and then ROIs were selected and encoded using lossless JPEG2000 algorithm. To non-ROIs, SPIHT was applied to achieve a high compression ratio. Then all bitstreams were merged to get the final image. In this, multi-ROIs of rectangular shape are selected manually from MRI images. The compression results of this method were better than traditional SPIHT in terms of PSNR and visual quality.

The selective medical image compression techniques for ROI-based compression of digital angiograms and lung CT images were proposed (Bruckmann and Uhl, 2000). They investigated the impact of wavelet transforms and JPEG as direct ROI coding algorithm for medical images. Authors argued that an automatic technique can never know the salient regions in an image. Hence ROI was selected interactively by marking the regions. The PSNR and compression ratio obtained with basic compression algorithm were compared with PSNR and CR of the selective compression algorithm. It has been analyzed that algorithm based on wavelets performed better in terms of rate-distortion performance as compared to the JPEG. In the experiment, ROI was selected with interactive marking and the size of ROI was 20% of the original image. It has been concluded that arbitrarily shaped ROI is not supported by JPEG because of the fixed block size and in case of wavelets; additional border data of ROI is required.

DWT bands-cluster and DWT texture-cluster image compression schemes using the DWT were presented (Karras et al., 2000). The image was divided into two regions: significant and nonsignificant textural regions using fuzzy C-means (FCM) clustering technique. The raster scanning with sliding windows of 8×8 dimensions was performed on the image. A texture identification analysis based on co-occurrence matrices was performed on each window to compute the feature vector.

Grayscale image was converted to black and white to label the significant and nonsignificant partitions. These DWT-based compression techniques were tested on two colon carcinoma images of patients with cancer. Reconstruction results showed that DWT texture-cluster method performed better than DWT but introduced blocking artifacts in the boundaries of the partition. Feed-forward neural network (FFN) and SPIHT were combined for compression of ultrasound images (Kumar, 2012). The ROI was selected manually and compressed with FFN and SPIHT was used for compression of the background. Compressed ROI and compressed background were then combined to yield an image with the highly compressed background without effecting the image resolution of ROI. Table 10.2 summarizes the supervised techniques for ROI-based coding.

Table 10.2 Overview of supervised medical image compression techniques.

Compression methods used	Image modality (size)	Segmentation technique	Shape of ROI (ROI size)	References (database used)
Modified JPEG 2000	Mammogram (512 × 512) (number of processed images)	Fractal-based segmentation	Less than 15% of the mammogram	Grinstead et al. (2000); Chan et al. (2014) (Collected from four different hospitals) 35 normal and 45 abnormal cases; 12 images were used for evaluation
FEZW	MRI brain tumors and fluorescence images of the eye	Automatic (ANN and IDFM)	Irregular spider hexagon ROI contours	Abdou and Tayel (2008)
For the ROI part: JPEG2000 For non-ROI part: SPIHT	MR (head and chest) (512 × 512)(24)	Manual segmentation	Rectangular shape	Hu et al. (2008)
DWT	Cancerous abdomen images 256 × 256	FCM clustering	Image divided into texturally significant and nonsignificant regions	Karras et al. (2000)
FFN for ROI part and SPIHT for non-ROI part compression	Ultrasound image (256 × 256)	Manual	Arbitrary	Kumar (2012)

FCM, Fuzzy C-means; FFN, feed-forward neural network; FEZW, fast and reduced bit embedded zerotree wavelet algorithm; IDFM, introduced the difference fuzzy model.

10.4 Comparative analysis of segmentation techniques

For comparative analysis of various techniques, the results taken from Sumithra (2016) are presented in this section. The techniques chosen in this comparative analysis include the supervised and unsupervised techniques, that is, thresholding by histogram (ThH), support vector machine (SVM), mean shift (MS), fuzzy c-means, Hough transform, and normalized graph cut were considered for performance analysis. It was fathomed out from the results that both ThH and SVM performed well for brain MR images as a segmentation methodology. MS method suffered from over-segmentation in comparison to other methods whereas the SVM technique incurred in a low value of over, under, or incorrect segmentation. It means MS algorithm captured the structure that was not considered salient by human observers. The NGC and MS methods resulted in high negative values and SVM and ThH methods have low negative values. The ThH and SVM techniques segmented performed well in extracting the boundaries of the tumor when compared to the unsupervised techniques. However, the desired results entail either a large amount of training data or a complex prior model that makes the technique application-specific. In this experiment, 60 images were used to train the SVM and 50 images were used for testing. It is evident that existing fully automated algorithms are highly effective but require large manually demarcated datasets for prior training or supervision to identify the tumorous area.

10.5 New trends

10.5.1 Deep learning

Deep learning appertains to deep neural networks with multiple layers for extracting the features from input images. It is a part of machine learning techniques that can be applied for complex tasks due to their self-learning ability as divergent to challenging feature engineering stage of existing algorithms. They attain remarkable outcome and generalizability by training on a large quantity of data (Akkus et al., 2017). Deep learning has a vast significance in computer vision problems, particularly in medical image processing. It is considered that in the coming 15 years, techniques developed with deep learning will gain control over humans and the diagnosis will be conducted by smart machines (Razzak et al., 2017).

However, dissemination of deep learning in image analysis specifically in medical imaging is quite sluggish as compared to other real-world applications. The current growth on other applications showed that a large amount of data results in better results; however, the use of large datasets in the domain of medical is still an issue. One of the big hurdles is a dearth of the annotated dataset. It is easy to annotate other data collected for real-world applications but annotation of medical imaging data is costly, plodding, and lingering as it takes a large amount of time of experts (Lundervold and Lundervold, 2019). Moreover, existing deep learning frameworks rely on supervised learning and need manual labeling of ground truths, which is a tiresome job on a large amount of data. Therefore, there is a great need for unsupervised learning-based deep learning models to decrease the burden of labeling on ground truths. For data-hungry deep learning methods, alternative techniques like transfer learning (Chang and Park, 2017; Zhao et al., 2018) and data augmentation (Eaton-Rosen and Bragman, 2018; Hussain et al., 2018) can also be applied to increase the size of the dataset.

10.5.2 Visual saliency Mmodels

The technological breakthroughs in the field of medical image analysis entail that the efficacies of the human visual system are taken into consideration for identification and extraction of ROI. The key idea of these techniques is to achieve a higher accuracy rate and lower computational overheads (Sran et al., 2017). For the most recent decade, hybrid approaches for segmentation in medical images are being developed. Segmentation techniques comprising visual saliency play a significant role in improving the results for ROI extraction in medical images (Sran et al., 2019). Some studies based on visual saliency are discussed here.

A method to extract ROI from brain MR images was presented in Zhang and Xiao (2008). A modified version of Itti's model was used to create the saliency map, and then dynamic thresholding was applied to extract ROI. The model was evaluated on 100 biomedical images and results were compared with Itti and Hou's method. The subjective evaluation revealed that the ROI was extracted efficiently with this method. To form the Gaussian pyramid of feature maps, the texture features from liver regions were extracted (Ma et al., 2009). Then edge effects of each component maps were removed and the saliency map was generated by feature fusions. Finally, all ROIs were located by a statistical method and false positives were removed. Experimental results showed that the ROI detected by saliency map was more accurate and efficient than FCM clustering. Mendi and Milanova (2010) applied selective visual attention for ROI extraction. Image segmentation was done by applying Chan-Vese active contour model and attended locations were determined by Itti's saliency model. This hybrid technique resulted in minimizing user interaction and made the entire segmentation process fast. An inverse difference pyramid approach was applied for image compression to achieve a high compression ratio and good image quality. This study has not conducted any result evaluation.

The vigorous developments of saliency detection models have almost clinched a human-like accuracy when it comes to performing recognition tasks (Raghu et al., 2019). The saliency models are the next game-changer for future projects in the field of computer vision and image processing. It is also viable to implement the visual attention mechanisms in deep learning architectures (Heess and Graves, 2014; Xu et al., 2014), empowering them to spotlight their resources on the most informative components of each layer input. It will help them to surmount the issue of a large data set and to improve the performance.

10.6 Challenges and future scope

The main difficulty in testing an image compression system is to make a decision on selecting the test images to use for performance evaluations. For a fair and correct evaluation of different algorithms, a comparative analysis must be performed on the same database. However, some standard medical image databases are available to the public but most of the work in this field is performed by using their own databases. It is very significant to realize that the characteristics of data acquired from different machines under variable conditions extensively affect the performance of compression methods. Hence, it is hard to analyze the performance of any algorithm as they are not evaluated on a standardized dataset. The sizes of images and selected ROIs are different for each algorithm. For instance, in Ansari and Anand (2009) results are compared with Yang et al. (2005) although modalities are the same (ultrasound images), image size and size of ROI are different. Even shapes of ROIs are also different. The former algorithm is evaluated on the image of size 667×505 where ROI is of arbitrary shape and in later, image size is 512×512 and ROI is of rectangular shape.

There is no provision to specify the size and shape of ROI as the requirement of ROI is entirely dependent on the application under analysis. In the standard database, ROI should be marked because the size and shape of ROI affect the compressing ratio of an algorithm. Researchers must specify the size of the ROI extracted so that comparative analysis can be easily done.

In this chapter, it has been observed that most of the work done is based on mammograms, MRI, and ultrasound images only. Algorithms are required to be developed for other modalities as well.

During the literature survey, it has been further observed that the time complexity has not been addressed by any researcher. Medical images are used for telemedicine, so time complexity also needs to be evaluated.

A large number of research publications in the field of segmentation-based medical image compression, especially in recent years show that it is a very active research area and that it is starting to gain more attention. This chapter presents a detailed summary of segmentation-based image coding techniques reported in compression of medical images. It has been analyzed that compression techniques using soft computing techniques for segmentation like fuzzy theory, SVM, atlas-based methods, and neural networks perform better as compared to conventional methods. However, desired results require either a large amount of training data or a complex prior model which makes the technique application-specific. It has been observed that fully automated algorithms require prior training or supervision to identify the tumorous area. As an alternative, the use of visual saliency models in segmentation task could open new avenues for developing robust, automatic, unsupervised, and less complex systems. This chapter is an attempt to focus the attention of researchers for improving the image quality and attaining a high compression ratio in segmentation-based medical image coding. The available research requires human interaction for ROI extraction that is error-prone and tedious. Future research in the ROI extraction of medical images will strive toward the accuracy and speed of segmentation techniques as well as reduce manual interaction. ROI-based medical image compression requires automatic segmentation, improved fidelity, and higher compression ratio.

The merits and limitations of segmentation techniques are also highlighted and these will provide a vision for the researchers who are involved in designing new ROI-based coding techniques for medical images. Additionally, this analysis can help to select the best segmentation technique for segmentation-based image compression.

References

Abdou, M.A., Tayel, M.B., 2008. An automatic bichannel compression technique for medical images. Int. J. Robot. Autom. 23 (1), 15−21. Available from: https://doi.org/10.2316/Journal.206.2008.1.206-2970.

Akkus, Z., Galimzianova, A., Hoogi, A., Rubin, D.L., Erickson, B.J., 2017. Deep learning for brain MRI segmentation: state of the art and future directions. 449−459. https://doi.org/10.1007/s10278-017-9983-4.

Ansari, M.A., Anand, R.S., 2009. Context based medical image compression for ultrasound images with contextual set partitioning in hierarchical trees algorithm. Adv. Eng. Softw. 40 (7), 487−496. Available from: https://doi.org/10.1016/j.advengsoft.2008.08.004.

Bai, X., Jin, J.S., Feng, D.D., 2003. Segmentation-based multilayer diagnosis lossless medical image compression. In: Proceedings of Pan-Sydney Area Workshop on Visual Information Processing, 9−14, Sydney. Conferences in Research and Practice in Information Technology, (VIP 2003), vol. 36.

Bairagi, V.K., Sapkal, A.M., 2013. ROI-based DICOM image compression for telemedicine. Sadhana Acad. Proc. Eng. Sci. 38 (1), 123−131. Available from: https://doi.org/10.1007/s12046-013-0126-4.

Bartrina-Rapesta, J., Serra-sagrist, J., 2009. JPEG2000 ROI coding method with perfect fine-grain accuracy and lossless recovery. 558−562.

Bartrina-Rapesta, J., Serra-sagristà, J., Aulí-llinàs, F., 2011. JPEG2000 ROI coding through component priority for digital mammography. Computer Vis. Image Underst. 115 (1), 59−68. Available from: https://doi.org/10.1016/j.cviu.2010.09.008.

Bhavani, S., 2010. A survey on coding algorithms in medical image compression. Int J. Comput. Sci. Eng. 2 (5), 1429−1434.

Bruckmann, A., Uhl, A., 2000. Selective medical image compression techniques for telemedical and archiving applications. Comput. Biol. Med. 30, 153−169.

Chan, H., Grinstead, B.I., Gleason, S.S., 2014. Content-based compression of mammograms with customized fractal encoding and a modified JPEG2000. Opt Eng 43 (12), Avaliable from: https://doi.org/10.1117/1.1810529.

Chang, J., Park, E., 2017. A method for classifying medical images using transfer learning: a pilot study on histopathology of breast cancer. EEE 19th International Conference on e-Health Networking, Applications and Services (Healthcom), Dalian, pp. 1−4.

Chen, C.W., Zhang, Y.-Q., Parker, K.J., 1994. Subband analysis and synthesis of volumetric medical images using wavelet. Vis. Commun. Image Process. 94, 1544−1555. Available from: https://doi.org/10.1117/12.185913.

Chen, C.W., Zhang, Y., Luo, J., Parker, K.J., 1858. Medical image compression with structure-preserving adaptive quantization., Proc. SPIE 2501, Visual Communications and Image Processing '95, (21 April 1995); Avaliable from: https://doi.org/10.1117/12.206631, 983−994.

Cosman, P.C., 1996. Wavelet/TSVQ image coding with segmentation. In: Twenty-Ninth Asilomar Conference on Signals, Systems and Computers, pp. 494−498.

Du, X., Li, H., Ahalt, S.C., 2001. Content-based image compression. In: Proceedings of the 2001 SPIE Aerosense Conference: Algorithms for Synthetic Aperture Radar Imagery VIII, Orlando.

Eaton-Rosen, Z., Bragman, F., 2018. Improving data augmentation for medical image segmentation. In: International Conference on Medical Imaging with Deep Learning, (Midl), 1−3.

Grinstead, B., Sarraf, H.S., Gleason, S., Mitra, S., 2000. Content-based compression of mammograms for telecommunication and archiving.

In: Proceedings 13th IEEE Symposium on Computer-Based Medical Systems. CBMS 2000.

Hannachi, E., Ahmed, S., 2017. Adaptive medical image compression based on lossy and adaptive medical image compression based on lossy and lossless embedded zerotree methods. (December). https://doi.org/10.3745/JIPS.02.0052.

Hu, M., Zhang, C., Lu, J., Zhou, B., 2008. A multi-ROIs medical image compression algorithm with edge feature preserving. 3rd International Conference on Intelligent System and Knowledge Engineering, Xiamen, pp. 1075-1080.

Hussain, Z., Gimenez, F., Yi, D., Rubin, D., (2018). Differential data augmentation techniques for medical imaging classification tasks. Annual Symposium proceedings. AMIA Symposium, 2017, 979–984.

Jangbari, P., Patel, D., 2016. Review on region of interest coding techniques for medical image compression. Int. J. Comput. Appl. 134(10):1-5. Published by Foundation of Computer Science (FCS), NY, USA.

Karras, D.A., Karkanis, S.A., Maroulis, D.E., Administration, B., Athens, A.I., 2000. Efficient image compression of medical images using the wavelet transform and fuzzy c-means clustering on regions of interest. In: EUROMICRO Conference.vol. 2, pp. 469–473.

Kim, M., Cho, Y., Kim, D., Ha, N., 1995. Compression of medical images with regions of interest (ROIs). SPIE Proceedings Volume 2501, Visual Communications and Image Processing '95; pp. 733–744, Avaliable from: https://doi.org/10.1117/12.206715.

Krishnamoorthy, R., 2012. A new adaptive medical image coding with orthogonal polynomials. Int. J. Comput. Appl. 46 (1), 5–12.

Kumar, V.,Sharma, J., Ayub, S., 2012. Image compression using FFN for ROI and SPIHT for background. Int. J. Comput. Appl. 46 (18), 30–34.

Liu, Z., Member, S., Xiong, Z., Wu, Q., 2002. Cascaded differential and wavelet compression of chromosome images. 49 (4), 372–383.

Lundervold, A.S., Lundervold, A., 2019. An overview of deep learning in medical imaging focusing on. Z. Fßr Medizinische Phys. 29 (2), 102–127. Available from: https://doi.org/10.1016/j.zemedi.2018.11.002.

Ma, L., Wang, W., Zou, S., Zhang, J., 2009. Liver focus detections based on visual attention model. In: 3rd International Conference on Bioinformatics and Biomedical Engineering, ICBBE 2009, pp. 1-5.

Mendi, E., Milanova, M., 2010. Contour-based image segmentation using selective visual attention. J. Softw. Eng. Appl. 3 (08), 796–802. Available from: https://doi.org/10.4236/jsea.2010.38092.

Mohan, V., Venkataramani, Y., 2014. Coding of clinical ROI using S-FCM and WBCT. J Appl Sci 14 (21), 2713–2721. Available from: https://doi.org/10.3923/jas.2014.2713.2721.

Mnih, V., Heess, N., Graves, A., et al., 2014. Recurrent models of visual attention. In: Advances in Neural Information Processing Systems, pp. 2204–2212.

Namuduri, K.R., Ramaswamy, V.N., 2003. Feature preserving image compression. 24, 2767–2776. https://doi.org/10.1016/S0167-8655(03)00120-X.

Ohiaki, Y., 1993. Data compression method of left ventricular cineangiograms. In: Proceedings of IEEE Pacific Rim Conference on Communications Computers and Signal Processing, Victoria, BC, Canada, vol.2, pp.602–605.

Penedo, M., Vidal, J.J., Pearlman, W.A., Tahoces, P.G., Souto, M., (2003). Region-based wavelet coding methods for digital mammography. In: IEEE Transactions on Medical Imaging, vol. 22, no. 10, pp. 1288–1296.

Perlmutter, S.M., Perlmutter, K., Cosman, P.C., Riskint, E.A., Olshent, R.A., Gray, R.M., et al., 1992. Tree-structured vector quantization with region-based classification. In: Conference Record of the Twenty-Sixth Asilomar

Conference on Signals, Systems & Computers, Pacific Grove, CA, USA, 1992, vol.2, pp. 691–695.

Pham, D.L., Xu, C., Prince, J.L., 2000. Current methods in medical image segmentation. Annu. Rev. Biomed. Eng. 2(1), 315–337.

Poggi, G., Olshen, R.A., 1995. Pruned tree-structured vector quantization of medical images with segmentation and improved prediction. 4 (6).

Raghu, M., Zhang, C., Kleinberg, J., Bengio, S., 2019. Transfusion: understanding transfer learning for medical imaging. In: 33rd Conference on Neural Information Processing Systems (NeurIPS 2019), Vancouver, Canada, 1(c), pp 3342–3352, arXiv:1902.07208.

Razzak, M.I., Naz, S., Zaib, A., 2017. Deep learning for medical image processing: overview, challenges and future. arXiv preprint arXiv:1704.06825.

Revathi, M., Shenbagavalli, R., Scholar, P.D., No, F.R., 2018. Comparative analysis and implementation of ROI based. Int. J. Sci. Res. Rev. 7 (11), 189–196.

Rupa, S., Mohan, V., Venkataramani, Y., 2014. MRI brain image compression using spatial fuzzy clustering technique. In: International Conference on Communication and Signal Processing, Melmaruvathur, pp. 915–919.

Shukla, J., 2010. A survey on lossless image compression methods. In: 2nd International Conference on Computer Engineering and Technology, Chengdu, pp. V6-136-V6-141.

Sophia, P.E., Anitha, J., Sophia, P.E., Anitha, J., 2017. Contextual medical image compression using normalized wavelet-transform coefficients and prediction contextual medical image compression using normalized wavelet-transform. 2063 (June). https://doi.org/10.1080/03772063.2017.1309998.

Sran, P.K., Gupta, S., Singh, S., 2013. Content based medical image coding with fuzzy level set segmentation algorithm. In: Lecture Notes in Electrical Engineering. https://doi.org/10.1007/978-81-322-0997-3_15.

Sran, P.K., Gupta, S., Singh, S., 2017. Recent advances and perspective of studies on visual attention models for ROI extraction in medical images. Int. J. Control Theory Appl. Retrieved from: <https://www.researchgate.net/publication/316580693>.

Sran, P.K., Gupta, S., Singh, S., 2019. Affect of visual saliency algorithm in hybrid segmentation techniques for ROI extraction in medical images. In: Lecture Notes in Electrical Engineering (LNEE). Springer.

Sumithra, M.G., 2016. Performance analysis of various segmentation techniques for detection of brain abnormality. In: IEEE Region 10 Conference (TENCON)—Proceedings of the International Conference, Singapore, pp. 2056-2061.

Tasdoken, S., Cuhadar, A., 2003. ROI coding with integer wavelet transforms and unbalanced spatial orientation trees. In: Proceedings of the 25th Annual International Conference of the IEEE Engineering in Medicine and Biology Society (IEEE Cat. No.03CH37439), Cancun, Vol.1, pp. 841-844.

Thangavelu, K., Krishnan, T., 2013. Lossless color medical image compression using adaptive block-based encoding for human computed tomographic images. https://doi.org/10.1002/ima.22056.

Thomas, D.S., Moorthi, M., Muthalagu, R., 2014. Medical image compression based on automated ROI selection for telemedicine application. 3 (1), 3638–3642.

Vilas, H.R., Shreesha, N., Chiranth, H., Bhille, M., 2016. Segmentation and compression of 2D brain MRI images for efficient teleradiological applications. In: International Conference on Electrical, Electronics, and Optimization Techniques (ICEEOT) - 2016, Chennai, pp. 1426–1431.

Vlaicu, A.M., Lungu, S., Crisan, N., Persa, S., 1995. New compression techniques for storage and transmission of 2-D and 3-D medical images. Adv. Image Video Commun. Storage Technol. 2451, 370–377.

Wong, S., Zaremba, L., Gooden, D., Huang, H.K., 1995. Radiologic image compression—a review. In: Proceedings of the IEEE, vol. 83, no. 2, pp. 194-219.

Xu, K., Courville, A., Zemel, R.S., Bengio, Y., 2014. Show, attend and tell: neural image caption generation with visual attention.In: Proc. International Conference on Learning Representations, Avaliable from: https://arxiv.org/abs/1502.03044.

Xu, Z., Bartrina-Rapesta, J., Blanes, I., Sanchez, V., Serra-Sagristà, J., García-Bach, M., et al., 2016. Diagnostically lossless coding of X-ray angiography images based on background suppression. Comput. Electr. Eng. Available from: https://doi.org/10.1016/j.compeleceng.2016.02.014.

Yang, H., Long, M., Tai, H., 2005. Region-of-interest image coding based on EBCOT. October 152 (5). Available from: https://doi.org/10.1049/ip-vis.

Zhang, Q., Xiao, H., 2008. Extracting regions of interest in biomedical images. https://doi.org/10.1109/FBIE.2008.8.

Zhao, J., Li, J., Sim, T., Yan, S., 2018. Understanding humans in crowded scenes: deep nested adversarial learning and a new benchmark for multi-human parsing. Comput. Vis. Pattern Recognit. 2016, 1–22.

Zuo, Z., Lan, X., Deng, L., Yao, S., Wang, X., 2015. An improved medical image compression technique with lossless region of interest. Opt. Int. J. Light. Electron. Opt. Available from: https://doi.org/10.1016/j.ijleo.2015.07.005.

11

Systematic survey of compression algorithms in medical imaging

Sartajvir Singh[1], Vishakha Sood[2] and Bhisham Sharma[1]

[1]*Chitkara University School of Engineering and Technology, Chitkara University, Himachal Pradesh, India* [2]*Chitkara University Institute of Engineering and Technology, Chitkara University, Rajpura, India*

Chapter Outline

11.1   Introduction

With the developments in digital image processing, the demand for digital medical images is growing day by day in hospitals and medical centers for different research and diagnostic purposes (Shang et al., 2011). Despite the numerous advantages, the data generated from medical images such as through magnetic resonance imaging (MRI) (Liang and Lauterbur, 2000), computed tomography (CT) (Pambrun and Noumeir, 2015) require a larger storage capacity to store the information of the human body in digital format (Paul and Anitha, 2019). Moreover, the key requirement of communication

Advances in Computational Techniques for Biomedical Image Analysis. DOI: https://doi.org/10.1016/B978-0-12-820024-7.00011-6

is to generate the data in a compact form that can be easily transferred from source to destination via the guided or unguided medium (Anitha et al., 2019). In order to meet such requirements of storage systems and communication networks, medical images need to be compressed before storage or transmission (Zhang et al., 2016). Therefore different compression techniques were developed with the objectives: (1) reduction in data size as per strict requirement in medical imaging, (2) cost-effective solution to network bandwidth utilization, and (3) enhancement in the storage capacity (Chen, 2007). During the past decade, a series of developments have been made in medical image compression algorithms to enhance the efficiency of storage and transmission (Liu et al., 2017). The compression techniques take advantage of redundant or repetitive information and attempt to compress the information before storage or transmission and decompress to retrieve the actual information. Such concepts offer efficient storage capacity as well as transmission (Jiang et al., 2012).

An image is acquired by a sensor (or camera) which converts the radiance information (or reflected electromagnetic energy) into digital numbers, called digital images. The digital images are generally categorized as (1) coding redundancies, (2) interpixel redundancies, and (3) psychovisual redundancies (Karadimitriou and Fenstermacher, 1997; Avramović, 2011). In coding redundancy, the variable-length code (VLC) represents the information in the form of code symbols. With natural coding, the same number of code symbols are used to represent the high and low probability of gray level occurrence (Starosolski, 2005). Using a fewer bits to high probable gray levels and a greater number of bits to low probable gray levels leads to effective compression. On the other hand, interpixel redundancy offers the correlation between the neighborhood pixels in which gray levels are not consistent and the value is predicted on the basis of the high correlation. The psychovisual redundancy is based on human perception because from a visual perspective, some information is more important than other information in an image (Grgic et al., 2001). But this type of redundancy cannot be utilized in lossless (LS) image compression because it introduces the noise in the uncompressed image (Zuo et al., 2015).

The compression algorithms are generally divided into two categories: (a) lossy compression and (b) LS compression. The lossy compression is accomplished with an acceptable degree of deterioration in the retrieved image such as joint photographic expert group (JPEG) (Wallace, 1992), JPEG2000 (9/7)

(Santa-Cruz et al., 2000; Skodras et al., 2001), transform coding, and wavelet-based (Schelkens et al., 2003). Lossy techniques offer a high compression ratio but the same percentage of input information can't be retrieved from the compressed image (Zuo et al., 2015). The image retrieved from lossy compression leads to degradation of the actual information in an original image (Kerensky et al., 2000). However, it eliminates unnecessary or redundant information from an image. Whereas in the case of LS compression, the same percentage of input information can be retrieved from the compressed image without any impact on the quality of an image (Ukrit and Suresh, 2013) such as joint photographic experts group lossless (JPEG-LS) (Weinberger et al., 2000) and JPEG2000 (5/3) (Wu and Lin, 2005). The LS techniques play a very vital role in medical image compression where each and every detail is important for diagnosis (Zuo et al., 2015).

In this chapter, we present a systematic comparison of recent advancements in image compression algorithms. This comprehensive literature also covers the details of image compression algorithms specially designed for medical images. In Section 11.2, the literature review on various modalities in medical imaging with their attributes is presented. In Section 11.3 produce the different parameters and file formats for medical image communications. In Section 11.4 of different medical image compression algorithms are presented. Finally, Section 11.5 the detailed summary and discussion on present as well as future trends.

11.2 Modalities of medical imaging

Before diving into compression of medical images, it is essential to understand the unique attributes in various types of medical images. Medical images are utilized for diagnosis, monitor, and treatment of the human body and each medical image has its own physical principles. Research activities in the field of medical imaging offer advancements or improvements in existing modalities (Liu et al., 2017). Table 11.1 represents the various attributes concerned with the common modalities. In this table, we have covered only limited medical imaging techniques which are most commonly used in clinical practices. However, the detailed information can be found in different studies (Cavaro-Ménard et al., 2008; Liu et al., 2017). It may be beneficial to understand which type of compression is best suitable for medical images.

Table 11.1 Summary of various attributes related to common medical imaging modalities.

Modality	Working principle	Characteristics	Field of view (x, y)/bit-depth/size	Use	Examples
Radiography	X-ray or gamma rays	• Single projection plane is acquired on to detector plane • The generation of flat two-dimensional (2D) images with protentional radiography	• 18 × 24—35 × 43 • 10—14 bits/pixel • 8—32 MB	• Cancer • Bone fractures • Chest	Kasban et al. (2015) and Liu et al. (2017)
CT	X-ray	• Acquires three-dimensional (3D) image on the basis of several projections at various angles • Dynamic imaging can be achieved using the advanced CT scanners	• 512 × 512 • 12—16 bits/pixel • 250—1000 GB	• Cancer • Heart disease • Emphysema • Liver masses	Gurdeep et al. (2010)
Mammography	Low-energy X-rays	• Enhances the characterization of breast lesions • Thin sections (breast tissue) are rebuilt with various projections over specific arc angles	• 6000 × 4500 • 10—14 bits/pixel • 8.8—52 MB/view • Required four views (minimum)	• Breast tissues • Breast cancer	Helvie (2010) and Clunie (2012)
MRI	Radio waves	• The scanner is based on a very strong magnetic field (0.2—3 Tesla) • The radiofrequency current that generates a varying magnetic field	• 512 × 512 • 12—16 bits/pixel • 50—250 GB	• Brain and brain stem • Cardiac • Joint disease, soft tissue, and tumors	Gudbjartsson and Patz (1995), Liang and Lauterbur (2000), and Li et al. (2011)
Ultrasound	HF sound waves	• The waves travel into the human body and strike with an edge between tissues	• 512 × 512 • 24 bits (RGB) • 38 MB/s	• Abdominal pain • Abnormal sounds and lump	Wagner (1983) and Hill et al. (2004)

(Continued)

Table 11.1 (Continued)

Modality	Working principle	Characteristics	Field of view (x, y)/bit-depth/size	Use	Examples
PET[5]	Gamma rays	• Based on (1) piezoelectric effect and (2) pulse-echo • Detection of two time-coincident highly energized photons from the emission of a positron-emitting radioisotope • Helps to reveal how your tissues and organs are functioning	• 512 × 512 • 16 bits • 1−6 MB	• Soft-tissue structures • Oncological • Cardiovascular • Neurological applications	Omami et al. (2014), Vaquero and Kinahan (2015), and Jones and Townsend (2017)
Digital pathology	Optical microscopy	• Thin slices of biological tissue are scanned to generate slide image • Study of the causes and effects of disease or injury	• 80,000 × 60,000 • 24 bits (RGB) • 4.8 GB	• Tissues • Body fluids • Cells • Molecules	Rothstein (1979), Lett (2007), and Harris and McCormick (2010)

CT, Computed tomography; *MRI*, magnetic resonance imaging; *HF*, high frequency; *RGB*, red green blue; *PET*, positron emission tomography.

11.3 File formats in medical imaging

11.3.1 Parameters

The image file format is a standardized form to save information in a computer storage device. The file format describes the organization of data in an image pixel. Generally, a medical image can be planar imaging or comprise one or more images which can be represented in the form of multislice imaging such as two-dimensional (2D), three-dimensional (3D), and four-dimensional (Larobina and Murino, 2014).

The essential elements of medical image file format comprise of (1) pixel depth, (2) photometric interpretation, (3) metadata, and (4) pixel data. Pixel depth represents the number of bits involved in the encoding of data for each pixel. For instance, an image has a size of 128×128 pixels with a pixel depth of 10 bits, it means the capacity required to store the information is $128 \times 128 \times 10 = 163,840$ bits or 20,480 bytes (on the computer). The pixel depth of 10 bits (2^{10}) is representing the integer range from 0 to 2047 ($2^{10}-1$) or it can also be represented in the form of a signed number (-1024 to $+1023$) in which the first bit fit is used to represent the sign and the rest of the bits (9) are used to represent the real number. To encode the information in floating-point numbers, file formats can be single-precision (32-bit) or the double-precision (64-bit) which is created by IEEE-754.

Another parameter, photometric interpretation, describes the representation of pixel information on true color or monochrome display. Monochrome images require one sample or channel per pixel such as CT and MRI whereas color images require multiple (three) samples or channels per pixels such as positron emission tomography (PET) (Verhaeghe et al., 2006) and single-photon emission tomography (National Research Council, 1996) to represent the information (Rahmim and Zaidi, 2008). In color images, multiple samples are assigned to a specific pixel on the basis of the color model, that is, red green blue (RGB) which represents the color combinations. The capacity required to store a single-color image is three-times the monochrome image. For instance, an image has a size of 128×128 pixels with a pixel depth of 10 bits and three samples or channels, meaning the total capacity required to store the image is $128 \times 128 \times 10 \times 3 = 491,520$ bits or 61,440 bytes (on the computer). The main advantage of the color image is that it shows the additional information as compared to the monochrome image which includes important applications such as encoding blood flow direction or velocity (Larobina and Murino, 2014).

The metadata as header contains the information associated with an image such as dimensions, spatial resolution, depth, and photometric interpretation which describe the images. For instance, MRI provides the actual information regarding the pulses such as timing, flip angle, and a number of acquisitions (Bladowska et al., 2010). To obtain the metadata, special or application-oriented software are used to convert actual information into standardized uptake values and post-processing file-formats (Rosset et al., 2004). Metadata is one of the most important parameters that provides essential data for research purposes. The parameter pixel-data deals with the bytes essential to represent the values in the form of integers or floating-point numbers. The actual size of the uncompressed image is multiplication of rows, columns, pixel depths, number of frames, and headers.

11.3.2 Formats

In medical imaging, the file formats can be described in one of two formats: (1) standardization of medical images such as Dicom (Bidgood et al., 1997; Rosset et al., 2004; Clunie, 2012), and (2) strengthening the post-processing analysis such as Analyze (Robb et al., 1989), Nifti (NIFTI documentation, 2004; Patel et al., 2010), and Minc (MINC software library and tools, 2000). These formats are specified either as a single file that contains metadata and image data (Dicom, Nifti, and Minc) or as two files, that is, one for metadata and another for image (Analyze). Table 11.2 represents the characteristics of most commonly used file formats in medical imaging. Amongst others, the main advantage of Dicom is that it supports a variety of compression techniques such as JPEG, run length coding (RLC), JPEG-LS, JPEG-2000 (Larobina and Murino, 2014), and joint photographic experts group extended range (JPEG-XR) (Dufaux et al., 2009).

11.4 Different compression techniques

In order to achieve effective storage and transmission, medical images are required to be compressed with the help of the compression technique (lossy and LS).

The lossy (irreversible) compression offers the advantage of greater compression at the cost of loss of some information whereas, LS (reversible) compression offers the moderate gain without any loss of information (Erickson, 2002). In medical imaging, there are a lot of controversies in the usage of lossy compression techniques (Koff and Shulman, 2006). Therefore it may be better to go for the adoption of LS compression in medical imaging instead of using a lossy compression technique with marginal loss of information. In the past few decades, a series of developments have been made in medical image compression and transmission techniques such as the LS-based region of interest (ROI) (Kaur and Wasson, 2015; Roček et al., 2017), Ripplet transform (RT)-based compression (Anitha et al

Table 11.2 Summary of most commonly used file formats in medical imaging.

Format	Created/company	Characteristics	Advantages	Disadvantages	Header	Configuration/extension	Data types
Analyze	1980s/Mayo Clinic	• Used for the medical imaging post-processing. • Designed for multidimensional data	• Possible to store three-dimensional (3D) or four-dimensional (4D) data in one file	• In some cases, scale factor is required to switch the pixel depth	Fixed length	Single file (image file in .img and header file in .hdr)	• Unsigned • Signed • Float • Complex
Nifti	2000s/National Institutes of Health	• Offers a format for neuroimaging • Offers a double method to store the orientation of the image in the space	• Potential to manage larger data set • Removes the requirement of size limit (32,767)	• Comprised with 544 bytes of header	Fixed length	Multiple files (image and header files in .nii)	• Unsigned • Signed • Float • Complex
Minc	1992/Montreal Neurological Institute (MNI)	• Provide a flexible data format for medical imaging	• Overcame the limit of supporting large files. • Provide other new features	• Compatibility issues with existing versions	Extensible binary	Multiple files (image and header files in .mnc)	• Unsigned • Signed • Float • Complex
Dicom	1990s/National Electric Manufacturers Association	• Act as a network communication protocol • Can store pixel values as integers	• Supported compression schemes • JPEG • RLE • JPEG-LS /2000	• Float values are not supported	Variable-length	Multiple files (image and header files in .dcm)	• Unsigned • Signed

JPEG, Joint Photographic Experts Group; *RLE*, run length encoding; *JPEG-LS*, joint photographic experts group lossless.

2019), ROI-based compression (Zuo et al., 2015), partial or selective encryption-based discrete cosine transform (DCT) (Wu and Tai, 2001), wavelet-based volumetric (Khatami et al., 2017), and many more (Liu et al., 2017). However, each compression technique has its own advantages and disadvantages and cannot be applied in every case. This section is followed by three subsections to describe the different advancements of compression algorithms in medical imaging, that is, LS, lossy, and advanced (a combination of both lossy and LS).

11.4.1 Lossless compression methods

The main objective of LS image compression is to achieve effective compression without compromising the quality of an image. Thus the compressed file could be transmitted and stored easily with the minimum requirements. These methods can reproduce the original image without any loss, also known as reversible. This is an important feature that makes these techniques appropriate for medical image compression systems. However, the compression ratio of the LS methods is moderate and less effective as compared to lossy compression. The main part of LS compression algorithms is encoder which encodes the information in a way to reduce the number of bits as much as possible (Hashemi-Berenjabad and Mojarrad, 2016).

11.4.1.1 Joint photographic experts group lossless

JPEG-LS is one of the efficient algorithms that provides the compression of images at very low computational complexity and with excellent coding (Weinberger et al., 2000; Brunello et al., 2003). Fig. 11.1A represents the methodology of JPEG-LS which can be performed in three basic steps such as (1) modeling, (2) prediction, and (3) coding (Liu et al., 2017). In JPEG-LS, there are two modes of operations, that is, (1) regular mode and (2) run mode (Zuo et al., 2015). However, the selection of mode is made as follows:

$$\text{Mode} = \begin{cases} \text{Run,} & \text{if } D \le \delta \\ \text{Regular else} \end{cases} \quad (11.1)$$

Where D is representing the difference between neighbor pixels. The coefficient δ is representing the maximum allowed deviation of the pixel. However, it must be set to zero in case of LS encoding. Or in other words, if the sample pixels are existing in the smooth region then pixels are encoded using run mode otherwise, pixels are encoded using a regular mode

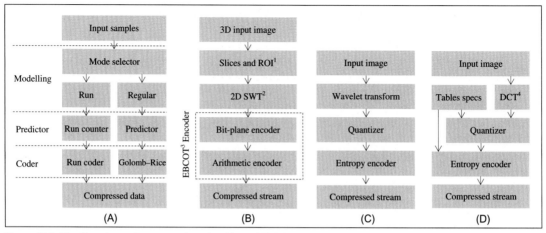

Figure 11.1 The flowchart of compression algorithms: (A) joint photographic experts group lossless (JPEG-LS) compression; (B) SWT-based lossless (LS) compression; (C) Wavelet transform (WT) based lossy compression; and (D) joint photographic experts group (JPEG) lossy compression. [1]*ROI*, region of interest; [2]*SWT*, stationary wavelet transform; [3]*EMBCOT*, embedded block coding with optimized truncation; and [4]*DCT*, discrete cosine transform.

which act as LS compression. A specific pixel in a sample is encoded as follow:

1. Selected pixel $\overline{P}$ is predicted with the help of median edge detector as follows:

$$\overline{P} = \begin{cases} \min(a, b), & c \ge \max(a, b) \\ \max(a, b), & c \ge \min(a, b) \\ a + b - c, & \text{Otherwise} \end{cases} \quad (11.2)$$

Where, variables a, b, and c are three neighboring pixels.

2. The predictor is used to compute the error e according to the following equation:

$$e = P - \overline{P} \quad (11.3)$$

Where P is representing the current values of the pixel.

3. To compute the context based on neighbor pixels (a, b, c, and d), differences (D_1, D_2, and D_3) are quantized as follow:

$$D_1 = d - b; D_2 = b - c; D_3 = c - a \quad (11.4)$$

This step helps to estimate the statistical behaviors of predicted errors.

4. At last, predicted error e will be encoded with the Golomb-Rice code in which e is varying from -2^{n-1} to $2^{n-1} - 1$, where n is a bit precision of a pixel. On the other hand,

smooth pixels are encoded using run coder to generate the compressed bitstream.

11.4.1.2 Stationary wavelet transform-based lossless compression

Stationary wavelet transform (SWT) compression technique is specially developed to overcome the nonexistence of translation-invariance in discrete wavelet transform (DWT) (Anusuya et al., 2014). In this algorithm, the 3D images are extracted into 2D slices and decimated using 2D SWT in parallel to embedded block coding with optimized truncation (EBCOT) of the bitstream (Taubman, 2000). The flowchart of the SWT compression algorithm is shown in Fig. 11.1B.

Steps to execute ROI-based compression algorithm are as follows:

1. In the first phase, the 3D medical image is provided as an input and transformed into 2D slices.
2. The ROI extracted the important information from the image and eliminated the rest of the unimportant information with the help of threshold methods (Zhang et al., 2005; Bai et al., 2004).
3. Then, the information will be extracted from slices with the help of SWT transform. SWT offers the ease to recover the relationship between the sub-bands. The wavelets contain the redundant data which may help in the reduction of image size (Nashat et al., 2011).
4. Afterwards, information is encoded with the help of EBCOT which involves the following coders:
   a. Bit-plane coder: It converts the signal into a set of bits which is represented in binary numbers. This process is initiated from the least significant bit toward the maximum significant bit and provides a better approximation to signal.
   b. Arithmetic coding: It is based on variable-length entropy which converts one form of string into another type of string. The resultant string comprises a fewer number of bits as compared to the original string. It offers better compression results as compared to Huffman coding (Gonzalez and Woods, 2002).

In SWT-based compression, the arithmetic coding is implemented over the outcomes of the bit-plane encoder. In order to solve the problems of data-intensive, parallel computing can be used to implement the arithmetic coding with the help of the multicore processor.

11.4.2 Lossy compression methods

Lossy compression algorithm is also referred to as near-LS compression in which a very small level of compression occurred. Such methods provide the greater compression ratio with compromise in a certain amount of loss of information. Other advantages of lossy compression involve the low requirement of storage capacity and transmission bandwidth (Koff and Shulman, 2006). It is noteworthy that there is still a lot of debate on the usage of lossy compression algorithms in the medical image because each and every detail in the medical image is important for a diagnosis.

11.4.2.1 Wavelet transform-based lossy compression

Wavelet transform (WT) is the most important computational tool, and is also referred to as short wavelike functions that can be scaled and translated (Padmaja and Nirupama, 2012; Bruylants et al., 2015). Wavelets offer the storage of images in many scales of resolution (Loganathan and Kumaraswamy, 2010). It decomposes an image into a large number of details and smooth variations (Sudhakar et al., 2005). The smooth variations are called low-frequency (LF) components and sharp variations are called high-frequency (HF) components (Fowler and Pesquet-Popescu, 2007). The methodology of WT-based loss compression is shown in Fig. 11.1C.

Steps to execute the WT-based compassion algorithm are as follows:

1. In the first phase, an input image is extracted into coefficients, called sub-bands with the help of WT.
2. To obtain the quantized output, the low pass filter is implemented over each row of an image to extract the LF components and then, high pass filter is implemented over the same row of an image to extract the HF components (Sudhakar et al., 2005).
3. To encode the sub-bands for better compression results, a variety of wavelet-based coding schemes are available such as embedded zero-tree wavelet which can be applied to generate compressed bitstream (Shapiro, 1993).

11.4.2.2 Joint photographic experts group lossy compression

The JPEG standard is one of the most common and well-defined lossy compression algorithms that deal with color images up to 24 bits per pixel and offer a greater level of compression ratio (Wallace, 1992; Neelamani et al., 2006). JPEG can be defined in a variety of lossy or LS encoding modes (Liu et al.,

2017). However, most of the modes support lossy coding algorithm. The compression level can be increased with a compromise in storage size and image quality. The basic block diagram of the JPEG standard is shown in Fig. 11.1D.

Steps to execute the JPEG compression algorithm are as follow:

1. In the first step, the image is segmented into 8×8 blocks.
2. Then, each block is converted with the help of a DCT. In DCT, coefficients that belong to zero frequency are called direct current (DC) coefficients and the rest of the coefficients are called alternating current (AC) coefficients.
3. Afterwards, coefficients of DCT are quantized using uniform scaler quantizer whose step size is varying with respect to frequency and array using table specs (Chouhan and Nigam, 2016).
4. At last, redundancy is exploited with the help of differential pulse code modulation encoding which will be followed by an encoding scheme such as VLC and Huffman coding (Liu et al., 2017). It is noteworthy that after quantization, AC coefficients become zero and can be encoded efficiently using RLC and VLC.

11.4.3 Advanced compression method

In order to take the advantages of both lossy and LS compression algorithm, various advanced algorithms have been developed and improved since the past decade (Zuo et al., 2015; Liu et al., 2017; Anitha et al., 2019). This section covers some advanced compression algorithms which are based on both lossy and LS compression algorithm to improve the compression ratio without compromising the important information in an image.

11.4.3.1 Region of interest-based compression algorithm

To achieve better compression results, an advanced medical image compression algorithm was developed with the combination of LS and lossy compression algorithms (Zuo et al., 2015). From Fig. 11.2A, the basic concept of ROI-based compression algorithm is to apply the LS compression algorithm to the ROI region and lossy compression algorithm to the non-ROI region. This process helps in achieving better results without losing the important information in an image.

Steps to execute ROI-based compassion algorithm:

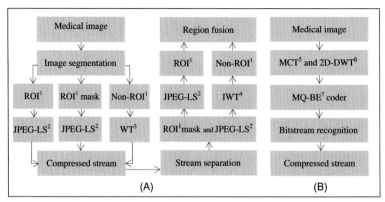

Figure 11.2 The flowchart of advanced compression algorithms: (A) ROI based compression; (B) joint photographic experts group 2000 (JPEG2000). [1]*ROI*, region of interest; [2]*JPEG-LS*, joint photographic experts group lossless; [3]*WT*, wavelet transform; [4]*IWT*, inverse WT; [5]*MCT*, multicomponent transformation; [6]*DWT*, discrete WT; and [7]*BE*, bit encoder.

1. The input image is partitioned into two separate regions, that is, ROI and non-ROI.
2. In an image, the compression is achieved by utilizing one of the following two algorithms to each ROI and non-ROI region.
   a. JPEG-LS algorithm is implemented on an ROI region because it carries important information available in an image.
   b. Wavelet-based lossy compression is implemented on a non-ROI region because it carries the less important information available in an image.
3. Afterwards, compression is achieved by combining the output from a different algorithm which can be decompressed at the receiver.
4. In the case of non-ROI, semi-blind deconvolution is implemented to recover the actual image.

11.4.3.2 Joint photographic experts group 2000

JPEG2000 standard is based on wavelet technology and delivers an extremely high level of scalability and accessibility (Clunie, 2002). The standard JPEG2000 as ISO/IEC JTC 1 and ITU-T (formerly CCITT) offers advantages like, a better performance at low bit-rates, low memory utilization, robustness toward errors (JPEG 2000 Image Coding System, 2005). Fig. 11.2B represents the essential steps of the JPEG2000 algorithm.

In order to implement this compression scheme, the following steps can be followed:

1. In the initial stage, the multicomponent transformation (MCT) is used to remove the redundancies between various image elements and enhances the performance of coding for the compression of images (Tzannes, 2003; Lee et al., 2010). MCT can effectively enhance storage and transmission by transforming each pixel independently.

2. In order to remove the spatial decorrelation of each component, 2D DWT is computed as follow:
   a. A $N \times M$ image is divided into an array of coefficients that contain four bands of data, each termed as low-low (LL), high-low (HL), low-high (LH), and high-high (HH).
   b. The bands HL, LH, and HH comprise HF components whereas, LL comprises LF components.
   c. It is noted that in the LS process, transformed coefficients are in an integer form which may not be quantized. But in lossy compression, DWT components must process through dead-zone quantization.

3. Then, an adaptive arithmetic coder, termed as MQ coder is used to coding each block with a size of 64×64.

4. At last, bitstream can be progressively transmitted with offering the resolution, spatial, quality, or component scalability.

11.4.3.3 Joint photographic experts group extended range

JPEG-XR supports both lossy and LS image compressions up to 32 bits per color plate. It has been designed with an objective of compression of continuous-tone images and provides better perceptual quality (Srinivasan et al., 2007). It offers high compression efficiency with low level of complexity but more complicated than JPEG (Hua et al., 2019). JPEG-XR utilizes the two-stages lapped biorthogonal transform (LBT) to reduce the block-boundary artifacts as in JPEG image (Liu et al., 2017). In the JPEG-XR algorithm (Fig. 11.3A), an image is separated into different macroblocks which are in the spatial domain and converted into the frequency domain. Afterwards, these bands are quantized and encoded.

Steps to execute JPEG-XR compression algorithm are as follows:

1. The input image is transformed by 2-stage LBT, that is, photo overlap transformation (POT) as first stage transformation and photo core transformation (PCT) as second stage transformation (Chen et al., 2016). It exploits the spatial correlation with a fixed size of blocks. The resultant transformed

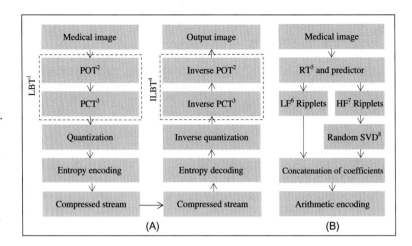

Figure 11.3 The flowchart of advanced compression algorithms: (A) joint photographic experts group extended range (JPEG-XR); and (B) RT-based compression. [1]*LBT*, lapped biorthogonal transform; [2]*POT*, photo overlap transformation; [3]*PCT*, photo core transformation; [4]*ILBT*, inverse LBT; [5]*RT*, Ripplet transform; [6]*LF*, low frequency; [7]*HF*, high frequency; and [8]*SVD*, singular value decomposition.

bands comprise the compressed independent multiresolution hierarchy.

2. Then, input transformed bands are quantized in which quantization steps can be varied across the different frequency bands.

3. Quantization is further followed by the inter-block prediction phase. This process eliminates the dependencies between the quantized transformed coefficients across blocks.

4. At last, compressed bitstream is generated via entropy encoding. In JPEG-XR, adaptive VLC can be utilized to achieve better results (Liu et al., 2017).

5. In order to decompress bitstream, entropy decoding, inverse quantization, and inverse LBT can be used.

11.4.3.4 Ripplet transform-based compression

Ripplet transform (RT) offers the efficient in-depth spatial representation of images at low compression rates (Xu et al., 2010). In order to improve the performance, it comprises the LS-based prediction and lossy singular value decomposition (SVD) of Ripplet coefficients (Rufai et al., 2014). The prediction phase provides information regarding the correlation between pixels of an image. This procedure offers improved performance with low level of complexity (Anitha et al., 2019). The methodology of RT-based compression is shown in Fig. 11.3B.

Steps to execute RT-based compassion algorithm as follow:

1. The LS predictor is used to express the correlation between the image pixels and generates the predicted error which will be encoded instead of the entire image. On the receiver end,

the decoder has knowledge of predictor function and predicted error is used to retrieve the original image.

2. Then, RT generates the ripples like shape in the spatial domain and represents the image in various scales as well as in various directions. In the frequency domain, it is computed as follow (Xu et al., 2010):

$$\rho_a = \frac{1}{\sqrt{c}} a^{\frac{d+1}{2d}} W(a \cdot r) V\left(\frac{ad}{c \cdot a}\right) \tag{11.5}$$

where ρ_a is the Fourier transform of Ripplet function; the parameters W and V are representing the radial and angular window, respectively. The parameters c and d are representing the scaling variables in r Ripplets functions. The scaling factor c measures the support and d is representing the degree of Ripplets. These parameters impact the dimensions of Ripplets in spatial domain and separate the HF and LF components.

3. The coefficients of discrete Ripplet transform R for an image function $f(m, n)$ is achieved as follows:

$$R_{j,\bar{k},l} = \sum_{m=0}^{a-1} \sum_{n=0}^{b-1} f(m, n) \overline{\rho_{j,\bar{k},l}(m, n)} \tag{11.6}$$

where $\rho_{j,\bar{k},l}$ is representing the Ripplet components with scale j. The parameters k and l are representing the position index and angle index.

4. Then, random SVD is used to reduce the dimensionality and image compression. This process offers a fast and efficient way to compute an image.

5. At last, both LF components and decomposed data are concatenated and arithmetic coding is performed on it to generate a compressed bitstream.

11.5 Summary and discussion

Since the past few decades, various lossy and LS compression techniques have been developed for medical imaging (Zuo et al., 2015). The main problem associated with medical imaging is achieving the higher level of compression ratio because LS algorithms provide less compression ratio such as JPEG-LS and SWT whereas, lossy algorithms provide a greater compression with compromise in quality of an image such as JPEG, wavelet-based compression. From a medical perspective, both algorithms are not providing satisfactory results because medical imaging requires a higher level of compression without compromise in quality. To overcome this problem, various developments have been made in medical image compression by adding the features of both lossy and LS compression algorithms together. The main idea behind such advanced integrated techniques is to apply the lossy compression algorithm to compress the unimportant information and LS compression algorithm to compress the important information in a medical image. In the past few years, various advancements have been made on this specific idea such as in RT-based compression (Anitha et al., 2019), ROI-based compression and JPEG-XR (Hua et al., 2019). Data compression in any form facilitates the effective transmission and storage.

Table 11.3 has shown the comparison of different compression algorithms in terms of characteristics, advantages, and disadvantages. It may provide the reader with a systematic comparison of different medical image compression algorithms which can be used to acquire a sense of variability in medical image compression. The transmission of images on the web servers associated with picture archiving and communication system (PACS) also utilizes the compression in which algorithms and rate will be decided by the PACS (Foos et al., 2000). So, on the web servers, the rate of compression is also a major concern with the utilization of those medical images in the diagnostic. However, with the advanced compression algorithm, higher compression rates can be achieved while preserving the important information in an image (Liu et al., 2017). The compression is one of the most important elements in teleradiology in which radiologists can send the compressed files and read the decompressed files.

Several authors (Liu et al., 2017; Tummala and Marni, 2017) have found that JPEG is one of the oldest lossy standards and originally designed for 2D images. For 3D images, it is less suitable as compared to JPEG2000 and JPEG-XR. Among JPEG2000 and JPEG-XR, JPEG2000 is more preferable as compared to JPEG-XR (Liu et al., 2017). The lossy compression algorithms like JPEG and SWT are less suitable as compared to LS compression and advanced (a combination of lossy and LS) compression algorithms (Tummala and Marni, 2017). From this perspective, advanced algorithms like RT-based and ROI-based compression are more suitable to achieve higher compression with fine details (without compromising important information in an image). It is also noteworthy that each algorithm has its own features and limitations which may depend on the input sample (medical image) so it is necessary to evaluate all advanced algorithms on different sets of medical images. Such analysis may provide future directions toward the effective

Table 11.3 Comparison between different compression algorithms.

Format	Category	Characteristics	Advantages	Disadvantages	Encoder	References
JPEG	Lossy	• The compression ratio is high • Simple in execution • Recognized standard • Based on DCT transform	• Better in telepathology diagnostics • Stores color information in 24 bits per pixel	• Not suitable for all types of medical images • Not suitable for 3D image volumes	• RLE • Huffman coding • DCT	Haque and Ahmed (2005), Koff and Shulman (2006), Anusuya et al. (2014), and Liu et al. (2017)
JPEG2000	Lossy and lossless (LS)	• Based on wavelet technology • Good in removing redundant information	• Most suitable for 3D simulation • More storage efficient • Prioritize the ROI	• Not suitable for contouring • Requires more processing power	• DWT • Multilevel DWT	Rabbani and Joshi (2002), Koff and Shulman (2006), Zuo et al. (2015), and Liu et al. (2017)
JPEG-LS	LS	• Based on the HP-LOCO codec • Can be used to compress elevation data	• Simple and easy • Offers a low level of computational complexity	• Not suitable for smaller images • Not widely adopted as compared to other JPEGs	• Arithmetic coding • Golomb • RLE	Rane and Sapiro (2001), Zuo et al. (2015), and Liu et al. (2017)
JPEG-XR	Lossy and LS	• Based on block-transform image compression • Implemented in two-stage LBT (POT and PCT)	• High compression efficiency • Low complexity in implementations	• Less suitable for all datasets of medical images • Output image includes blocking artifacts	• VLC	Liu et al. (2017) and Hua et al. (2019)
Wavelet-based compression	Lossy	• Also known as DWT • It treats the image as a signal or wave • Allows gradual transmission without any blocking	• Offers a better-quality image • Fast computation • Usable where scalability and tolerable degradation is of prime importance	• This technique generates a low-resolution version of waves in initial steps	• Entropy coding • Adaptive arithmetic coding	Koff and Shulman (2006), Chen and Tseng (2007), Anusuya et al. (2014), Zuo et al. (2015), and Anitha et al. (2019)

(Continued)

Table 11.3 (Continued)

Format	Category	Characteristics	Advantages	Disadvantages	Encoder	References
SWT-based compression	LS	• It is a time-invariant wavelet decomposition method • Works by averaging the variants of DWT	• Resolution retained • Image noise eliminated • Easier to get the relationship among the sub-bands	• For accurate results, measurements at the site of interest are required	• Arithmetic coding • VLC	Anusuya et al. (2014)
ROI-based compression	Lossy and LS	• Lossy compression for unimportant data • LS compression for important data	• Offers higher compression rates • Easy in implementation	• The background quality is lowered as compared to the foreground	• VLC	Zuo et al. (2015)
RT-based compression	Lossy and LS	• All the spatial details of the image are retained • Generalization of the curvelet transform	• Representation in high directional features • Efficient in image denoising applications	• Time-consuming process in case of large images • RT degrades the performance with an increase in the coefficient		Anitha et al. (2019)

JPEG, joint photographic experts group; *RLE*, run length encoding; *DCT*, discrete cosine transform; *ROI*, region of interest; *DWT*, discrete wavelet transform; *JPEG-LS*, joint photographic experts group lossless; *HP-LOCO*, Hewlett-Packard-low complexity lossless compression; *JPEG-XR*, joint photographic experts group extended range; *LBT*, lapped biorthogonal transform; *POT*, photo overlap transformation; *PCT*, photo core transformation; *VLC*, variable-length coding; and *RT* Ripplets transform.

storage and transmission of medical images and enhance its application range.

11.6 Conclusion and future directions

Data compression plays a vital role in meeting the requirements of modern medical practices with respect to efficient storage and transmission. Various standards are available to exchange the compressed medical images such as DICOM which supports many compression standards such as JPEG-LS, JPEG2000, and RLE. However, the most important consideration must be given to compression ratio and image quality. To meet such requirements, advanced (combination of lossy and LS) compression algorithms offer a significant way to compress the image with less compromise in quality as compared to lossy and LS compression algorithms. It is expected that this chapter will give effective guidance toward the comprehensive knowledge of advanced compression algorithms and also provide many challenges and opportunities in the field of medical image compression algorithms.

It is noted that there is significant variability in the medical imaging and advanced methods are not yet explored over different medical image sets. So, this may restrict the applicability of advanced compression algorithms because they have been designed to optimize image compression based on the properties and capabilities of a specific medical image. A large-scale evaluation of different medical images using advanced compression algorithms is one of the future requirements to establish guidelines for effective utilization of lossy and LS compression schemes together in different types of modalities and organ systems.

Disclosure statement

There is no potential conflict of interest declared by the authors.

References

Anitha, J., Sophia, P.E., de Albuquerque, V.H.C., 2019. Performance enhanced ripplet transform based compression method for medical images. Measurement 144, 203–213.

Anusuya, V., Raghavan, V.S., Kavitha, G., 2014. Lossless compression on MRI images using SWT. J. Digit. Imaging 27 (5), 594–600.

Avramović, A., 2011, November. Lossless compression of medical images based on gradient edge detection. In: 2011 19thTelecommunications Forum (TELFOR) Proceedings of Papers. IEEE, pp. 1199–1202.

Bai, X., Jin, J.S., Feng, D., 2004. Segmentation-based multilayer diagnosis lossless medical image compression. Proceedings of the Pan-Sydney Area Workshop on Visual Information Processing. Australian Computer Society, Inc, pp. 9–14.

Bidgood Jr, W.D., Horii, S.C., Prior, F.W., Van Syckle, D.E., 1997. Understanding and using DICOM, the data interchange standard for biomedical imaging. J. Am. Med. Inform. Assoc. 4 (3), 199–212.

Bladowska, J., Bednarek-Tupikowska, G., Sokolska, V., Badowski, R., Moroń, K., Bonicki, W., et al., 2010. MRI image characteristics of materials implanted at sellar region after transsphenoidal resection of pituitary tumours. Pol. J. Radiol. 75 (2), 46.

Brunello, D., Calvagno, G., Mian, G.A., Rinaldo, R., 2003. Lossless compression of video using temporal information. IEEE Trans. Image Process. 12 (2), 132–139.

Bruylants, T., Munteanu, A., Schelkens, P., 2015. Wavelet based volumetric medical image compression. Signal. Process. Image Commun. 31, 112–133.

Cavaro-Ménard, C., Naït-Ali, A., Tanguy, J.Y., Angelini, E., Bozec, C.L., Le Jeune, J.J., 2008. Specificities of physiological signals and medical images. In: Compression of Biomedical Images and Signals. Wiley-ISTE, London, pp. 266–290.

Chen, Y.Y., 2007. Medical image compression using DCT-based subband decomposition and modified SPIHT data organization. Int. J. Med. Inform. 76 (10), 717–725.

Chen, Y.T., Tseng, D.C., 2007. Wavelet-based medical image compression with adaptive prediction. Comput. Med. Imaging Graph. 31 (1), 1–8.

Chen, H., Guo, X., and Zhang, Y., 2016, July. Implantion of onboard JPEG XR compression on a low clock frequency FPGA. In: 2016 IEEE International Geoscience and Remote Sensing Symposium (IGARSS). IEEE, pp. 2811–2814.

Chouhan, A. and Nigam, M.J., 2016, July. Double compression of JPEG image using DCT with estimated quality factor. In: 2016 IEEE 1st International Conference on Power Electronics, Intelligent Control and Energy Systems (ICPEICES). IEEE, pp. 1–3.

Clunie, D.A., 2002. DICOM Supplement 61: JPEG 2000 Transfer Syntaxes. <ftp://medical.nema.org/medical/dicom/final/sup61_ft.pdf>.

Clunie, D.A. 2012. Lossless compression of breast tomosynthesis: objects to maximize dicom transmission speed and review performance and minimize storage space. In: Radiological Society of North America 2012 Scientific Assembly and Annual Meeting, Chicago, IL, USA.

Dufaux, F., Sullivan, G.J., Ebrahimi, T., 2009. The JPEG XR image coding standard [Standards in a Nutshell]. IEEE Signal. Process. Mag. 26 (6), 195–204.

Erickson, B.J., 2002. Irreversible compression of medical images. J. Digit. Imaging 15 (1), 5–14.

Foos, D.H., Muka, E., Slone, R.M., Erickson, B.J., Flynn, M.J., Clunie, D.A., et al., 2000. JPEG 2000 compression of medical imagery, Medical Imaging 2000: PACS Design and Evaluation: Engineering and Clinical Issues, 3980. International Society for Optics and Photonics, pp. 85–96.

Fowler, J., Pesquet-Popescu, B., 2007. An overview on wavelets in source coding, communications, and networks. EURASIP J. Image Video Process. 2007 (1), 060539.

Gonzalez, R.C., Woods, R.E., 2002. Digital Image Processing. Pearson Education, Upper Saddle River.

Grgic, S., Grgic, M., Zovko-Cihlar, B., 2001. Performance analysis of image compression using wavelets. IEEE Trans. Ind. Electron. 48 (3), 682–695.

Gudbjartsson, H., Patz, S., 1995. The Rician distribution of noisy MRI data. Magn. Reson. Med. 34 (6), 910–914.

Gurdeep, K., Khandelwal, N., Jasuja, O.P., 2010. *Computed tomographic studies on ossification status of medial epiphysis of clavicle: effect of slice thickness and dose distribution*. Gov. Counc. 2010–2012 32, 298.

Haque, M.R., Ahmed, F., 2005. Image data compression with JPEG and JPEG2000. In: 8th International Confrrence on Computer and Information Technology, pp. 1064–1069.

Harris, T.J., McCormick, F., 2010. The molecular pathology of cancer. Nat. Rev. Clin. Oncol. 7 (5), 251.

Hashemi-Berenjabad, S., Mojarrad, S., 2016. A review on medical image compression techniques. Int. J. Emerg. Technol. Eng. Res. (IJETER) 4 (1), 88–91.

Helvie, M.A., 2010. Digital mammography imaging: breast tomosynthesis and advanced applications. Radiol. Clin. Ns. Am. 48 (5), 917.

Hill, C.R., Bamber, J.C., ter Haar, G.R., 2004. Physical Principles of Medical Ultrasonics. Wiley, Chichester.

Hua, K.L., Trang, H.T., Srinivasan, K., Chen, Y.Y., Chen, C.H., Sharma, V., et al., 2019. Reduction of artefacts in JPEG-XR compressed images. Sensors 19 (5), 1214.

Jiang, H., Ma, Z., Hu, Y., Yang, B., Zhang, L., 2012. Medical image compression based on vector quantization with variable block sizes in wavelet domain. Comput. Intell. Neurosci. 2012, 5.

Jones, T., Townsend, D.W., 2017. History and future technical innovation in positron emission tomography. J. Med. Imaging 4 (1), 011013.

JPEG 2000 Image Coding System, 2005. Interactivity tools, APIs and Protocols; ISO/IEC IS 15444-9. ISO, Geneva.

Karadimitriou, K., Fenstermacher, M., 1997, March. Image compression in medical image databases using set redundancy. In: Proceedings DCC'97. Data Compression Conference. IEEE, p. 445.

Kasban, H., El-Bendary, M.A.M., Salama, D.H., 2015. A comparative study of medical imaging techniques. Int. J. Inf. Sci. Intell. Syst. 4 (2), 37–58.

Kaur, M., Wasson, V., 2015. ROI based medical image compression for telemedicine application. Procedia Comput. Sci. 70, 579–585.

Kerensky, R.A., Cusma, J.T., Kubilis, P., Simon, R., Bashore, T.M., Hirshfeld, J.W., et al., 2000. American College of Cardiology/European Society of Cardiology international study of angiographic data compression phase I: the effects of lossy data compression on recognition of diagnostic features in digital coronary angiography. J. Am. Coll. Cardiol. 35 (5), 1370–1379.

Khatami, A., Khosravi, A., Nguyen, T., Lim, C.P., Nahavandi, S., 2017. Medical image analysis using wavelet transform and deep belief networks. Expert Syst. Appl. 86, 190–198.

Koff, D.A., Shulman, H., 2006. An overview of digital compression of medical images: can we use lossy image compression in radiology? J. Can. Assoc. Radiol. 57 (4), 211.

Larobina, M., Murino, L., 2014. Medical image file formats. J. Digit. Imaging 27 (2), 200–206.

Lee, H., Lee, K.H., Kim, K.J., Park, S., Seo, J., Shin, Y.G., et al., 2010. Advantage in image fidelity and additional computing time of JPEG2000 3D in comparison to JPEG2000 in compressing abdomen CT image datasets of different section thicknesses. Med. Phys. 37 (8), 4238–4248.

Lett, D., 2007. National standards for forensic pathology training slow to develop. Can. Med. Assoc. J. 117 (3), 240–241.

Li, C., Huang, R., Ding, Z., Gatenby, J.C., Metaxas, D.N., Gore, J.C., 2011. A level set method for image segmentation in the presence of intensity inhomogeneities with application to MRI. IEEE Trans. Image Process. 20 (7), 2007–2016.

Liang, Z.P., Lauterbur, P.C., 2000. Principles of Magnetic Resonance Imaging: A Signal Processing Perspective. SPIE Optical Engineering Press.

Liu, F., Hernandez-Cabronero, M., Sanchez, V., Marcellin, M., Bilgin, A., 2017. The current role of image compression standards in medical imaging. Information 8 (4), 131.

Loganathan, R., Kumaraswamy, Y.S., 2010. Medical image compression using biorthogonal spline wavelet with different decomposition. IJCSE Int. J. Comput. Sci. Eng. 2 (9), 3003–3006.

MINC software library and tools, 2000. <http://www.bic.mni.mcgill.ca/>.

Nashat, S., Abdullah, A., Abdullah, M.Z., 2011. A Stationary Wavelet Edge Detection Algorithm for Noisy Images. School of Electrical & Electronics University Sains Malaysia Engineering Campus.

National Research Council, 1996. Mathematics and Physics of Emerging Biomedical Imaging. National Academies Press.

Neelamani, R., De Queiroz, R., Fan, Z., Dash, S., Baraniuk, R.G., 2006. JPEG compression history estimation for color images. IEEE Trans. Image Process. 15 (6), 1365–1378.

NIFTI documentation, 2004. <http://nifti.nimh.nih.gov/nifti-1/documentation>.

Omami, G., Tamimi, D., Branstetter, B.F., 2014. Basic principles and applications of 18F-FDG-PET/CT in oral and maxillofacial imaging: a pictorial essay. Imaging Sci. Dent. 44 (4), 325–332.

Padmaja, G.M., Nirupama, P., 2012. Analysis of various image compression techniques. ARPN J. Sci. Technol. 2 (4), 371–376.

Pambrun, J.F., Noumeir, R., 2015. Computed tomography image compressibility and limitations of compression ratio-based guidelines. J. Digit. Imaging 28 (6), 636–645.

Patel, V., Dinov, I.D., Van Horn, J.D., Thompson, P.M., Toga, A.W., 2010. LONI MiND: metadata in NIfTI for DWI. Neuroimage 51 (2), 665–676.

Paul, E.S., Anitha, J., 2019. Analysis of transform-based compression techniques for MRI and CT images. Intelligent Data Analysis for Biomedical Applications. *Academic Press*, pp. 103–120.

Rabbani, M., Joshi, R., 2002. An overview of the JPEG 2000 still image compression standard. Signal. Process Image Commun. 17 (1), 3–48.

Rahmim, A., Zaidi, H., 2008. PET versus SPECT: strengths, limitations and challenges. Nucl. Med. Commun. 29 (3), 193–207.

Rane, S.D., Sapiro, G., 2001. Evaluation of JPEG-LS, the new lossless and controlled-lossy still image compression standard, for compression of high-resolution elevation data. IEEE Trans. Geosci. Remote Sens. 39 (10), 2298–2306.

Robb, R.A., Hanson, D.P., Karwoski, R.A., Larson, A.G., Workman, E.L., Stacy, M.C., 1989. Analyze: a comprehensive, operator-interactive software package for multidimensional medical image display and analysis. Comput. Med. Imaging Graph. 13 (6), 433–454.

Roček, A., Javorník, M., Slavíček, K., Dostál, O., 2017, December. Reversible watermarking in medical imaging with zero distortion in ROI. In: 2017 24th IEEE International Conference on Electronics, Circuits and Systems (ICECS). IEEE, pp. 356–359.

Rosset, A., Spadola, L., Ratib, O., 2004. OsiriX: an open-source software for navigating in multidimensional DICOM images. J. Digit. Imaging 17 (3), 205–216.

Rothstein, W.G., 1979. Pathology: the evolution of a specialty in American medicine. Med. Care 17 (10), 975–988.

Rufai, A.M., Anbarjafari, G., Demirel, H., 2014. Lossy image compression using singular value decomposition and wavelet difference reduction. Digit. Signal Process. 24, 117–123.

Santa-Cruz, D., Ebrahimi, T., Askelof, J., Larsson, M., Christopoulos, C.A., 2000. JPEG 2000 still image coding versus other standards, Applications of Digital Image Processing XXIII, vol. 4115. International Society for Optics and Photonics, pp. 446–454.

Schelkens, P., Munteanu, A., Barbarien, J., Galca, M., Giro-Nieto, X., Cornelis, J., 2003. Wavelet coding of volumetric medical datasets. IEEE Trans. Med. Imaging 22 (3), 441–458.

Shang, Y., Niu, H., Ma, S., Hou, X., Chen, C., 2011. Design and implementation for JPEG-LS algorithm based on FPGA. International Conference on Information and Management Engineering. Springer, Berlin, pp. 369–375.

Shapiro, J.M., 1993. Embedded image coding using zerotrees of wavelet coefficients. IEEE Trans. Signal. Process. 41 (12), 3445–3462.

Skodras, A., Christopoulos, C., Ebrahimi, T., 2001. The jpeg 2000 still image compression standard. IEEE Signal. Process. Mag. 18 (5), 36–58.

Srinivasan, S., Tu, C., Regunathan, S.L., Sullivan, G.J., 2007. HD Photo: a new image coding technology for digital photography, Applications of Digital Image Processing XXX, vol. 6696. International Society for Optics and Photonics, p. 66960A.

Starosolski, R., 2005. Performance evaluation of lossless medical and natural continuous tone image compression algorithms, Medical Imaging, vol. 5959. International Society for Optics and Photonics, pp. 116–127, p. 59590L.

Sudhakar, R., Karthiga, R., Jayaraman, S., 2005. Image compression using coding of wavelet coefficients—a survey. ICGST-GVIP J. 5 (6), 25–38.

Taubman, D., 2000. High performance scalable image compression with EBCOT. IEEE Trans. Image Process. 9 (7), 1158–1170.

Tummala, S.V., Marni, V., 2017. Comparison of Image Compression and Enhancement Techniques for Image Quality in Medical Images (Master Thesis). Department of Applied Signal Processing Blekinge Institute of Technology.

Tzannes, A., 2003. Compression of 3-Dimensional Medical Image Data Using Part 2 of JPEG 2000. Aware. Inc.

Ukrit, M.F., Suresh, G.R., 2013. Effective lossless compression for medical image sequences using composite algorithm. 2013 International Conference on Circuits, Power and Computing Technologies (ICCPCT). IEEE, pp. 1122–1126.

Vaquero, J.J., Kinahan, P., 2015. Positron emission tomography: current challenges and opportunities for technological advances in clinical and preclinical imaging systems. Annu. Rev. Biomed. Eng. 17, 385–414.

Verhaeghe, J., D'Asseler, Y., Staelens, S., Lemahieu, I., 2006. Optimization of temporal basis functions in dynamic PET imaging. Nucl. Instrum. Methods Phys. Res. Sect. A: Accel. Spectrom. Detect. Assoc. Equip. 569 (2), 425–428.

Wagner, R.F., 1983. Statistics of speckle in ultrasound B-scans. IEEE Trans. Sonics Ultrason. 30 (3), 156–163.

Wallace, G.K., 1992. The JPEG still picture compression standard. IEEE Trans. Consum. Electron. 38 (1), xviii–xxxiv.

Weinberger, M.J., Seroussi, G., Sapiro, G., 2000. The LOCO-I lossless image compression algorithm: principles and standardization into JPEG-LS. IEEE Trans. Image Process. 9 (8), 1309−1324.

Wu, B.F., Lin, C.F., 2005. A high-performance and memory-efficient pipeline architecture for the 5/3 and 9/7 discrete wavelet transform of JPEG2000 codec. IEEE Trans. Circuits Syst. Video Technol. 15 (12), 1615−1628.

Wu, Y.G., Tai, S.C., 2001. Medical image compression by discrete cosine transform spectral similarity strategy. IEEE Trans. Inf. Technol. Biomed. 5 (3), 236−243.

Xu, J., Yang, L., Wu, D., 2010. Ripplet: A new transform for image processing. J. Vis. Commun. Image Represent. 21 (7), 627−639.

Zhang, N., Wu, M., Forchhammer, S., Wu, X., 2005. Joint compression-segmentation of functional MRI data sets, Medical Imaging 2005: PACS and Imaging Informatics, vol. 5748. International Society for Optics and Photonics, pp. 190−201.

Zhang, F., Song, Y., Cai, W., Hauptmann, A.G., Liu, S., Pujol, S., et al., 2016. Dictionary pruning with visual word significance for medical image retrieval. Neurocomputing 177, 75−88.

Zuo, Z., Lan, X., Deng, L., Yao, S., Wang, X., 2015. An improved medical image compression technique with lossless region of interest. Optik 126 (21), 2825−2831.

Biomedical Image Security

12

Multilevel medical image encryption for secure communication

Shoaib Amin Banday[1], Ajaz Hussain Mir[2] and Shakeel Malik[1]

[1]Department of Electronics and Communication Engineering, School of Engineering and Technology (SoE&T), Islamic University of Science & Technology (IUST), Jammu and Kashmir, India [2]Department of Electronics and Communication Engineering, National Institute of Technology Srinagar, Srinagar, Jammu and Kashmir, India

12.1 Introduction

Among all the areas of research worldwide, healthcare is of prime focus. This is reflected from the development of medical imaging modalities like computed tomography, magnetic resonance imaging, functional-MRI, ultrasound imaging, positron emission tomography, single positron emission tomography, etc. These medical imaging tools are being extensively used as they provide noninvasive, easy, and quick access inside a human

Advances in Computational Techniques for Biomedical Image Analysis. DOI: https://doi.org/10.1016/B978-0-12-820024-7.00012-8

body. With the continuous advancements in the field of imaging tools, we have been able to image a human body organ or any specific site precisely with a high resolution. Therefore the number of images pertaining to a single organ or an anatomical site under study can be huge. One of the potential reasons for this huge amount of image data is that, a medical expert may want to extract detailed diagnostic information from these images. The downside of this huge amount of image data is the increasing challenge of storing and securing transmission for the purpose of image analysis which may include processes like segmentation, data hiding, feature selection, image enhancement, and restoration (Mitra and Uma Shankar, 2015; Phophalia et al., 2014; Ji et al., 2015; Wu et al., 2015; Jung et al., 2009). On the other hand, telemedicine has evolved significantly for detection and diagnosis of diseases remotely, which means more frequent transmission of medical images over the network. Since medical organizations must comply to Health Insurance Portability and Accountability Act, it becomes crucial that medical images be secured from any unauthorized access over the network. The security of any medical image is characterized as its integrity, confidentiality, and authentication (Lou et al., 2009; Hu and Han, 2009; Lin et al., 2009). These short comings limit the development of mobile pervasive healthcare solutions intended solely for enhancing the performance of secure medical image transmission. Therefore like other sensitive data, medical images must be secured while transmitting them over an insecure channel.

12.2 Related work

The most commonly adopted architecture for medical image cryptosystem is the confusion−diffusion architecture or permutation−substitution architecture (see Fig. 12.1). Confusion is a term used widely in encryption terminology and is defined as a property wherein we hide the relationship among the key and cipher image. This implies that even with a minute deviation in the encryption key, there should be a huge change in the cipher image. The other term being diffusion is defined as a property wherein we hide the relationship between plain input image and the cipher image. This implies that a minuscule change in the original input image should hugely change the output image.

Cryptographic systems have been one of the common ways of securing the sensitive data applying symmetric key or an asymmetric key mechanism (Hongjun et al., 2016). Some conventional block ciphers have been extensively used in the past

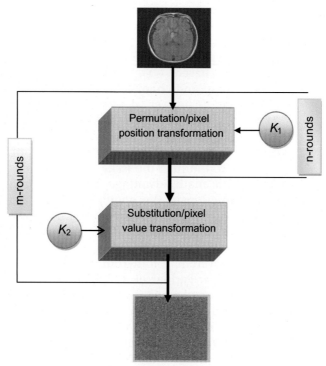

Figure 12.1 Conventional permutation—substitution architecture.

decade for the encryption of medical images like data encryption standard, International Data Encryption Algorithm (IDEA), and advanced encryption standard (Menezes et al., 1996). However, considering the sizable images to be encrypted and the need for fast encryption mechanisms for use in real time medical health applications, these block ciphers have shown unacceptable results. To obtain this balance of performance and speed in medical image encryption, a plethora of encryption mechanisms have been proposed and implemented from time to time. In a number of research papers, chaos theory-based algorithms are being proposed and implemented (Diaconu, 2016; Abdmouleh and Bouhlel, 2013; Ashtiyani et al., 2008; Fu et al., 2013). The major advantage of these techniques comes from their extreme sensitivity to initial conditions, key space, and improved diffusion and confusion capabilities. These chaotic cryptosystems are driven by chaotic dynamical systems whose preliminaries are associated with control and synchronization (Sarker and Parvez, 2005).

A two-dimensional (2D) chaotic map and key stream-based confusion—diffusion architecture is presented by Fridrich

(1998). The work reported in Scharinger (1998) used chaotic Kolmogorov and shift register-based pseudo random number generator to hide the relationship between the input image and the cipher image. Some of the researchers have suggested strategies based on permutation of pixels by employing Baker's map and chaotic cat map to obtain three-dimensional (3D) map (Chen et al., 2004; Mao et al., 2004). Similarly (Belkhouche et al., 2005) discussed a permutation strategy for the encryption of medical images. The literature of medical image encryption also reports the use of chaotic sequence sorting to diminish the issue of periodicity (Belkhouche et al., 2005). The main advantage of this technique is the considerable reduction in the encryption time. The work introduced by Behnia et al. (2008) employs a hierarchical chaotic system that uses one-dimensional chaotic maps. The overall coupled chaotic system can be thought of as a high dimensional dynamic system. A four-round symmetric image cryptosystem presented in Patidar et al. (2009) achieves confusion and diffusion by employing chaotic standard map and logistic maps respectively. The literature also reports the application of two chaotic image ciphers: first, the image pixels are shuffled in the entirety of the image and later the confusion is achieved by using hyper-chaotic system to hide the relationship between the cipher image and the plain image (Gao and Chen, 2008a,b). A spatial chaos-based cryptosystem is proposed in Sun et al. (2008). In this paper, a spatial chaos map is used to encrypt an image on per pixel basis. In recent times, the idea of selective image encryption has received a great amount of attention. The selective image encryption considerably reduces the computational burden of the cryptosystem in terms of time without considerable compromise on the level of security (Puech and Rodrigues, 2005; Zhou et al., 2009; Rao et al., 2006; Panduranga and Naveen Kumar, 2013a,b; Ou et al., 2007; Brahimi et al., 2008; Xiang et al., 2007; Liu, 2006; Som and Sen, 2013). The selective image encryption algorithms work on specific portions of the images only of which are in contrast to the conventional encryption schemes. The encryption based on the selective approach makes it appropriate for some real time medical imaging tasks.

In this work, a multilevel chaotic encryption technique for medical images is proposed. This technique utilizes multiple chaotic maps as a means for substitution via the use of sine, cubic, and logistic maps. In addition to this, the permutation (confusion) is realized by the use of the Arnold cat map on the medical images.

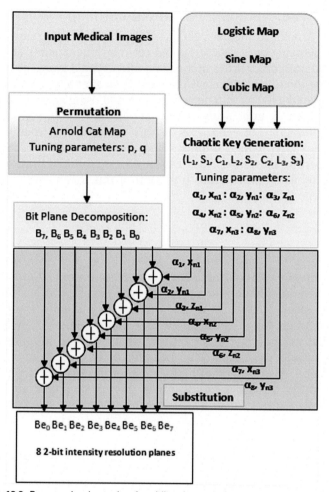

Figure 12.2 Proposed schematic of multilevel encryption.

12.3 Materials and methods

The proposed medical image encryption methodology follows a permutation–substitution framework and is shown in Fig. 12.2. As can be seen from the diagram, the encryption begins with the controlled shuffling of the pixel positions by employing Arnold cat map transformation. After permuting the pixel positions of the original medical images, we extract all the bit planes of the original input image. All the bit planes are then encrypted separately by unique chaotic keys to ensure security at the bit plane level of the image.

12.3.1 Permutation via Arnold cat map

The Arnold cat map is a 2D invertible chaotic map (Shang et al., 2008; Liehuang et al., 2006). Arnold cat map mainly aims at shuffling the position of pixels of the plain unencrypted image in such a way that the original image is obtained back after a specified number of iterations. This can be better illustrated using an example:

Consider a gray scale image of size $n \times m$ ($n = m$; for a square image). Let each pixel in this image be represented by the index (x,y), which implies that x can take values from 1 to n and y can take values from 1 to m. Given an initial index value of a pixel as (x,y), the transformation of this index can be done as per the following:

$$A(x,y) = \begin{bmatrix} 1 & r \\ s & rs+1 \end{bmatrix} \begin{bmatrix} x \\ y \end{bmatrix} mod\ n \qquad (12.1)$$

where $A(x,y)$ is the transformed index of the pixel with original index of (x,y). From the above generalized expression of the Arnold transformation, it can be inferred that a pixel has undergone a shear factor of $\mathbf{s}$ in the x-direction. Similarly, the transformed index has a shear factor of $\mathbf{r}$ in y-direction. Now let us consider an image of 216×216 size that needs to be permuted using Arnold cat map by a shear factor of 1 both in x- and y-direction. Also the initial index value of the pixel is ($x = y = 5$). This reduces the above expression for pixel positioned at (5,5) to:

$$A(5,5) = \begin{bmatrix} 1 & 1 \\ 1 & 2 \end{bmatrix} \begin{bmatrix} 5 \\ 5 \end{bmatrix} mod\ (256) = (10, 15)$$

In the next two iterations, the pixel is permuted to positions given by:

$$A(10,15) = \begin{bmatrix} 1 & 1 \\ 1 & 2 \end{bmatrix} \begin{bmatrix} 10 \\ 15 \end{bmatrix} mod\ (256) = (25, 40)$$

$$A(25,40) = \begin{bmatrix} 1 & 1 \\ 1 & 2 \end{bmatrix} \begin{bmatrix} 25 \\ 40 \end{bmatrix} mod\ (256) = (65, 105)$$

Similarly all other pixel indexes are permuted by the same factor. This shuffling continues up to a point that is determined by the values of r, s, and n. In general, the procedure for Arnold cat transformation is given in Fig. 12.3. The inverse of this transformation can be easily found out and is given as:

$$A'(x,y) = \begin{bmatrix} rs+1 & -r \\ -s & 1 \end{bmatrix} \begin{bmatrix} x \\ y \end{bmatrix} mod\ n \qquad (12.2)$$

Procedure for Arnold cat map transformation

Step 1: Input a medical image and extract image details

$I_{original}$ ⟵ *Read an original medical image*

I_{height} ⟵ *Obtain no. of columns from $I_{original}$*

I_{width} ⟵ *Obtain no. of rows from $I_{original}$*

ArnoldCatImg ⟵ *Initialize an empty (I_{width}, I_{height})*

i ⟵ *ArnoldCatImg*

Counter ⟵ *1*

Step 2: Arnold cat map transformation

while counter ≠ x **do**
    for x = 1 to I_{width}**do**
        for y = 1 to I_{height}**do**
            $X_{new} = Mod (x+y, I_{width})$
            $Y_{new} = Mod (x+2y, I_{height})$
            ArnoldCatImg $(X_{new}, Y_{new}) = I_{original}$
        end
    end
end
    Output: $I_{original}$, ArnoldCatImg

Figure 12.3 Pseudo-code for Arnold cat map transformation.

where $A'(x,y)$ is the inverse transformation of a pixel.

Fig. 12.4 shows an Arnold cat map transformation of a left ventricle heart MR image. Fig. 12.4B shows the permuted ventricle image. As can be observed, the image appears skewed after three iterations. As we proceed with more iterations of the original image, Fig. 12.4C−E, the original image pixels are completely shuffled. Figs. 12.4F−I are now reverse permutations and as evident, the original left ventricle heart image begins to appear again. Starting with the initial values of *r* and *s*, the original will have different permuted images at different iteration numbers. For the above case, the original image is retrieved back after 68 iterations as can be seen from Fig. 12.4J.

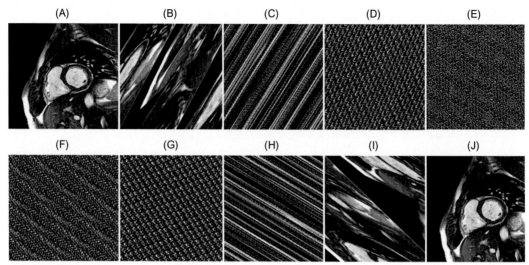

Figure 12.4 (A) Original left ventricle magnetic resonance (MR) image followed by Arnold cat mapped images after: (B) 1 iteration, (C) 3 iterations, (D) 10 iterations, (E) 15 iterations, (F) 40 iterations, (G) 54 iterations, (H) 65 iterations, (I) 67 iterations, and (J) 68 iterations.

12.3.2   Proposed multiple chaotic map transformation

From the past few decades, symmetric key-based chaotic systems have been explored for secure image storage and transmission via enhanced pixel diffusion and confusion frameworks (Alvarez et al., 1999; Wong et al., 2000; Wong, 2002; Khan and Zhang, 2008; Pareek et al., 2003). One of the possible ways to illustrate chaotic systems is to employ the use of logistic map which may be mathematically put as:

$$x(n + 1) = rx_n(1 - x_n) \tag{12.3}$$

Eq. (12.3) defines a mathematical function that generates a random chaotic sequence whose values lie between 0 and 1. It characterizes an evolving process in time x_{n+1} depending on values of x_n, r is a constant. Different values of r, show chaotic behavior of the map. For some initial value of the variable x, the sequence will develop in a very specific way which completes differentiates from an evolving process that has been initiated differently. This indicates that the presence of the randomness as the present determines the future value but any close approximation of the initial value does not determine the future.

In the proposed work, we employ the use of three chaotic functions viz.: logistic, sine, and cubic to obtain eight keys for encrypting the original image and are given from Eqs. (12.4) to (12.11).

$$x_{n1} + 1 = \alpha_1 x_{n1}(1 - x_{n1}) \tag{12.4}$$

$$y_{n1} + 1 = \alpha_2 sin(\pi y_{n1}) \tag{12.5}$$

$$z_{n1} + 1 = \alpha_3 z_{n1}(1 - (z_{n1})^2) \tag{12.6}$$

$$x_{n2} + 1 = \alpha_4 x_{n2}(1 - x_{n2}) \tag{12.7}$$

$$y_{n2} + 1 = \alpha_5 sin(\pi y_{n2}) \tag{12.8}$$

$$z_{n2} + 1 = \alpha_6 z_{n2}(1 - (z_{n2})^2) \tag{12.9}$$

$$x_{n3} + 1 = \alpha_7 x_{n3}(1 - x_{n3}) \tag{12.10}$$

$$y_{n3} + 1 = \alpha_8 sin(\pi y_{n3}) \tag{12.11}$$

To investigate the potential of using chaotic maps, we start tuning the parameters of the chaotic equations given from Eqs. (12.4)–(12.11). For the logistic equation given in Eq. (12.3), we have two tunable parameters α_1 and x_{n1}. These two parameters can be randomly chosen to obtain a random output sequence (encryption key) that can be used for encrypting the image. As an illustration, we proceed with the following two cases:

1. We change the value of α_1 in the range of 2−3.99.
2. Keeping α_1 constant, we change the values of x_{n1}.

Case 1: Studying the impact on the periodicity of the generated key sequence, we change the values of α_1 which correspond to the values of *r* (Eq. 12.3) from 2.0 to 3.99 and obtain the chaotic sequences as shown in Fig. 12.5A−F. The plots show the nature of generated output sequences. At the start, when we choose the value of *r* as 2.0 keeping the initial condition fixed, we observe a simple sequence at the output. As the value of *r* is increased to three, the generated output sequence becomes more chaotic in nature as shown in Fig. 12.5C. Since a strong image encryption method demands the use of a random sequence as its key, it can easily be observed from Fig. 12.5D and E that the generated sequence becomes more and more

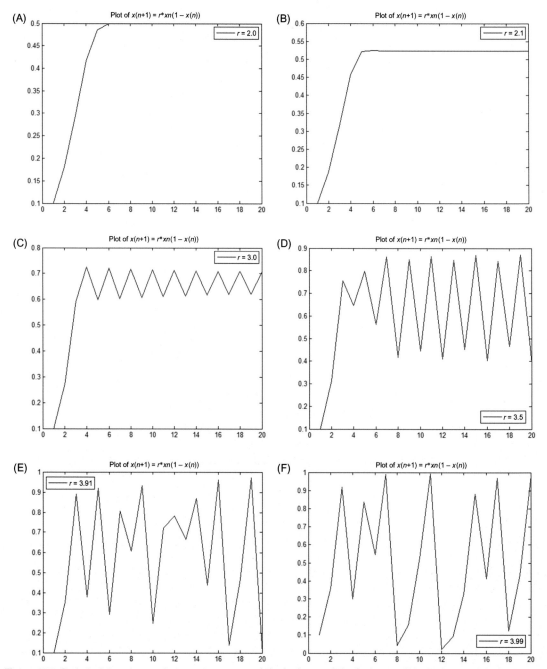

Figure 12.5 Period of the generated output sequence at (A) $r(\alpha_1) = 2.0$, (B) $r(\alpha_1) = 2.1$, (C) $r(\alpha_1) = 3.0$, (D) $r(\alpha_1) = 3.5$, (E) $r(\alpha_1) = 3.91$, and (F) $r(\alpha_1) = 3.99$.

random as we approach the value of 3.99. The completely random sequence can be observed in the last plot corresponding to Fig. 12.5F. It can be concluded from Fig. 12.5A–F that the period of the generated output sequence becomes infinite at the r value of 3.99

Case 2: Studying the impact of the second tuneable parameter x_{n1} (same as x_n of Eq. (12.3)) on the generated output sequence. Here, we would like to observe the effect of changing the basic initial condition of the chaotic map equation. Since a good encryption method needs to be highly sensitive to the initial conditions, we consider two different initial conditions for generating the chaotic sequences:

1. $x_{n1} = 0.100000$
2. $x_{n1} = 0.100001$

From the two values of x_{n1}, a subtle difference appears between the two starting (initial) conditions. Output key sequence generated for encryption is shown in Fig. 12.6. The plot in blue and red corresponds to the output sequences with initial conditions set at 0.100000 and 0.100001 respectively. Although the initial conditions are just slightly different, the obtained output sequence has varied significantly. This depicts the sensitiveness of the chaotic maps on the initial conditions. For the above two values of x_{n1}, Fig. 12.7 shows the absolute error of the two chaotic sequences shown in Fig. 12.6.

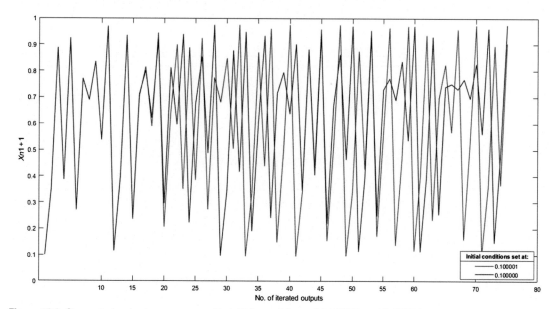

Figure 12.6 Generated output sequences with initial conditions of 0.100000 and 0.100001.

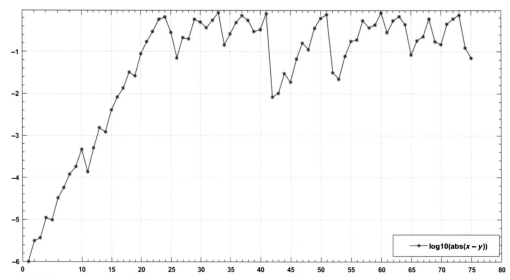

Figure 12.7 Plot showing absolute error between two sequences (Fig. 12.6).

From Figs. 12.5−12.7, it is evident that the key generated from the first chaotic map (logistic map) is a random key sequence which is one of the significant aspects of a good key generation scheme. Secondly, the obtained random sequence is sensitive to the basic initial conditions governing the chaotic equation. Using appropriate values of α_1 and x_{n1}, we encrypt the first bit plane slice of the medical image obtained after the Arnold cat transformation. Similarly, the other seven keys are generated using different chaotic equations to encrypt the remaining seven bit plane images. The governing chaotic equations and their tunable parameters are summarized in Table 12.1.

12.4 Results and analysis

The experimentation has been carried out using MATLAB on a windows machine (core i7−8550U @ 1.80 GHz 1.99 GHz). The medical images used in this work have been taken from a dataset of brain tumors, consisting of 3064 T1-weighted MR images with brain tumors like: glioma (1426), pituitary tumor (930), and meningioma (708) taken from 233 patients. Out of 3064 T1-weighted contrast images, 1000 have been used for experimentation. In addition to brain tumor dataset, a locally obtained database of heart images is used during the course of experimentation

Table 12.1 Summary of key generation from chaotic functions.

Key no.	Chaotic function	Governing chaotic equation	Tunable parameters	Parameter values to chaos	Used to encrypt
1	Logistic	$x_{n1} + 1 = \alpha_1 x_{n1}(1 - x_{n1})$	α_1 and x_{n1}	$\alpha_1 = 3.99$	Bit plane 1
2	Sine	$y_{n1} + 1 = \alpha_2 sin(\pi y_{n1})$	α_2 and y_{n1}	$\alpha_2 = 0.99$	Bit plane 2
3	Cubic	$z_{n1} + 1 = \alpha_3 z_{n1}(1 - (z_{n1})^2)$	α_3 and z_{n1}	$\alpha_3 = 2.55$	Bit plane 3
4	Logistic	$x_{n2} + 1 = \alpha_4 x_{n2}(1 - x_{n2})$	α_4 and x_{n2}	$\alpha_1 = 3.99$	Bit plane 4
5	Sine	$y_{n2} + 1 = \alpha_5 sin(\pi y_{n2})$	α_5 and y_{n2}	$\alpha_2 = 0.99$	Bit plane 5
6	Cubic	$z_{n2} + 1 = \alpha_6 z_{n2}(1 - (z_{n2})^2)$	α_6 and z_{n2}	$\alpha_3 = 2.55$	Bit plane 6
7	Logistic	$x_{n3} + 1 = \alpha_7 x_{n3}(1 - x_{n3})$	α_7 and x_{n3}	$\alpha_1 = 3.99$	Bit plane 7
8	Sine	$y_{n3} + 1 = \alpha_8 sin(\pi y_{n3})$	α_8 and y_{n3}	$\alpha_2 = 0.99 \cdot$	Bit plane 8

and analysis. The analysis is carried out using image parameters like: entropy, histogram, line profiles, correlation coefficient and key space.

12.4.1 Histogram analysis

Histogram is one of the simplest but an effective way of comparing the two images. Given an image encryption technique, the histograms of original input image and an encrypted image should be completely different and the histograms of the original input image and the decrypted image should be same. The top row of Fig. 12.8 shows an original brain tumor image and its corresponding histogram. After processing the original input image, an encrypted image is obtained; the same along with the corresponding histogram is shown in the middle row of Fig. 12.8. As apparent, the histogram plot of input image and the histogram plot of encrypted brain image are completely different. Similarly, the bottom row of Fig. 12.8 shows the histogram of the decrypted brain image which exactly resembles input brain image histogram.

12.4.2 Image entropy

The second parameter that has been used for illustrating the difference between the plain medical image and the secret image to be transmitted is the image entropy. Image entropy refers to image information and is also defined as the randomness in an image, which is the average uncertainty of the source of information. In the image, entropy is defined as the states of

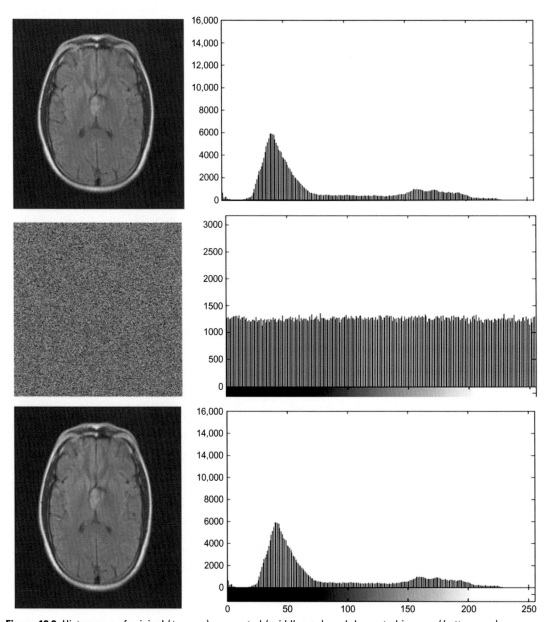

Figure 12.8 Histograms of original (*top row*), encrypted (*middle row*), and decrypted images (*bottom row*).

intensity level which pixels can adapt to. A medical image cryptosystem is considered to be a strong one when the entropy difference between the plain medical image and the secret image is significantly large. The average entropy difference between

Table 12.2 Entropy difference between plain input medical image and its encrypted version.

Entropy			
Image	Original image	Encrypted image	Decrypted image
Entropy ($r = 0.1$)	5.7516	7.9932	5.7516
Entropy ($r = 0.01$)	5.7516	7.9931	5.7516

the plain medical input image and its corresponding encrypted version is tabulated in Table 12.2. The entropy difference between the plain medical image and its encrypted version is significantly larger.

12.4.3 Line profile

The third parameter used in the analysis is the line profile. It is the set of intensity values of pixels taken along the horizontal stretch (row-wise) or vertical stretch (column-wise) regularly spaced. For the two dissimilar images the line profile plots would be significantly different while as the line profile plots of the two similar images would be alike. The same is illustrated in Fig. 12.9. It shows a plain input medical image and its line profile which corresponds to its third row on the top row of the Fig. 12.9. The middle row shows an encrypted brain image and its line profile which again corresponds to the third row. However, it can be observed that the two plots are completely different. Similarly, the bottom row of Fig. 12.9 shows the decrypted image and its line profile for the third row. The line profile of the plain input medical image and its decrypted version is exactly the same.

12.4.4 Correlation coefficient

Correlation coefficient is the fourth metric used in the analysis. It is a statistical measure that condenses the comparison of two 2D images down to a single scalar value. For two identical images, the correlation coefficient is computed as one and for two completely dissimilar images, the correlation coefficient is zero. A good image encryption method must ensure minimal correlation between the plain input medical image and its encrypted version. Similarly, correlation coefficient between the plain input image and its decrypted version must be close to

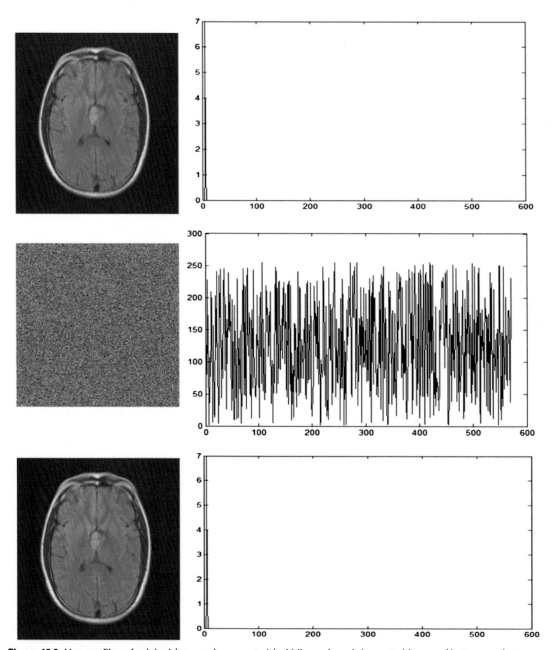

Figure 12.9 Line profiles of original (*top row*), encrypted (*middle row*), and decrypted images (*bottom row*).

one. Table 12.3 shows correlation of 10 originals and their encrypted versions. It can be observed that the value of correlation between the original image and their corresponding

Table 12.3 Correlation between 10 originals and their encrypted versions.

Correlation coefficient										
Images	E_1	E_2	E_3	E_4	E_5	E_6	E_7	E_8	E_9	E_10
O_1	0.0500	0.0459	0.0426	0.0499	0.0374	0.0422	0.0440	0.0380	0.0505	0.0530
O_2	0.0404	0.0560	0.0505	0.0522	0.0399	0.0441	0.0465	0.0433	0.0485	0.0587
O_3	0.0371	0.0506	0.0581	0.0496	0.0371	0.0433	0.0439	0.0437	0.0476	0.0555
O_4	0.0424	0.0510	0.0479	0.0571	0.0408	0.0436	0.0485	0.0411	0.0490	0.0581
O_5	0.0402	0.0495	0.0448	0.0514	0.0459	0.0394	0.0459	0.0402	0.0460	0.0460
O_6	0.0417	0.0487	0.0489	0.0499	0.0352	0.0492	0.0436	0.0371	0.0472	0.0573
O_7	0.0416	0.0516	0.0480	0.0540	0.0404	0.0432	0.0511	0.0411	0.0482	0.0568
O_8	0.0357	0.0464	0.0471	0.0441	0.0325	0.0359	0.0395	0.0529	0.0466	0.0507
O_9	0.0447	0.0501	0.0493	0.0512	0.0377	0.0430	0.0455	0.0453	0.0562	0.0557
O_10	0.0410	0.0522	0.0496	0.0523	0.0376	0.0454	0.0465	0.0422	0.0482	0.0647

encrypted versions is nearly zero which signifies no correlation between the two.

12.4.5 Key space of the proposed cryptosystem

The set of all the keys that can cipher determines the key space of that cipher. A good medical image encryption must have a key space large enough to avoid brute force attacks and small enough for real time ciphering and deciphering. Since the proposed medical image cryptosystem uses two key spaces, one coming from the use of the Arnold cat transformation and the other comes from the use of chaotic maps. The Arnold cat map transformation uses two tunable parameters (p and q) and chaotic maps employ 16 tunable parameters. Therefore the key space offered by this cryptosystem is significantly large to avoid a brute force attack.

12.5 Conclusion

This paper is fundamentally based on the application of multiple chaotic maps for secure medical image transmission. The proposed scheme employs position transformation-value transformation architecture to encrypt medical images. The position transformation is carried using Arnold cat transformation. The transformed pixel position image is undertaken through a bit plane extraction, each of which is encrypted using a unique key stream produced from the eight chaotic equations. The experimental results and their evaluation via: analysis of key in terms of its sensitivity, statistics, and its key space show the efficacy of the proposed work. The results obtained and their analysis, show the potential and suitability of the proposed methodology for secure medical image transmissions.

References

Abdmouleh, A. K. M. K., Bouhlel, M. S., 2013, Dynamicchaotic look-up table for MRI medical image encryption. In: Proceedings of the 2013 International Conference on Systems, Control, Signal Processing and Informatics, pp. 241–246.

Alvarez, E., Fernandez, A., Jimenez, G.P., Marcano, A., 1999. New approach to chaotic encryption. Phys. Lett. A 263, 373–375.

Ashtiyani, M., Birgani, P.M., Hosseini, H.M., 2008. Chaos based medical image encryption using symmetric cryptography. In: 3rd International Conference on Information and Communication Technologies: From Theory to Applications, ICTTA 2008. IEEE, pp. 1–5, 2008.

Behnia, S., Akhshani, A., Mahmodi, H., 2008. A novel algorithm for image encryption based on mixture of chaotic maps. Chaos Solitons Fractals 35 (2), 408–419.

Belkhouche, F., Gokcen, I., Qidwai, U., 2005. Chaotic gray-level image transformation. J. Electron. Imaging 14 (4), 043001.

Brahimi, Z., Bessalah, H., Tarabet, A., Kholladi, M.K., 2008. Selective encryption techniques of JPEG2000 codestream for medical images transmission. WSEAS Trans. Circuits Syst. 7 (7), 718–727.

Chen, G.R., Mao, Y.B., Chui, C.K., 2004. Asymmetric image encryption scheme based on 3D chaotic cat maps. Chaos Solitons Fractals 21 (3), 749–761.

Diaconu, A.V., 2016. Circular inter–intra pixels bit-level permutation and chaos-based image encryption. Inf. Sci. 355, 314–327.

Fridrich, J., 1998. Symmetric ciphers based on two-dimensional chaotic maps. Int. J. Bifurc. Chaos 8 (6), 1259–1284.

Fu, C., et al., 2013. An efficient and secure medical imageprotection scheme based on chaotic maps. Comput. Biol. Med. 43 (8), 1000–1010.

Gao, T.G., Chen, Z.Q., 2008a. A new image encryption algorithm based on hyper-chaos. Phys. Lett. A 372 (4), 394–400.

Gao, T.G., Chen, Z.Q., 2008b. Image encryption based on a new total shuffling algorithm. Chaos Solitons Fractals 38 (1), 213–220.

Hongjun, L., Abdurahman, K., Yangling, L., 2016. Asymmetric color pathological image encryption scheme based on complex hyper chaotic system. Optik 127, 5812–5819.

Hu, J.K., Han, F.L., 2009. A pixel-based scrambling scheme for digital medical images protection. J. Netw. Comput. Appl 32 (4), 788–794.

Ji, Z., Xia, Y., Sun, Q., Cao, G., Chen, Q., 2015. Active contours driven by local likelihoodimage fitting energy for image segmentation. Inf. Sci. 301, 285–304.

Jung, H., Sung, K., Nayak, K.S., Kim, E.Y., Ye, J.C., 2009. k-t focus: a general compressed sensing framework for high resolution dynamic MRI. Magn. Reson. 61, 103–116.

Khan, M.K., Zhang, J., 2008. Multimodal face and fingerprint biometrics authentication on space-limited tokens. Neurocomputing 71 (13–15), 3026–3031.

Liehuang, Z., Wenzhuo, L., Lejian, L., Hong, L., 2006. A novel algorithm for scrambling digital image based on cat chaotic mapping. In: Proceedings of the 2006 International Conference on Intelligent Information Hiding and Multimedia Signal Processing (IIH-MSP'06). IEEE, ISBN: 0-7695-2745-0/2006.

Lin, C.F., Chung, C.H., Lin, J.H., 2009. A chaos-based visual encryption mechanism for clinical EEG signals. Med. Biol. Eng. Comput 47 (7), 757–762.

Liu, J.L., 2006. Efficient selective encryption for JPEG 2000 images using private initial table. Pattern Recogn. 39 (8), 1509–1517.

Lou, L.D.C., Hua, M.C., Liua, J.L., 2009. Multiple layer data hiding scheme for medical images. Comput. Stand. Interfaces 31 (2), 329–335.

Mao, Y.B., Chen, G.R., Lian, S.G., 2004. A novel fast image encryption scheme based on 3D chaotic baker maps. Int. J. Bifurc. Chaos 14 (10), 3613–3624.

Menezes, A.J., van Oorschot, P.C., Vanstone, S.A., 1996. Handbook of Applied Cryptography. CRC Press.

Mitra, S., Uma Shankar, B., 2015. Medical image analysis for cancer management in natural computing framework. Inf. Sci. 306, 111–131.

Ou, Y., Sur, C., Rhee, K.H., 2007. Region-based selective encryption for medical imaging. Proceedings of the 1st Annual International Conference on Frontiers in Algorithmics. Springer, Berlin, pp. 62–73.

Panduranga, H.T., Naveen Kumar, S.K., 2013a. Selective image encryption for medical and satellite images. Int. J. Eng. Sci. Technol. 5 (2).

Panduranga H.T., Naveen Kumar S.K., 2013b. Partial image encryption using block wise shuffling and chaotic maps. In: 2013 International Conference on Optical Imaging Sensor and Security (ICOSS). IEEE, pp. 1–5.

Pareek, N.K., Patidar, V., Sud, K.K., 2003. Discrete chaotic cryptography using external key. Phys. Lett. A 309, 75–82.

Patidar, V., Pareek, N.K., Sud, K.K., 2009. A new substitution–diffusion based image cipher using chaotic standard and logistic maps. Commun. Nonlinear Sci. Numer. Simul. 14 (7), 3056–3075.

Phophalia, A., Rajwade, A., Mitra, S.K., 2014. Rough set based image denoising for brain MR images. Signal Process. 103, 24–35.

Puech, W., Rodrigues, J.M., 2005. Crypto-compression of medical Images by selective encryption of DCT. In: EUSIPCO'05: European Signal Processing Conference, Antalya, Turkey.

Rao, Y.S., Mitra, A., Prasanna, S.M., 2006. A partial image encryption method with pseudo random sequences. International Conference on Information Systems Security. Springer, Berlin, pp. 315–325.

Sarker, M.Z.H., Parvez, M.S., 2005. A cost effective symmetric key crypto-graphic algorithm for small amount of data. In: Proceedings of the 9th IEEE International Multitopic Conference, December 2005, pp. 1–6.

Scharinger, J., 1998. Fast encryption of image data using chaotic Kolmogorov flows. J. Electron. Imaging 7 (2), 318–325.

Shang, Z., Ren, H., Zhang, J., 2008. A block location scrambling algorithm of digital image based on Arnold transformation. In: 9th IEEE International Conference for Young Computer Scientists, ISBN: 978-0–7695-3398-8/08.

Som, S., Sen, S., 2013. A non-adaptive partial encryption of grayscale images based on chaos. Procedia Technol. 10, 663–671.

Sun, F.Y., Liu, S.T., Li, Z.Q., 2008. A novel image encryption scheme based on spatial chaos map. Chaos Solitons Fractals 38 (3), 631–640.

Wong, K.W., 2002. A fast chaotic cryptography scheme with dynamic look-up table. Phys. Lett. A 298, 238–242.

Wong, W.K., Lee, L.P., Wong, K.W., 2000. A modified chaotic cryptographic method. Comput. Phys. Commun. 138, 23−236.

Wu, H., Huang, J., Shi, Y., 2015. A reversible data hiding method with contrast enhancement for medical images. J. Vis. Commun. Image Represent. 31, 146−153.

Xiang, T., Wong, K.W., Liao, X., 2007. Selective image encryption using a spatiotemporal chaotic system. Chaos Interdiscip. J. Nonlinear Sci. 17 (2).

Zhou, Y., Panetta, K., Agaian, S., 2009. A lossless encryption method for medical images using edge maps. In: Annual International Conference of the IEEE Engineering in Medicine and Biology Society. IEEE, pp. 3707−3710.

13

A modified digital signature algorithm to improve the biomedical image integrity in cloud environment

Balasubramanian Prabhu Kavin[1,2], Sannasi Ganapathy[1,2], Pradeep Suthanthiramani[1,2] and Arputharaj Kannan[1,2]

[1]*School of Computing Science and Engineering, Vellore Institute of Technology, Chennai, India* [2]*Centre for Distance Education, Anna University, Guindy, Chennai, India*

Chapter Outline

13.1   Introduction

In this world, an enormous amount of data is generated every day and managing it is a serious threat to all IT industries. For this purpose, the cloud computing resource is adopted for managing the large volume of data efficiently, even though the duplicated data is occupying more extra memory space. For overcoming data duplication, a hashing technique is used for avoiding the data deduplication in cloud database. The duplication is checked by using two levels such as file level and content level. Here, the file level depends on the file name and the

Advances in Computational Techniques for Biomedical Image Analysis. DOI: https://doi.org/10.1016/B978-0-12-820024-7.00013-X

credentials, and the content level is also depending on the file content. These file levels and content levels are checked by applying the cryptographic techniques and hash algorithms. The various kinds of hashing algorithms are available in the survey to avoid the data deduplication such as secure hash algorithm-1 (SHA-1), secure hash algorithm-2 (SHA-2), and message digest algorithm-5 (MD5). The performance of these existing hashing techniques is varied in terms of hash values. Hence, the security level of the data is also varied according to the hash value of it. Here, the MD5 hash algorithm supports hash values up to 128 and SHA algorithm supports hash values up to 512, even though the proven work is available in the literature for breaking the digital signature of the MD5 algorithm easily (Raju et al., 2018).

13.1.1 Challenges

In recent days, medical data storage and data sharing techniques in cloud database are providing many advantages to physicians as well as patients in the healthcare industries. Though, there are numerous amounts of facilities available in the medical data sharing technique in cloud, data security becomes a very big challenge for the healthcare industries. When the data is stored in the local environment, the infrastructure is provided and maintained by the data owner. But, if the data owner needs to store in cloud database then the data is sent to the third-party cloud service provider (CSP) for storage and retrieval. Generally, problems occur in the medical image data while providing integrity and authenticity. Here, the data integrity is the assurance of the medical image that, it is not modified by the unauthorized users and authenticity is assured by its origin and the relevant patient identity. Accidently, the medical image data can be modified by an unauthorized person. For avoiding this kind of modification, the compression and decompression process can be done while transferring the image data through the Internet. As a result, the information modification or the information loss in the image will create a problem of misdiagnosis and improve the expenditure of the doctors. In this work, to overcome such problem we have proposed a new digital signature to ensure the originality of the magnetic resonance imaging (MRI) brain image which can be stored in the cloud database. If the storing signature and the verification signature are the same then the image is original or else it ensures that the image contains some modifications.

The contributions of this paper include: (1) the new proposal of a modified digital signature scheme to ensure data integrity and authenticity of the bio-medical image, (2) the third-party auditor checking the shared medical image whether it is damaged or modified by applying the proposed digital signature scheme, (3) an existing Adler32 hash function for creating digital signature with 8 bits and the proposed digital signature scheme providing 16 bits of output signature which is better than the existing digital signatures, and (4) proving the efficiency of the proposed model through their experiments. The remainder of this paper is formulated as below: Section 13.2 describes in detail the various cryptographic algorithms, digital signature schemes, and bio-medical applications. Section 13.3 explains clearly the proposed modified digital signature scheme. Section 13.4 is demonstrates the performance of the proposed digital signature scheme through various experimental results. Section 13.5 concludes the proposed work and future suggestions in this direction.

13.2 Literature survey

In the past, many works have been done in the direction of cryptographic algorithms, data deduplication, privacy preservation methods, healthcare and medical applications, and digital signature schemes which are proposed by different researchers. Moreover, the various intrusion detection systems have been developed by various researchers in the past (Ganapathy et al., 2012, 2013; Prabhu Kavin and Ganapathy, 2017) and researchers also developed the cryptography-based security models (Elumalaivasan et al., 2016; Padmanabhan et al., 2017; Prabhu Kavin et al., 2018; Prabhu Kavin and Ganapathy (2019a,b). Among them, Chawdhury and Habib (2008) suggested an effective technique for enhancing the security level of the passwords that are in the hashed format. They have used a mathematical function with a random key to encrypt the password that has been hashed. Cao and Yang (2010) presented a new analysis that ensures the data integrity in cloud. In their work, the MD5 algorithm was used for analyzing the need and it satisfies the secure auditing and management functionalities. Lin et al. (2011) developed a digital signature algorithm which is developed based on SHA in order to produce a message digest. Moreover, the key property of this algorithm contains the acceptable lengthy input and it generates an output with necessary length. In addition, they generated message digest that consists of a main body, constant values, initial values, parsing, and padding. Finally, the problem of length of hash value is resolved by using their digital signature algorithm. Sklavos (2012) developed a new hashing algorithm named as SHA-3, which is the successor of SHA-2. The SHA-3 is providing better security than the existing digital signature algorithms such as SHA-1 and SHA-2 which are breakable.

Ora (2015) presented a combined a scheme of partially homomorphic Rivets–Shamir–Adleman (RSA) and MD5 hashing algorithm to protect the user data in the cloud environment. Zhu et al. (2012) presented a new encryption scheme by incorporating the temporal access control for providing data integrity. In their scheme, the temporal attributes are defined in the access policy for enforcing the temporal constraints. Even though, after the utilization of temporal attributes also the integrity and the confidentiality of the user data are not sufficient. Chen et al. (2018) designed a new security architecture named as cyber DB for protecting the database processing in cloud. In their method, the complete user database stored in the cloud storage has been encrypted and the cipher texts are accessible using queries. Kiskani and Sadjadpour (2018) recommended a theoretical approach that will be useful for securing the data in cloud storage. They ensured that, a cloud user can download the data privately without the knowledge of servers. Moreover, the requested content of index is stored in the entire network with different combinations.

Bao et al. (2017) developed a new security technique for highly confidential medical data by using signal scrambling. These scrambled data are sent to the cloud for storing while the tiny data is kept locally for data retrieval. In the cloud database only, the jumbled data are stored, whereas in the local memory only the key terms that are required for retrieving the data are stored. Even though, their method did not achieve satisfied performance due to rises in the relevant data issues and data synchronization issues. Fu et al. (2018) constructed a flexible structure for resolving the security issues in data processing, collection, storage, and retrieval. According to the time latency requirements, the cloud server will do the processing and the storage of the gathered data. Moreover, the limited number data search methods are only presented so that the mining is not possible in the cloud server. Patel et al. (2016) proposed a new integrated cryptographic algorithm by combining the blowfish with elliptic curve cryptography (ECC) technique to protect the user data stored in the cloud. By integrating these two techniques the execution time has been reduced and the confidentiality level has been increased, along with this the authentication has also been provided. Finally, during the detection of attackers the computational complexity level was increased. Wang et al. (2016) suggested an enhanced key distribution agreement for the purpose of reducing the cost of storage and encryption. In their protocol, the secret key of the users will not be visible to the CSP or the key authority. Furthermore, there is a chance of failure due to the single point terminal access.

Yu et al. (2016) developed a new auditing system that is based on the identity for ensuring the integrity of the data. Their mechanism eliminates the complexity in the process of certificate management over the traditional schemes. Moreover, their system is vulnerable to various kinds of network attacks and privacy issues and achieved better performance in terms of providing data security and integrity. Pan et al. (2017) introduced a highly efficient signature generator server by using elliptic curve technique to secure the data. The different forms of ECC systems like encryption/decryption, key agreement, and digital signature were efficiently supported by this server. Finally, they proved that their server is useful for providing the sufficient data security. Ding et al. (2018) presented a new access control mechanism that depends upon attribute-based encryption. In addition, ECC has been used in this system. In this scheme, the computational difficulties have been reduced by using scalar multiplication instead of bilinear pairing over elliptic curves. Moreover, the ECC increases the number of bits in its keys for achieving a higher security.

Kao et al. (2013) developed a novel key authority system that is centralized to the user and provides security for the cloud user data. This system uses the standard RSA for encrypting the cloud user's data indirectly by using the public keys of the users. Instead of storing the private keys in servers or user's computer they have been sent as two-dimensional barcode images to the user's mobile device. In case the cloud servers have been compromised, the user's data is also secured. The users can store their secret key in their mobile device and they can be displayed in two-dimensional barcodes. This user centric key management key is proven to be practically possible by using it in storage for company, storage for individual, and even in surveillance for home. In this work, a hierarchic architecture of sharing data and primary key alternate has been designed. Ningning and Yueyun (2014) developed a novel integrated public key authority scheme which depends on the hyper elliptic curve cryptosystem. The proposed system is suitable for the scattered storages in a cloud environment. The key management processes have been enhanced with key agreement, distribution of keys, and updating of key, etc. The problem of extensive key authority and managing storage can be effectively solved by this system. On account of resisting collusion attack the cloud storage system can provide service with security and reliability. By the way, the efficiency and the scalability have been increased. Chen et al. (2016a,b) suggested an efficient security scheme for securing the system from the insider attack. The traditional public-key based encryption process with key term search framework is inherently vulnerable of inside attack. Moreover, this genetic security scheme has been constructed by importing a hashing technique. By utilizing the problem of Diffie–Hellman the author has increased the efficiency of the scheme. Zhu et al. (2017) proposed an integrated encryption methodology by combining the equality testing methodology and the public key encryption technique. This system provides secure access permission to the cipher text and also protects the user's identities. Testing of the encrypted cipher text by various public keys is done in this scheme to check the similarity of information. This framework is against chosen cipher text attack due to the assumptions that are made by the Diffie–Hellman which is bilinear. The security of this scheme is enhanced as strong as the decision bi-linear with the support of double decision bilinear. The efficiency of this technique is proven in the random oracle standard.

Yu et al. (2018) presented a bit wise encryption scheme that is based over the parity learning that has noise issue. The single bit encryption has been improved to multi bit encryption and along with this the error occurrence during decryption has been solved in this scheme. In addition, the accuracy and chosen plain text attack security have been provided. Only minimum range of cipher-text space and computational overhead has been improved by this scheme while comparing with the existing scheme. Along with resisting quantum attack this scheme also provides high security. Zhang et al. (2018) proposed a powerful audit technique for cloud database by utilizing the lattice-based assumptions. This system is secured from post quantum cryptography and establishing of public key infrastructure is not required. The private key of the user is maintained constantly and updated by using lattice basis delegation technique. Using lattice assumptions provides security and accuracy for the cloud storage and prevented against third-party auditors. Yan et al. (2018) proposed an efficient dynamic integrity verification system to boost up the privacy of the signature information. In this work the third-party auditor (TPA) will receive the protected digital signature, user file, and the user data from the cloud service provider (CSP). The quantum computer attacks have been resisted and cloud storage space has been utilized by employing lattice and bloom filter techniques.

Yu et al. (2016) recommended a user identity-based auditing agreement policy for removing the complexity of certificate management in protocols. This RSA-based system will support files with different block sizes and public integrity checking. Security is also provided for the suggested construction RSA assumption. Yang et al. (2017) suggested a new algorithm for reducing the communication expenses in cloud. Strip, improved strip, and cyclic are the three types of partitioning techniques incorporated in this algorithm. In improved strip partitioning different steps are accelerated parallel way. Comparing with other existing algorithms the performance of general number field sieve has enhanced speed.

The various types of the security mechanisms which were presented by various researchers have been discussed in detail in the literature review section. All these mechanisms perform well while comparing with the existing approached to which they had compared. Although, different types of new techniques were suggested by the researchers for providing the security for the medical data, improving the integrity of the confidential medical images is very much important for the user in the cloud environment.

13.3 Proposed work

This section explains the newly developed digital signature algorithm which is developed for handling the medical images containing a dataset that ensures the data integrity and the confidentiality of medical image data that are stored in the cloud database. For improving the check sum property of the proposed digital signature algorithm, an existing Adler32 is utilized for generating the hashed message in this work and explained in the consecutive subsections. Moreover, a new formula is also introduced for performing signing process and the verification process of the proposed digital signature algorithm. The newly introduced formula is derived from proposed base formula which is explained in the first subsection of this section.

13.3.1 Base formula

This base formula in Eq. (13.1) is constructed according to the mathematical concepts of trigonometry and rational function.

Generally, trigonometry is used for calculating the relationships between the length and the angles for the certain time period. Moreover, the key parameters that create a trigonometric $=$ based digital signature are P, $H(m)$, and K where, P indicates a random prime number for setting the Galois field size and the $H(m)$ indicates that the hashed message that is used as an angle of cosine value and the k represents the public key value which selects randomly.

The base formula for this methodology is:

$$\sum_{i=1}^{k} cos(i \times H(m)) mod \ P = \frac{cos\left[(k+1) \times \frac{H(m)}{2}\right] \times sin\left[\frac{k \times H(m)}{2}\right]}{sin\left[\frac{H(m)}{2}\right]} mod \ P$$

(13.1)

where, P denotes that the random prime number within the limit "L", $H(m)$ denotes hashed message using Adler32 hash function, k denotes the public key, and i is the parameter within the limit value of the public key k. In this base formula, the left-hand side is used for performing signing process and the opposite part is taking care of the verification process of the signature. These operations are under taken by the TPA. So, the CSP is not aware about the data that is already available in the cloud database.

13.3.2 Adler32

The Adler-32 checksum is taken into consideration by computing two 16-bit checksums named as X and Y which are concatenating the two 16 bits into a 32-bit integer. Here, the checksum X is the total number of bytes and B is the total number of individual values of X from every steps. In Adler-32, initially X holds the value of 1 and the Y holds the value of 0. The modulo sum 65,521 which is the biggest prime number that is less than the value of 2^{16}. Here, the bytes are stored based on the big endian in network and Y occupied the most significant bytes. The function is expressed as below:

$$X = 1 + E1 + E2 + \cdots + En(mod \ 65521)$$
$$Y = (1 + E1) + (1 + E1 + E2) + \cdots + (1 + E1 + E2 + \cdots + En)$$
$$(mod \ 65521)$$
$$= n \times E1 + (n-1) \times E2 + (n-2) \times E3 + \cdots + En + n$$
$$(mod \ 6521)$$
$$\text{Alder-32}(E) = C \times 65536 + A$$

where, E indicates the string of bytes for the checksum can be computed, and n indicates the length of E. The Alder-32 is a checksum and this working nature is totally different from MD5. Moreover, the MD5 is a message digest which is secure. The Adler32 is used to perform hashing quickly and it has a small bit space and simple algorithm with less collision rate and security. In addition, the MD5, SHA, and other cryptographic/secure hashing techniques have the biggest bit spaces with more complexity. Compare SHA-2 with 256 bits for Adler32's measly 32 bits. Adler32 is also used in hash tables for performing data integrity checking process, and it is not designed like MD5 algorithm or other secured message digests.

13.3.3 Modified digital signature algorithm

The proposed modified DSA has four different phases namely key generation, signature, verification, and the comparison phases. Here, the key generation phase is used to generate keys for the input dataset which contains the MRI images, the signature phase generates the signatures, verification phase is used to verify the original data and the received data and the comparison phase compares the values and ensures the data integrity. This subsection is explained in detail about all the four phases.

Phase 1: Key generation

Input: MRI image, storage limit value per day
Output: Numerical values of P, $H(m)$, and k
Step 1: A value for limit "L" is supplied by CSP (Where L is the value of the limit provided to the cloud user for storing the images for the day).
Step 2: Choose a Prime number "P" from within the fixed limit "L".
Step 3: Generate $H(m)$ value (i.e.) hashed message by applying Adler32 hash function to the MRI image that is to be saved in the cloud data base.
Step 4: A public key "k" is generated randomly with in the "P" value.
Step 5: Choose a value for the parameter "i" whose values will be inside limit of "k" value.
Step 6: The generated keys will be sent to the signing phase.

Phase 2: Signature.

Input: Numerical values of P, k, $H(m)$ and i that are generated from the key generation phase.
Output: Digital signature for the MRI image.

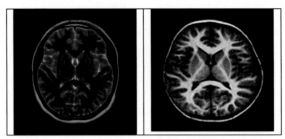

Figure 13.1 Sample magnetic resonance imaging (MRI) images.

Step 7: Apply the values of *i*, $H(m)$ and *P* in the signing formula Eq. (13.2) "*V*"

$$V = \left[\sum cos\left(i \times H(m)\right)\right] mod \ P \tag{13.2}$$

Step 8: Add the generated signature value "*V*" to the MRI image which is to be stored in the cloud storage.

Phase 3: Verification.
   Input: Public key *k*, MRI image.
   Output: Verification signature of the image.
   Step 9: Generate $H(m)$ value (i.e.) hashed message by applying Adler32 hash function to the MRI Image.
   Step 10: Get the public key "*k*" from the key generation phase.
   Step 11: Apply public key value "*k*" and hashed message value $H(m)$ in the proposed formula Eq. (13.3) "*S*". (Where "*S*" is one of the parameters for generating the verification signature).

$$S = cos\left[(k + 1) \times \frac{H(m)}{2}\right] \tag{13.3}$$

Step 12: Apply public key value "*k*" and hashed message value $H(m)$ in the proposed formula Eq. (13.4) "*T*". (Where "*T*" is also one of the parameters for the generating the verification signature).

$$T = sin\left[\frac{k \times H(m)}{2}\right] \tag{13.4}$$

Step 13: By substituting the value of $H(m)$ in the proposed Eq. (13.5) "*U*" formula the value of "*U*" will be generated.

$$U = sin\left[\frac{H(m)}{2}\right] \tag{13.5}$$

Table 13.1 Caesar cipher table.

R1	A	B	C	D	E	F	G	H	I	J	K	L	M	N	O	P	Q	R
R2	05	07	09	10	02	04	06	08	03	04	01	24	14	29	17	23	12	30

R1	S	T	U	V	W	X	Y	Z	0	1	2	3	4	5	6	7	8	9
R2	25	13	34	19	31	35	16	26	18	32	20	27	21	33	15	22	28	11

Step 14: The generated values of "S", "T", and "U" are applied in Eq. (13.6) "R". (Where "R" gives the value of verification signature).

$$R = \left[\frac{S \times T}{U}\right] \bmod P \tag{13.6}$$

Step 15: Send the computed value "R" (i.e.) verification signature to the comparison phase.

Phase 4: Comparison
Input: Signed signature "V" present with the MRI image and verification signature "R".
Output: The image is "original" or "fake".
Step 16: The digital signature of "V" and the verification signature "R" are compared and checked for similarity.
Step 17: If both the signatures match exactly then display "original".
Step 18: If both the signatures do not match with each other then display "fake".

The medical MRI image dataset is used as an input for this modified digital signature algorithm and it will be checked with the cloud database through the TPA in this work. The content or image originality is ensured after checking with the received image from the user side which is recommended or processed through CSP. In the cloud, an enormous medical data is being handled today, and also an increase in the volume of medical data in the form of numerical and non-numerical data as an image. The proposed modified digital signature algorithm is used by a TPA for ensuring the data integrity.

13.3.4   Mathematical proof

This proposed digital signature algorithm is explained briefly in this section by applying the value in the above-mentioned algorithmic steps. The numerical value that is generated from the key generation part is utilized in the signing, verification, and comparison phases.

13.3.4.1   Key generation part

The key parameters that are required for creating digital signature are P, $H(m)$, and k. Where, P is the random prime number chosen within the fixed limit "L", $H(m)$ is hashed message using Adler32, and k is the randomly chosen public key with in the limit of "P".

13.3.4.2   Adler32 hash function

The MRI brain image is considered the input value as hash value and also generated the hash function by using Adler32 for the image. The hashed value of Adler32 is considered as the input value for the proposed algorithm. Fig. 13.1 is the input image of the Adler32 hash function and *AE7A555D* is the message digest of the hash function.

$$H(m) = AE7A555D$$

13.3.4.3   Caesar cipher table

The Caesar cipher table used in this work comprises of all *26* alphabets and all numbers as the plain text. Here, we use the Caesar cipher table in which the key values are random numbers. This random number keys will increase the complexity of the third-party user to guess the serialized key values. It will protect the system from the known cipher text attack.

Input: *AE7A555D*

In Table 13.1 *R1* row represents the plain text and *R2* row represents cipher text value that are random. By comparing the 8 bits message digest value with the table above, the cipher text value is generated.

$$AE7A555D = 05\ 02\ 22\ 05\ 33\ 33\ 33\ 10 = H(m)$$

Then 8 bits plain text value is converted in to 16 bits cipher text by comparing with the key values of Caesar cipher table. First two bits are taken and processed to generate the 2 bits of the digital signature. Likewise, all the 16 bits of the message digest are processed.

Table 13.2 Values to signature table.

D1	05	07	09	10	02	04	06	08	03	04	01	24	14	29	17	23	12	30
D2	3	,	l	.	9	–	0	+	x	@	2	$	4	%	5	^	7	!
D1	25	13	34	19	31	35	16	26	18	32	20	27	21	33	15	22	28	11
D2	8	<	A	;	b	?	C	&	d	/	E	"	f	'	G	>	h	*

$$P = 13$$

$$H(m) = 05$$

$$k = 4$$

$$i = 1 \text{ to } k$$

13.3.4.4 Signing formula

The values of the key parameters P, $H(m)$, k, and i which are generated by the key generation phase will be used for creating the signature by applying the generated values in the formula.

$$V = \left[\sum \cos\left(i \times H(m)\right)\right] \bmod P$$

Therefore:

$$\sum \cos(i \times H(m)) = \cos(1 \times 5) + \cos(2 \times 5) + \cos(3 \times 5) + \cos(4 \times 5)$$

$$\sum \cos(i \times H(m)) = 0.283662 + (-0.83907) + (-0.75969) + 0.408082$$

$$\sum \cos(i \times H(m)) = -0.907015 \bmod 13$$

$$V = 12$$

This V is the signature value of the MRI image. Likewise all the values will be applied and a complete signature will be generated for the image.

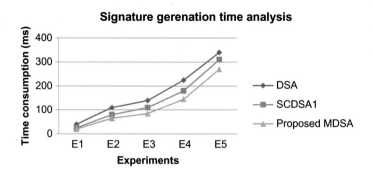

Figure 13.2 Signature generation time analysis.

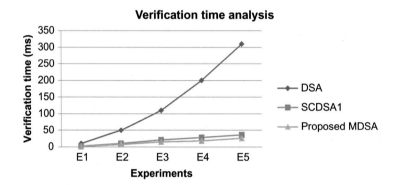

Figure 13.3 Signature verification time analysis.

13.3.4.5   Verification formula

The values of the key parameters P, $H(m)$, k, and i which are generated by the key generation phase will be used for creating the verification by applying the generated values in the formula.

$$S = cos\left[(k+1) \times \frac{H(m)}{2}\right]$$

$$S = cos\left[(4+1) \times \frac{5}{2}\right]$$

$$S = cos\left[\frac{25}{2}\right]$$

$$S = \mathbf{0.997798}$$

$$T = sin\left[\frac{k \times H(m)}{2}\right]$$

$$T = sin\left[\frac{4 \times 5}{2}\right]$$

Table 13.3 Character analysis report.

S. No.	Methodology	Signature	Uppercase	Lowercase	Digits	Symbols	Characters
1.	CRC16	a0a1	No	2	2	No	4
2.	CRC32	347570ab	No	2	6	No	8
3.	Adler32	AE7A555D	4	No	3	No	8
4.	Proposed work	7Ix7***3	1	1	3	3	8

$$T = sin[10]$$

$$T = \mathbf{0.54402}$$

$$U = sin\left[\frac{H(m)}{2}\right]$$

$$U = sin\left[\frac{5}{2}\right]$$

$$\boldsymbol{U = 0.598472}$$

$$R = \left[\frac{S \times T}{U}\right] mod \ P$$

$$S \times T = -0.542823$$

$$R = \left[\frac{-0.542823}{0.598472}\right] mod \ 13$$

$$R = -0.907015 \ mod \ 13$$

$$\boldsymbol{R = 12}$$

This R is the verification value of the MRI image. Likewise, all the values will be applied and complete verification signature will be generated for the MRI Image.

13.3.4.6 Comparison

The signed value V and the verification signature vale R will be compared with each other in this comparison phase.

$$V = R$$

$$12 = 12$$

In this case the value of the signed signature and the verification signature are the same. So, it proves that the image that has been downloaded for the cloud database is a genuine image without any errors and modification.

13.3.4.7 Values to signature table

The only purpose of this table is to create digital signature using the given values. The *D1* represents the cipher text values which are derived from *R2* row of Table 13.1. *D2* represents the cipher text key values that comprise of symbols, numbers, uppercase and lowercase alphabets. This mixed character keys will improve the predictive complexity of identifying the key values.

If all the values are applied to the algorithm, the sample output will be like *12 09 03 12 11 11 11 05*. These values will be converted into a complete signature for comparing with Table 13.2 values to signature table, then the output will be of the form complete digital signature *7Ix7***3*.

13.4 Experimental results

The proposed model has been implemented by using J2EE7, JSDK 8.1 version software, MySQL8.0, Apache Tomcat 8.0.27, and public cloud service for storage. Here, the MRI image dataset is used as input for validating the performance of the proposed model. The sample MRI images that are considered as input data in this work are shown in Fig. 13.1.

Fig. 13.2 demonstrates the signature generation time analysis between the newly proposed model and the existing digital signature algorithms. Here, five different experiments have been conducted.

From Fig. 13.2, it is observed that the proposed model performance is well rather than the existing DSAs namely digital signature algorithm (DSA) (Mughal et al., 2018), and the shortened complex digital signature algorithms (SCDSA) (Mughal et al., 2018) that are available in the literature in this direction. This is due to the use of a new formula which is used in this proposed DSA.

The verification time analysis is shown in Fig. 13.3 which is considered the newly developed DSA model and the available DSAs such as DSA (Mughal et al., 2018) and SCDSA (Mughal et al., 2018). Here, five different experiments such as E1, E2, E3, E4, and E5 have been conducted. The verification time is calculated in the unit of milliseconds in all five different experiments.

From Fig. 13.3, it declared that the efficiency of the modified DSA is greater than the existing DSAs namely DSA (Mughal et al., 2018) and the SCDSA (Mughal et al., 2018) which are available in the literature in this direction. This is due to the use of a new formula which is used in this proposed digital signature algorithm for performing signature verification process.

Table 13.3 displays the comparative analysis of the character in the digital signature of different methodologies. The comparison has been done among the methodologies like cyclic redundancy check 16 (CRC16) (Huo et al., 2015), cyclic redundancy check 32 (CRC32) (Huo et al., 2015), Adler32 (Sachin Tripathi and Biswas (2011), along with the proposed work. The comparative parameters are uppercase, lowercase, digits, symbols, and characters. This analysis report demonstrates that the newly developed DSA performed well according to the characters while compared with other existing methodologies.

13.5 Conclusion and future works

This paper developed a modified digital signature scheme for ensuring data integrity and authenticity of the bio-medical image data, which is shared in the cloud through the Internet. Here, the TPA checks the shared medical image whether it is damaged or modified by applying the proposed digital signature scheme. Moreover, an existing Adler32 hash function is used for creating digital signature with 8 bits and the proposed digital signature scheme provides 16 bits of output signature which is better than the existing digital signatures. Finally, the proposed scheme proves the efficiency according to the signature generation and verification times by conducting five different experiments. This model can be improved further with a new hash function instead of Adler32.

References

Bao, S.-D., Chen, M., Yang, G.-Z., 2017. A method of signal scrambling to secure data storage for healthcare applications. IEEE J. Biomed. Health Inform. 21 (6), 1487–1494.

Cao, D., Yang, B., 2010. Design and implementation for MD5-based data integrity checking system. In: 2010 2nd IEEE International Conference on Information Management and Engineering, Chengdu, pp. 608–611.

Chawdhury, M.D.A., Habib, A.H.M.A., 2008. Security enhancement of MD5 hashed passwords by using the unused bits of TCP header. In: 2008 11th

International Conference on Computer and Information Technology, Khulna, pp. 714−717.

Chen, R., Mu, Y., Yang, G., Guo, F., Wang, X., 2016a. Dual-server public-key encryption with keyword search for secure cloud storage. IEEE Trans. Inf. Forensics Security 11 (4), 789−798.

Chen, R., Mu, Y., Yang, G., Member, F.G., Huang, X., Wang, X., et al., 2016b. Server-aided public key encryption with keyword search. IEEE Trans. Inf. Forensics Security 11 (12), 2833−2842.

Chen, B.H.K., Cheung, P.Y.S., Cheung, P.Y.K., Kwok, Y.-K., 2018. CypherDB: a novel architecture for outsourcing secure database processing. IEEE Trans. Cloud Comput. 6 (2), 372−386.

Ding, S., Li, C., Li, H., 2018. A novel efficient pairing-free CP-ABE based on elliptic curve cryptography for IoT. Special section on security and trusted computing for industrial Internet of Things, IEEE Access, vol. 6, pp. 27336−27345.

Elumalaivasan, P., Kulothungan, K., Ganapathy, S., Kannan, A., 2016. Trust based ciphertext policy attribute based encryption techniques for decentralized disruption tolerant networks. Aust. J. Basic Appl. Sci. 10 (2), 18−26.

Fu, J.-S., Liu, Y., Chao, H.-C., Bhargava, B.K., Zhang, Z.-J., 2018. Secure data storage and searching for industrial IoT by integrating fog computing and cloud computing. IEEE Trans. Ind. Inform. 14 (10), 4519−4528.

Ganapathy, S., Yogesh, P., Kannan, A., 2012. Intelligent agent-based intrusion detection system using enhanced multiclass SVM. Comput. Intell. Neurosci. 2012, 1−9.

Ganapathy, S., Kulothungan, K., Muthuraj kumar, S., Vijayalakshmi, M., Yogesh, P., Kannan, A., 2013. Intelligent feature selection and classification techniques for intrusion detection in networks: a survey. EURASIP J. Wirel. Commun. Netw. 271 (1), 1−16.

Huo, Y., Li, X., Wang, W., Liu, D., 2015. High performance table-based architecture for parallel CRC calculation. In: The 21st IEEE International Workshop on Local and Metropolitan Area Networks, Beijing, pp. 1−6.

Kao, Y.W., Huang, K.-Y., Gu, H.-Z., Yuan, S.-M., 2013. uCloud: a user-centric key management scheme for cloud data protection. IET Inf. Security 7 (2), 144−154.

Kiskani, M.K., Sadjadpour, H.R., 2018. Secure and private information retrieval (SAPIR) in cloud storage systems. IEEE Trans. Veh. Technol. 67 (12), 1−8.

Lin, C., Yeh, Y., Chien, S., Lee, C., Chien, H., 2011. Generalized secure hash algorithm: SHA-X. In: 2011 IEEE EUROCON—International Conference on Computer as a Tool, Lisbon, pp. 1−4.

Mughal, M.A., Luo, X., Ullah, A., Ullah, S., Mahmood, Z. 2018. A lightweight digital signature based security scheme for human-centered Internet of Things, Special section on human-centered smart systems and technologies, IEEE Access, vol. 6, Pp. 31630−31643.

Ningning, S., Yueyun, C., 2014. Novel hyper-combined public key-based cloud storage key management scheme. China Commun. no. 2, 185−194.

Ora, P., Pal, P.R., 2015. Data security and integrity in cloud computing based on RSA partial homomorphic and MD5 cryptography. In: 2015 International Conference on Computer, Communication and Control (IC4), Indore, pp. 1−6.

Padmanabhan, S., Sumathi, V., Ganapathy, S., 2017. Cloud based POS system for secured smart shopping CART using RFID. J. Adv. Res. Dyn. Control Syst. 9 (Sp-14), 2764−2777.

Pan, W., Zheng, F., Zhao, Y., Zhu, W.-T., Jing, J., 2017. An efficient elliptic curve cryptography signature server with GPU acceleration. IEEE Trans. Inf. Forensics Security 12 (1), 111−122.

Patel, P., Patel, R., Patel, N., 2016. Integrated ECC and blowfish for smartphone security, Procedia Comput. Sci., volume 78. Elsevier, pp. 210–216.

Prabhu Kavin, B., Ganapathy, S., 2017. Data mining techniques for providing network security through intrusion detection systems: a survey. Int. J. Adv. Comput. Electron. Eng. 2 (10), 1–6.

Prabhu Kavin, B., Ganapathy, S., 2019a. A novel M-commerce data security mechanism using elliptic curve cryptography. Int. J. Innov. Technol. Explor. Eng. (IJITEE) 8 (10), 847–851.

Prabhu kavin, B., Ganapathy, S., 2019b. A secured storage and privacy-preserving model using CRT for providing security on cloud and IoT based applications. Comput. Netw. 151, 181–190.

Prabhu Kavin, B., Ganapathy, S., Karman, A., 2018. An intelligent task scheduling approach for cloud using IPSO and A* search algorithm. In: 2018 Eleventh International Conference on Contemporary Computing (IC3), pp. 1–5.

Raju, R., Kumar, S.A., Manikandan, R., 2018. Avoiding data replication in cloud using SHA-2. In: 2018 International Conference on Computation of Power, Energy, Information and Communication (ICCPEIC), Chennai, pp. 210–214.

Sachin Tripathi, G.P., Biswas, S.K., 2011. Cryptographic keys generation using identity. In: 3rd International Conference on Advances in Recent Technologies in Communication and Computing (ARTCom 2011), Bangalore, pp. 148–151.

Sklavos, N., 2012. Towards to SHA-3 hashing standard for secure communications: on the hardware evaluation development. IEEE Lat. Am. Trans. 10 (1), 1433–1434.

Wang, S., Zhou, J., Liu, J.K., Yu, J., Chen, J., Xie, W., 2016. An efficient file hierarchy attribute-based encryption scheme in cloud computing. IEEE Trans. Inf. Forensics Security 11 (6), 1265–1277.

Yan, Y., Wu, L., Gao, G., Wang, H., Xu, W., 2018. A dynamic integrity verification scheme of cloud storage data based on lattice and Bloom filter. J. Inf. Security Appl. 39, 10–18.

Yang, L.T., Huang, G., Feng, J., Xu, L., 2017. Parallel GNFS algorithm integrated with parallel block Wiedemann algorithm for RSA security in cloud computing. Inf. Sci. 387, 254–265.

Yu, Y., Xue, L., Au, M.H., Susilo, W., Ni, J., Zhang, Y., et al., 2016. Cloud data integrity checking with an identity-based auditing mechanism from RSA. Fut. Gen. Comput. Syst. 62, 85–91.

Yu, Z.M., Gao, C.Z., Jing, Z.J., Gupta, B.B., Cai, Q.R., 2018. A practical public key encryption scheme based on learning parity with noise. IEEE Access 6, 31918–31923.

Zhang, X., Wang, H., Xu, C., Wang, H., Xu, C., 2018. Identity-based key-exposure resilient cloud storage public auditing scheme from lattices. Inf. Sci. 472, 223–234.

Zhu, Y., Hu, H., Ahn, G.-J., Huang, D., Wang, S., 2012. Towards temporal access control in cloud computing. In: The 31st Annual IEEE International Conference on Computer Communications: Mini-Conference, vol. 6, pp. 2576–2580.

Zhu, H., Wang, L., Ahmad, H., Niu, X., 2017. Key-policy attribute-based encryption with equality test in cloud computing. IEEE Access 5, 20428–20439.

14

Medical imaging security and forensics: a systematic literature review

Bhisham Sharma[1], Deepika Koundal[2] and Sartajvir Singh[1]

[1]*Chitkara University School of Engineering and Technology, Chitkara University, Himachal Pradesh, India* [2]*Department of Virtualization, School of Computer Science, University of Petroleum and Energy Studies, Dehradun, India*

Chapter Outline

14.1 Introduction

Clinical radiological imaging is used to give solutions to legitimate inquiries, for example, how or why the individual passed on or might be attempting to recognize the character and the individual who may professing to be more established or more youthful than he/she truly is. In prior days, activity must be performed to glance in the stomach area, though in the present situation, straightforward sweep is performed. The same innovation can be utilized to give answers about the dead without doing a postmortem examination (posthumous) by simply doing a sweep aside from certain instances of uncertain.

Advances in Computational Techniques for Biomedical Image Analysis. DOI: https://doi.org/10.1016/B978-0-12-820024-7.00014-1

Computed tomography (CT) is one of the favored assessments to be executed as it can give three-dimensional (3D) image, not at all like the X-ray, which gives a two-dimensional (2D) image. X-ray is additionally great, especially in instances of abrupt demise in infants and little kids. Be that as it may, this has an additional detriment, especially in measurable cases: if there is any ferrous (iron-containing) metal included, it will move in the scanner's huge magnet. The proportion of cutting-edge visual data (video, image, and 3D object) has been extended rapidly on the Internet. Security of visual data ends up being dynamically critical for certain applications, for example, video observation, mystery transmission, military, and helpful applications. Therefore there is a great need for secure and fast end transmission which is important in the real world. Nowadays, the transmission of visual data is a step-by-step timetable and it is imperative to find a gainful technique to transmit them over frameworks (Puech, 2008). The security of visual data should be conceivable by encrypting the data with the coverage of figures. To lessen the time of transmission, the data compression is basic. Up to this point, scarcely any courses of action have been introduced for combined image encryption and weight. Currently, other research is introduced which used data in encoded images. Since the entropy of mixed image is maximal, the embedding step, pondered-like disturbance, is over the top by standard data hiding estimations. Another idea is applied in reversible data hiding which counted on mixed images to empty the introduced data before the image is unscrambled (Puech, 2008).

Today, with the development of winning image altering programming, it is essentially conceivable to control computerized images with no expert information. Altering advanced images is typically stopped unpretentiously, with the goal that it isn't unmistakable by human visual framework. This may be used for assailants to abuse this property. To foresee access through illegal processes in the propelled images, mechanized watermarking of an image is familiar with embedding an inconspicuous sign into a host image to such a degree, the bits which include the line passed on wherever through the host record, are hard to be controlled while the watermark data can be removed by figuring. Huge necessities for mechanized watermarking are elusiveness, power, cutoff, and security. Regardless, dependent upon technology the centrality of all is increasingly spotlighted. Power is one of the basic features in the image line. For extending life, numerous structures are recommended in temporal and spatial spaces. One among these systems is singular value decomposition (SVD). The essentialness of the given procedure is a direct result of consistency of specific regards in experience with geometric and signal taking care of attacks (Araghi and Manaf, 2019).

Images have been an incredible media of correspondence. Individuals have doing image control utilizing cost-free altering software. An astounding model is Photoshop, Gimp, and so on. Photoshop is utilized for better and terrible image control. The alteration of images goes under awful control. The awful images can be seen under control in therapeutic field, imagery, and news media firms. A computerized image is put away in bits and can likewise be portrayed regarding bit profundity. Bit profundity is the quantity of bits that are utilized for storing one pixel. An image is combination of bit esteems 0 for dark and 1 for white (Arun Anoop, 2015; Bhatt et al., 2012; Carew and Errickson, 2019).

For around 10 years, a few reversible watermarking plans have been proposed for securing images of delicate substance, similar to medicinal or military images, for which any adjustment may affect their elucidation. These strategies enable the client to reestablish precisely the first image from its watermarked form by evacuating the watermark. Along these lines it becomes conceivable to refresh the watermark content, as security properties (e.g., one computerized signature or some validness codes), whenever without including new image contortions (Coatrieux et al., 2012).

As restorative gadgets gather and trade individual wellbeing information, verifying them is significant. Absence of security may prompt loss of patients' protection, yet may likewise physically hurt the patient by enabling enemies to present false information or adjusting/smothering real information, initiating wrong finding. Undoubtedly, ensuring wellbeing information is a legitimate prerequisite also. The Health Insurance Portability and Accountability Act (HIPAA) of 1996, has indicated the progression of specialized, managerial, and physical security methodology is required for secured substances to guarantee the classification of electronic ensured wellbeing data (Arney et al., 2011).

Image phony should be possible from multiple points of view, including at least one image. The most widely recognized image phonies are duplicate move imitation and joining. In duplicate move image imitation, one or a few sections are reordered into different parts in a similar image. This kind of fraud is mostly done to disguise some data in the image. In grafting, a few pieces of an image or more images are reordered into another image. This sort of phony is done for the most part to criticize an individual. In the medicinal services space, image fabrication can be not kidding. In the event that a mammogram is hacked, and the gatecrasher utilizes the duplicate move falsification to amplify the territory of disease, the finding will not be right, and the patient will be in a tough situation. On the off chance that there is an image fabrication identification framework in a medicinal services system, it can identify the phony before beginning the analytic procedure. On account of a fraud, the framework can request another example from the patient (Ghoneim et al., 2018).

Medicinal imaging assumes a critical job in the human services framework. Images bolster determination, treatment choice, and fill likewise looks into needs. Thus, any medicinal image seen and broke down must be dependable. Reliability can be categorized as two security parts "respectability" which guaranteed the information which is not changed by nonapproved people; and "validness" which affirmed the information birthplace and its connection to one patient. It is fundamental to guard images from any harm, additionally, to recognize an image that has been altered while considering the medico-lawful system. Medicinal images can be adjusted incidentally, as during correspondence, or purposely. In the later circumstance, images can be altered perniciously with the presentation or evacuation of discoveries. Whenever utilized, such an image will actuate as a mistake of the medicinal staff. As a model, in telemedicine applications, lossy image compression is endured in order to diminish the measure of data to be transmitted (Huang et al., 2011).

Worldwide image handling like sifting can be utilized by the doctor during their translation to raise up some particular bits of image data. Lossy image compression acts also in order to make conceivable image sharing on low piece rate stations like those experienced in telemedicine or to pick up away capacities. Reviews are normally led so as to decide the great tradeoff between compression rate and protection of the image quality for the finding. Contingent upon their degree or quality, these procedures may imperil the analysis estimation of images, by inciting loss of basic data (Huang et al., 2012).

Among the various answers for approving the realness of an image, "daze legal sciences" methods have as of late stood out. They take a gander at the location of an image change from the earlier information about the image under perception (e.g., a mark put away or imparted to the image). A huge gathering of "daze crime scene investigation" strategies depend on classifier instruments based on some images included in order to perceive change impressions (Huang et al., 2012).

Tattoos are potential features that can be used in these purposes. In any case, these are not exceptional and universal, and skin revealed in confirmation images probably won't have a satisfactory count of conspicuous tattoos for singular ID. For the most part, it was hard to use vein structures for criminological distinctive evidence, since they were for all intents and purposes imperceptible to independent eyes in concealing images clicked by customer camera (Tang et al., 2012).

Restorative image applications like telediagnosis need sharing of patient information over the Internet. Subsequently, the advanced clinical images just as picture archive and communication systems can be legally secure during transmission in emergency clinic data framework. Images can be modified by introducing or removing injuries by using some image processing techniques such as scaling, shifting, and lossy compression techniques like joint photographic experts group (JPEG). Contingent upon stretch out of the altering; there might be inadmissible data misfortune which brings a wrong diagnosis by the doctors. If the restoring image is transformed, then it will be easy to check the kind of modification which is made in image. Checking the decency of a therapeutic image is an assessment strategy that accomplices the three indisputable degrees of uprightness to be explicit modification recognizable proof, control, and wrongdoing scene examination assessment. Different strategies like watermarking, image digest, and astonish lawful sciences can be utilized for checking image dependability. Cryptographic hash limits, for instance, Secure Hash Algorithm-1, Message Digest Algorithm-5 will convey 128 and 160-piece single course hash regards independently that can be employed for uprightness examination (Joseph and Deepa, 2015).

In steganography, the primary design is to guarantee that the assailant doesn't question the presence of concealed information. This is accomplished by concealing any information on spread articles, for example, sound, video, image and so on. The primary reason for sending concealed information is to convey information from sender to recipient dependably without reach of the hands of outsiders/aggressors and with no weakening/adjustment. Various models for this were made previously. One old-style model is a hair of slave that had been scratched, a message had been composed on his head and the hair of slave was relied upon to develop. After the hair of slave developed, the slave had been sent to the beneficiary of the message. At that point, the hair of the slave had been re-scratched and the concealed message had been received (Karakus and Avci, 2019). Essentially, there are four segments in steganography: (1) Spread object: The earth wherein information is covered up. (2) Mystery information: The message that will be covered up in the spread article. (3) Stego object: The shrouded state in the spread object of mystery information. (4). Stego key: The concealing capacity that will be utilized to shroud information.

Tying down an image over the system to prevent unapproved spying and packing images dependent on lossless or lossy methodology, are the cardinal go for the analysts. With critical upgrade in visual insight and image examination techniques, image information is utilized in different delicate applications, for example, military reconnaissance, criminological examination, therapeutic consideration, and so on. In these applications, gigantic ordered image datasets are kept up that are at risk to be hacked by the assailants. Contingent on the application range, reasonable compression and security calculations ought to be executed (Mulla et al., 2015).

Wavelet decomposition is performed on images due to intrinsic multiresolution characteristics. The discrete wavelet transform is used for reducing the image size at each level, for example, a square image of size $n \times n$ pixels at level L has been decreased for estimating $n/2 \times n/2$ pixels at level $L+1$. The image is decomposed at each level into four subimages which have been acquired from a low-pass and a high-pass channel along the image lines and sections (Myna et al., 2007).

The objective of radiograph division is to limit the district of every tooth in an X-ray image. Dental radiographs may experience the ill effects of low quality, low differentiate, and uneven introduction which confuse the assignment of division. Dental X-beam images have three unique districts: delicate tissue locales and foundation with the least force esteems, bone areas with normal power esteems, and teeth areas with the most elevated force esteems. At times, the power of the bone zones is near the force of the teeth, which makes it hard to utilize a solitary limit for portioning the whole image (Nomir and Abdel-Mottaleb, 2007).

14.2 Related work

In this segment, a few techniques based on image security have been discussed.

Distinguishing proof of individual character is a noteworthy research exertion which has been used for the creation of palm-print, face, unique mark, and dental recognizable proof frameworks. These frameworks are utilized by law implementation specialists. However, they are flopped in instances of incomplete nonfacial skin of hoodlums or exploited people who are perceptible in image proofs. Prior it was hard to utilize vein designs for criminological distinguishing proof as they are generally undetectable to the unaided eye in shading images taken by cameras. A computational technique dependent on skin optics to reveal vein designs from shading images has been created. Be that as it may, its presentation is subject to the exactness of the skin optical model. It can extricate data from a couple of synchronized shading and close to infrared (NIR) images, with the utilization of a neural system to delineate qualities to NIR forces (Tang et al., 2012).

Astonish lawful sciences system for remedial images were introduced by (Huang et al., 2012). This structure isolated the modified images from one of the similar images that perceived the possibility of overall change. It used two image features that are histogram reorganized block-based discrete cosine transform coefficients (HRBD) and the histogram estimations of reorganized block-based Tchebichef minutes (HRBT). Using these features, improved images are requested into looking at classes by means of getting ready assorted combined support vector machines (SVMs). A multi-classifier is employed by the integration of decisions given by matched classifiers. The accuracy of multi-classifier with the integration of data features obtained from HRBD and HRBT together is more than 70%. Additionally, the performance of multi-classifier is better than other classifiers that used these features individually. This system didn't require any prior information or watermarking (Huang et al., 2012).

Gupta and Raval (2012) proposed the concept based on SVD and discrete wavelet transform (DWT). Eight bits' modernized imprint has been utilized to make a procedure to take out the imitated result. In this, peak signal-to-noise ratio (PSNR) is represented as 43.337 dB, and eventual outcomes to analyze the power varies depend upon attack's power between 0.4418 and 0.9994. Regardless, their performance essentially checked the tangibility to nonmedical images and to the extent security, it is now and again serviceable for every one of the 8 bits of the electronic imprint to be evacuated precisely in outrageous attacks (Gupta and Raval, 2012).

Another method was given by Ali et al., that was based on differential evolution and DWT + SVD in which perfect ruling component is located to alter the immaterialness and life. In spite of the way that this scheme expanded a high power, the cultivated PSNR is essentially declared as 33.357 dB (Ali et al., 2014). Researchers also proposed another DWT + SVD method based on self-adaptive differential evolution so that congruity among elusiveness and healthiness can be made. In any case, this method has given low PSNR proportional to 33.29 dB (Ali and Ahn, 2014). They suggested straight befuddled guide in pieces for security. Later SVD breaks down, U and S coefficients of the watermark image that are embedded to the specific estimation of low—low subband of DWT in the host image which is isolated into nonspread squares. The method was attempted in front of endless struggle and the fake helpful result is changed by using both U and S coefficients of SVD. However, improvement estimations like what it is proposed in this method decrease the straightforwardness of the figuring and in this way incorporates costs and lessens availability. This method similarly is checked for just images which are not therapeutic (Ali et al., 2016).

Ansari and Pant introduced the DWT + SVD methodology based on artificial bee colony (ABC) and achieved PSNR of 37.3179 dB. This technique is nonoutwardly weakened with the two sorts of helpful and nontherapeutic images attempted. In like way, the past technique, the ABC upgrade estimation lessens the ease of the count (Ansari and Pant, 2017). Makbol et al., imagined a blend image watermarking plan to empty the sham positive issue which utilizes the U fragments of the line image after specific worth breaking down (SVD) to be enclosed to the S coefficients of the spread. To maintain security, puzzle key by S and V line is used. To find a perfect scaling-factor, the multi-target underground creepy crawly state headway (MOACO) is used by the makers. The plan is outwardly weakened and to the extent independency from the sort of host image, makers simply checked it for unhelpful images (Makbol et al., 2017).

Vali et al., proposed a visually impaired image watermarking plan dependent on discrete wavelet transform and SVD. They inserted a dim scale watermark into the S coefficients of the host image after redundant discrete wavelet transform (RDWT) and SVD. To locate an ideal scaling factor so as to improve subtlety and power they utilized self-versatile differential advancement calculation, and to guarantee killing the bogus positive issue, they included a computerized mark notwithstanding watermark image to the host. Be that as it may, utilizing an 8-piece computerized signature can't shield the plan from bogus positive assault. Since the likelihood of extricating each of the 8 bits after extreme assaults securely is exceptionally low, thus, the plan can't guarantee security quite well. This plan is additionally imperiled with bogus negative issue in assaults with high force. Since this is only 8 twofold bits that ought to be extricated as 0 or 1, removing every one of the 8 bits after assaults is a troublesome issue (Vali et al., 2018).

In the methodology by Thakur et al., a violent-based secure helpful image line was given using non subanalyzed contourlet transform (NSCT), discrete wavelet transform to improve control similarly. Firstly, the source image is apportioned into subimages and then NSCT is applied on them. RDWT is applied to NSCT image and the particular vector of the DWT coefficient is taken care of. An identical structure is emphasized for both two watermark images. The solitary estimation of the two watermarks is brought into the particular lattice of the source. Therefore to guarantee security, a 2D key set up together with encryption was applied with respect to watermarked therapeutic image. In any case, in this system, the outcome of security test doesn't show up, while using two watermark images has decreased the indistinctness (Thakur et al., 2018).

Gangadhar et al., presented by an image watermarking count based on inverse discrete wavelet transform and particle swarm optimization (PSO). In this approach, therapeutic images are revealed on improved DWT to recoup the invariant wavelet space. The watermark is embedded into the picked area by changing the benchmarks of the coefficients in the image using edge work. By the help of the PSO computation, the scaling factors improved. The approach is basically investigated for restorative images and the PSNR for an ordinary six images is 45.2284 dB (Gangadhar et al., 2018).

In the strategy presented by researchers, image watermarking plan with DWT and two levels SVD were made. All past blend DWT + SVD plans are presented to only one level of SVD; subsequently, this strategy is novel for the sort of hybridization, wrapping up a colossal improvement in both nuance and power conversely with the customary DWT + SVD-based plans (Araghi, 2018).

To evacuate the watermark, a two-level check structure is presented which contained both propelled imprint and B test. The chief level is a propelled imprint and the consequent level is a test for counterfeit positive and sham negative effect coming about on account of attacks with high power. In outrageous ambushes, it is less useful for all 8 bits of modernized imprint to viably be removed keeping an eye out for counterfeit negative issue. On account of this, the approval system disavows the extraction approval with the second preliminary of affirmation (B test). Subsequently, if the imprint isn't isolated fittingly in perspective on ambush's earnestness (false N = negative) or aggressors fought to evade the essential checked level (false positive), it distinguished the continually level. In this approach, watermark is inserted precisely and openly from the kind of source image (Araghi, 2018).

Sharma et al. introduced a tampering technique for digital images that is a threat for security management. Different techniques and challenges related to modifying affirmation and image certification have been examined and legitimate proposals for security situation have been introduced. Authors clarified quickly in the medicinal field as masters and specialists explore dependent on imaging. Image adjusting is a moved workmanship which needed comprehension of image properties and phenomenal visual imaginative personality (Sharma and Abrol, 2013).

Anantharaj et al. proposed tampering and copy-move forgery detection scheme using sift feature. Channel framework is utilized to locate the near to part and assembling the close focuses, and changes related to geometry which are utilized to apparent the likeness and disparity of the photos. This tampering affirmation is utilized to perceive whether an image is authentic or not. Impelled image ordinarily utilized in different field like healing imaging, news consideration makes more issues on the genuine world. In most created image correspondence, the authors referenced the fundamental issue is its legitimacy (Anantharaj, 2014).

Sadeghi et al. proposed efficient copy-move forgery detection for digital images. Duplicate move creation is the most and the large saw sorts of distortion which duplicates some bit of the image and glues it to another bit of a practically identical image to cover a basic scene. Duplicate move counterfeit disclosure method proposed subject to Fourier transform to see produces. Image joining is the scheme of making a phony image by cutting one piece of an image and gluing it to a various image. A method is introduced to see the zone of duplicate move and to modify an image with the Fourier transform. To perceive a shaped region, the exact qualities of every single parts of the image chosen, and separated from each other (Sadeghi et al., 2012).

Murali et al. has presented the comparative analysis of forgery detection techniques for images. Image control has become dynamically standard in the hour of bleeding edge cameras and image evolving programming. Authors made a random selection of global threshold setting and evaluation utilized in JPEG for photo forgery detection. Authors presented a method based on JPEG compression analysis for forgery detection algorithm (Murali et al., 2013). Cozzolino et al. proposed estimation for duplicate move making affirmation and constraint dependent on the energetic figuring of a thick closest neighbor field. Patch match was utilized for randomized calculation for the closest neighbor, in which the search mauls the consistency of customary images for joining quickly to a near optimal and soft field (Cozzolino et al., 2014).

Singh et al. saw that a surgery may prompt adjustments in more than one facial locale. For instance, blepharoplasty is fundamentally performed to change temple however it likewise impacts the eyebrows. They likewise broke down that with huge varieties in the appearance, surface, and state of various facial districts, it is hard for face acknowledgment calculations to coordinate a postmedical procedure face image with premedical procedure face images. Past part-based face acknowledgment approaches may not give instruments to address the simultaneous varieties presented in different highlights in light of the fact that these methodologies, for the most part, underscore on investigating each element freely. Then again, it is seen that people take care of issues utilizing recognition and information spoken to at various levels of data granularity (Bhatt et al., 2012).

Facial maturing is an organic procedure that prompts slow changes in the geometry and surface of a face. In contrast to maturing, plastic medical procedure is an unconstrained procedure and its belongings are commonly in opposition to that of facial maturing. Since the varieties are caused because plastic medical procedure techniques are unconstrained, it is hard for face acknowledgment calculations to show such nonuniform face changes. Then again, camouflage is the way toward disguising one's personality by utilizing cosmetics and different frill. Both plastic medical procedure and mask can be abused by people attempting to cover their personality and dodge acknowledgment. Varieties are caused because camouflage is transitory and reversible; in any case, varieties are caused because plastic medical procedure is enduring and may not be reversible (Bhatt et al., 2012).

14.3 Feasible study to find essential factors

These significant elements are limiting the impact of sign handling assaults, upgrading the strength, and rectifying the bogus positive issue.

14.3.1 Handling of watermark

In watermark predealing with, the whole technique has been performed on both host and line images to set up the phase of line embedding. Before the insertion of watermark image, it has been duplicated unnecessarily till the weight of the line image is getting equal to the host image's size. With the watermark overabundance, the likelihood of losing evacuated watermark in specific ambushes like cutting attack is getting very low. This is because of the reiteration that the likelihood of including extra watermark or multi-watermarking by attackers is in truth lessened due to the quick effect on the idea of the watermarked image (Araghi and Manaf, 2019).

14.3.2 Model quality of imaging

The large number of model quality of imaging can be grouped with procurement type delineated in Fig. 14.1. Account forms investigated are not comparable here, and more distant ordered are either transmissive or intelligent, which are discussed beneath.

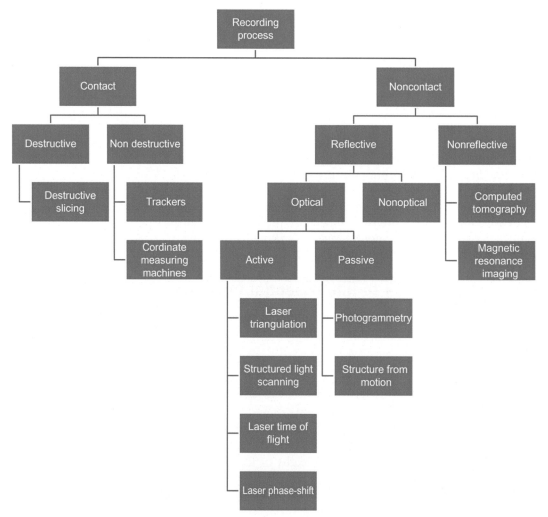

Figure 14.1 Distinctive imaging modalities accessible in scientific science documentation.

14.3.2.1 Intelligent

Intelligent systems try by reflecting a source of light on an affair and record the mirrored information. Accordingly, outside of an affair should be uncovered. The idea of the data captured is impacted by floor features and its current condition, for example, offering little appreciation to savage or wet surface to the temperature, shape, and availability of the subject.

14.3.2.2 Transmissive

Transmissive imaging frameworks are worked by experiencing a guide to get information which is volumetric, all things considered the significant bit of leeway is that an example shouldn't be revealed or unpackaged, or on account of human dead bodies, macerated. Transmissive imaging encourages survey of inner highlights, for example, bones or organs in humans, yet in addition protests inside different objects, for example, things in a bag. The outside of a subject may be accounted for differentiating the quality. The two transmissive systems are CT and magnetic resonance imaging (MRI). These require expert radiographers to play out the image getting, regardless, the image dealing with may be finished by skilled customers.

14.3.2.3 Multimodal imaging

Multimodal imaging is nowadays used in medical domain in order to enhance the quality and highlighting the features of image. It further builds up the utility of 3D modernized imaging by gathering information from diverse systems to shape one related model. For instance, some authors have combined various procedures without the necessity for acquiring or using reference markers simultaneously. Additionally, it is possible for joining surface and inside volumetric data, such as integration of photogrammetry with CT to make unedited 3D models that are relative and show real nature. Multimodal imaging was recognized as one of the four critical issues in imaging, further it has been prescribed that the simultaneous utilization of non-contact and contact methods may overwhelm the issues with precision. Moreover, fusion of noticeable imaging with infinitesimal or nuclear methodology is in high demand (Puech, 2008).

14.3.3 Tools for proving image authenticity

1. Fotoforensics

It is a gadget for image legitimate sciences. In this, the parameters such as Digest, JPEG, Metadata, original are inspected which are dependent on the image. Hash is a single heading encryption used as a message digest consisting of secure hash algorithm version and message digest forms. These days' hash respect discovering goals are accessible (decode) and it can be yielded based on estimation. *Source*: http://fotoforensics.com/ELA strategy could be used to choose whether image has been deliberately changed.

2. Tin Eye

    It is a switch image web index. It discovers where an image originates. It is the first image search device on the web for utilizing image ID development. Tin eye continually crawled the web and invigorated the image dataset routinely. It is not able to recognize the persons in the image. Tin eye program modules are open.

3. JPEG Snoop

    It is a type of JPEG file decoding utility. It is a free windows application that is used to investigate and disentangle the internal nuances of JPEG and motion JPEG records. It is used to analyze the origin of an image to test its validity.

4. Indexic

    Replaceable image record group (Exiting) is a determination for image document position utilizing computerized cameras.

5. Image forensic

    It is an image legal examining apparatus. Primary bit of leeway of this site for dissect error level analysis signature check. Furthermore, investigation results are confidential. Blunder analysis assesses the quality of level for networks inside the photos.

6. Get ghiro

    It is utilized for computerized image legal sciences. Get ghiro is a multi-client condition. Images consist of huge amounts of data. Get ghiro permit bunch image examination.

7. Belka soft Forgery Detection Plugin

    This robotizes genuineness examination of images. The detection of forgery module is dependably identified fashioned and altered images among a large number of records accessible on a PC. A one of kind element of this module is the capacity to identify controlled images dependent on examination of image compression and quantity relics. The module offers dependable identification of images and recordings that were altered, adjusted, or controlled on a computer after they have been taken still or camcorder.

14.3.4 Digital imaging techniques to different forensic applications

Various digital imaging techniques to several forensic applications have been given below. Table 14.1 also shows the various image tampering techniques.

1. Biological profiling

    Modernized image can be utilized for standard normal profiling systems to improve new strategies, for example cranial sinuses (Puech, 2008). There is countless composition on regular profiling in quantifiable humanities using mechanized data, basically from CT integrated with magnetic resonance image. For example, Martinez Vera analyzed MRI images of the manubrium for estimating age. This is particularly significant since MRI is a nonionizing method and offers an undeniably good response for age estimation (for instance in legal improvement cases).

2. Weapon distinguishing proof

    A weapon may be obtained from a 3D model of bones injury. This is developed morphologically by recognizing the condition, interpreting the volume rendering, or with the utilization of stereolithography. Different analysts made 3D models from bet mortem CT sweeps of an unfortunate casualty and examined speculated weapons, they effectively coordinated the damage example to an item utilizing 3D displaying to the show results. The precision of these strategies has since been tended to, and the probability of utilizing procedures, for example, small scale CT filtering to encourage quantitative information has been illustrated; which is profitable as it can possibly diminish translation predisposition.

3. Scene catch

    The collection of 3D recording techniques that are utilized for documentation, examination, and introduction of a wrongdoing scene. 3D information catch strategies give exact scene recording that doesn't experience the ill effects of the spatial contortion impacts related with 2D image chronicle. Scientists reports that in the course of recent decades, specialists have approached 3D imaging hardware yet were battling to utilize and apply the information. In any case, police powers can now consistently catch the wrongdoing scene documentation by using 3D information and with the ongoing advances in programming.

4. Surface wounds

    In 2000, photogrammetry was utilized to coordinate tire track facial damage with results that can be seen more prevalent as compared to customary 2D image overlay technique. Number of research work on 3D documentation related to surface injuries has been risen, injuries with shape, for instance, those from "weapons, devices, dental etchings, shoes, drugs, or delivered coins", can be composed with objects. Undoubtedly, photogrammetry is employed to arrange surface injuries with instruments and to repeat planned damages. It has been shown that this system can create high-goals, sensible, and 3D surface models. Case-report utilized laser filtering and imagery to archive proof of misuse and starvation. Besides, a measurable 3D approach [utilizing PC helped plan (computer-aided drafting) bolstered photogrammetry] was utilized to display skin damage and a weapon, encouraging example coordinating of damage with state of the weapon. Analysts have observed that wounds can be quantified more precisely with photogrammetry as compared to standard scientific images.

5. Taphonomy

Taphonomy vary in bodies that can be seen after some time. Though, customarily photos have been utilized to report these variations, as of late specialists have researched utilizing 3D recording systems. Authors utilized structure from motion (SfM) and geographic informations system (GIS) for reporting of deterioration on human corpses and saw these instruments as helpful and proficient for recording the disintegration and taphonomy.

6. Footwear marks

The restoring of impressions of footwear has been a normal procedure for police powers. In this way, three-dimensional imaging systems can be utilized to catch subtleties of such impression. Authors gave instances of suspected shoes and an impression using sand that was reported utilizing a laser scanner. They expressed that the product permits correlation between two databases and then the subsequent 3D model acted as a helpful instrument for court show. In any case, it has been noticed that further work is required before the organized light system can supplant conventional throwing procedures.

7. Finger-marks

It is conceivable to recoup edge detail utilizing 3D scanners for the assortment of after death fingerprints. In spite of the fact that this examination utilized prototyped gear for the documentation procedure, it affirmed that the recuperation of detail is conceivable. Also, caught finger edge detail just as shape utilizing organized light checking yet recognized that coordinating fingerprints through acknowledgment required future work. There is no research for distinguishing 3D imaging of a finger mark on a surface except microscopy or standard imagery. This may be due to some extent to finger-marks being 2D as there is no requirement for a third measurement (except if recouped from a bended surface). Additionally, the constrained goals of surface scanners may reduce the procedures unsatisfactory. Moreover, any finger mark should be noticeable all together for a surface scanner to catch it, in this manner, dormant imprints would not be obvious without upgrade.

8. Chomp marks

   Bitemark examination is one of the principal guides to show the use of laser filtering in bitemark investigation that might be tested in a court anyway. In their specialized note, the utilization of a digitized nibble was contrasted quantitatively with a maxillary model with the point of progressing in the direction of a less emotional examination. Since, tended to the inconstancy of dentition utilizing laser examining, which still showed that alert ought to be applied to bitemark investigation, and found effective coordinating of bitemarks on nibbled apples with cone-shaft CT filtered dental curves in a dataset. Authors introduced that bitemarks documentation utilizing a laser scanner ought to be judged close by customary conventions at a posthumous. In this examination, information is used as a 3D to print an imitation model of a bitemark expressing that 3D printing could be valuable for instructive purposes and court introductions.

9. Ballistics

   3D imaging can help criminological pathologists to give a precise and visual translation of slug direction which utilized the virtual postmortem approach. These systems regularly base on CT and MRI filtering, anyway contemplates have built up that despite the fact that this sort of imaging is helpful for getting dispersion, profundity and bearing of shots, it is likewise critical to consider the underlying postmortem examination assessment as contrasts in elucidation may emerge. In like manner, photogrammetry has been utilized in the reproduction of outer shot directions and in after death surface documentation. Photogrammetry imaging process is fast but inadequate at imaging certain body features like body hair, despondencies or surfaces with liquid.

10. Bloodstain pattern analysis

    Researchers has used 3D imaging in examination of bloodstain design to distinguish the direction and purpose of birthplace of blood beads. Authors have found that light filtering is a successful method for recording the blood stain. It is a nonobtrusive and faster method than traditional documentation methods. Also, an examination utilizing various 3D systems with contrasting goals include laser checking and organized light filtering has found that precise territory of causes and directions could be imagined and investigated precisely utilizing 3D models.

11. Road car accidents

    The advantage of 3D innovation to recording street car accidents was perceived early. Authors indicated that 3D information of a scene would help in recreating the occasions and delineation of this employing an individual case being hit by a vehicle. In this research, 3D laser filtering has been utilized. In this way, 3D mishap recreation has been accomplished and shown as helpful utilizing short proximity photogrammetry, laser filtering, and using still images and recordings to make 3D models.

12. Forensic prehistoric studies

    3D documentation has numerous applications in measurable paleontology, for example, recording stays in-situ and recording complex destinations including mass graves or mixing together. For instance, SfM has been shown for recording funerary taphonomy and mass grave documentation. Furthermore, photogrammetry is joined with GIS information to record and translate graves and stays in-situ. There are likewise instances of utilizing organized light filtering for recording human stays in graves while not carefully 'scientific' in nature.

13. Forensic building

    Scientific designing cases required 3D documentation systems. For instance, laser examining has been utilized to report the scene of the power station breakdown in Didcot, United Kingdom in 2016 ("Dr Karl Harrison at the Forensic Archaeology, Anthropology, and Ecology Symposium, London, United Kingdom, 12 June 2017"). Laser checking has been effectively employed for creating 3D models in two examples of building breakdown (a mind boggling structure breakdown of a shoring framework and an upset crane) an undertaking that would be "about outlandish" without advanced imaging. The authors have shown that they had remake the complex scenes for the assessment, effectively leading basic examination and procurement of measurements.

14.3.5 Classification of digital forensics

The aim of source classification is to arrange the images or recordings as per their cause, for example, Canon versus Nikon, and so forth. Gadget identification plans to demonstrate that the given image or video has been obtained by a specific gadget. Gadget linking is used to bunch the objects as indicated by their basic source, for example, in a given technique of images or in a given technique of recordings, which images or recordings were acquired utilizing an equivalent camera. Preparing history recovery's goal is to recuperate the handling tie applied to the image or the video. In this, we are keen on nonmalevolent preparing like separating, resizing, splendor, or differentiation change, compression, and so on. Uprightness verification, we planned for finding vindictive preparing like any item unequivocally added to the image or the video or any article expressly expelled from the video or the image. Oddity investigation manages clarifying inconsistencies found in an image or a video that might be an after effect of advanced preparing or other marvels explicit to computerized camera. Fig. 14.2 shows the grouping of computerized legal sciences.

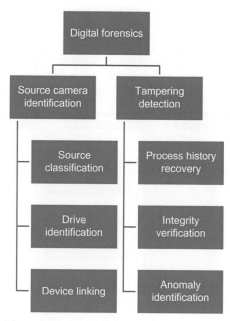

Figure 14.2 Classification of digital forensics.

14.3.6 Image forgery detection

Image phony identification strategies can be categorized as five classes:

Pixel-based systems are able to recognize the measurable inconsistencies that are presented at the pixel level. Configuration based strategies are used to influence the measurable relationships given by a particular lossy compression plot. Camera-based procedures are used to misuse the curios that are presented by the camera focal point, on-chip postpreparing or sensor. Physically based strategies express the model and distinguish the inconsistencies in three-dimensional cooperation between the camera, light and the physical articles. Geometric-based strategies are used to make estimations of an article on the planet and their positions with the camera (Pandey et al., 2016). Fig. 14.3

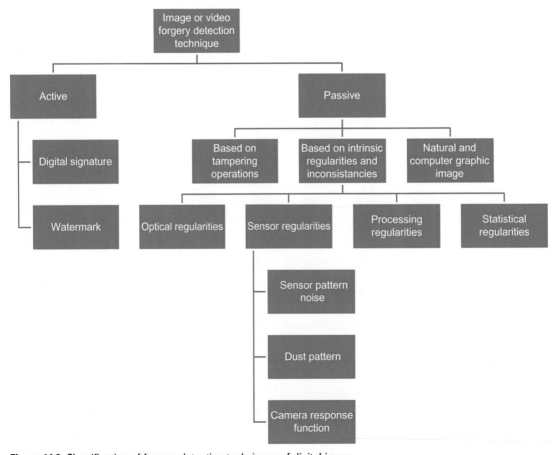

Figure 14.3 Classification of forgery detection techniques of digital image.

shows the grouping of advanced image falsification discovery procedures.

14.4   Comparative analysis and discussions

Table 14.1 Image tampering techniques analysis.

References	Image activity	System administration	Alter identification methods
Puech (2008)	Modifying, joining, duplicate glue, editing, and cloning	Accessibility	Edge obscuring
Araghi and Manaf (2019)	Duplicate move, resize, image cutting, noising, and obscuring	Accessibility verification	Laplace channel, PCA, DCT, DWT, and SVD
Tang et al. (2012)	Duplicate move, resize, image cutting, noising, and obscuring	Accessibility verification	Laplace filter, PCA, DCT, DWT, and SVD
Arun Anoop (2015)	Duplicate move, square component-based strategies	Accessibility verification	PCA, DCT, DWT, and SIFT
Bhatt et al. (2012)	Copy duplicate move and cutting	Accessibility verification	Multiscale WLD, LBP, LLB, and SVM
Carew and Errickson (2019)	Duplicate move and image joining	Accessibility verification	Measurable and square attributes
Coatrieux et al. (2012)	Duplicate move, joining, resize, and trimming cloning	Accessibility	Pixel, group, camera physically, and geometric based
Arney et al. (2011)	Duplicate move, duplicate make, and duplicate glue	Accessibility	JPEG compression examination, edge recognition, and confinement
Ghoneim et al. (2018)	Duplicate move	Accessibility	JPEG compression and square-based
Huang et al. (2011)	Mutilating, cancellation, inclusion, and image montage bogus inscribing	Nil	Computer-based intelligence (recognition duplication). Division grouping (ROI)
Makbol et al. (2017)	Image joining nearby/worldwide obscuring compression and resize	Nil	DCT SRM, and CASIA V2 dataset
Huang et al. (2012)	Division feature extraction	Accessibility	Structure semantic cosmology practical knowledge base
Ansari and Pant (2017)	Duplicate move	Trust Integrity	Area duplication
Ali et al. (2014)	Duplicate move	Verification	SPL and LBP
Ali and Ahn (2014)	Duplicate move	Accessibility	Confinement
Ali et al. (2016)	Duplicate move	Accessibility	Filter MIFT confinement

DCT, Discrete cosine transformation; *DWT*, discrete wavelet transform; *JPEG*, joint photographic experts group; *LBP*, local binary pattern; *LLB*, Landau–Lifshitz–Bloch; *PCA*, principal component analysis; *ROI*, region of interest; *SIFT*, scale-invariant feature transform; SVD, singular value decomposition; WLD, Weber local descriptor.

14.5 Future research challenges

1. A duplicate move imitation is made by reordering content inside a similar image, and possibly postpreparing it. In this time, the identification of duplicate move phonies has become one of the most effectively investigated points in dazzle image legal sciences (Arun Anoop, 2015).

2. When managing imaging information from living or perished people the desires and convictions of the individual and additionally the closest relative may be viewed when choosing whether to share the advanced information. Besides, these territories have a solid relationship to worldwide catastrophes, for example, the mass killings in fighting, as opposed to the 3D recuperation of a footwear mark (Carew and Errickson, 2019).

3. One of the primary issues in criminological casework is the unpredictable idea of breaking down and deciphering information. Because of the multifaceted nature of proofs, information is investigated and translated in the measurable sciences. The issue of acceptability of proof and researchers tribute accounts are raised (Carew and Errickson, 2019).

4. Training and institutionalization fluctuate between disciplines, research centers, and nations. The formation of standard methodology is recommended to guarantee reproducibility between research centers (Carew and Errickson, 2019).

5. These challenges incorporate radiographs of low quality that seriously influence the results as well as subsequently, the precision of the biometric framework. Another issue is that dental images may change over the long haul, particularly if the evening images were caught quite a while after the morning images which prompt trouble in coordinating (Myna et al., 2007).

14.6 Conclusions

The improvement and utilization of computerized images in criminological sciences has jumped further in recent years. Vivid 3D innovations and computerized imaging has been offered propelled abilities to record and examine wrongdoing scene and proof. A summary of imaging over legal matters has been discussed in this study in order to incorporate writing concentrated on humans, just as further subject sorts, for example, follow proof. Advanced image and video legal is one of the rapidly developing examination regions. A survey of advanced image and video measurable with the current references of detached legal strategies utilizing commotion highlights is displayed in this chapter. We had presented brief thought regarding types of imaging modalities, tools for proving image authenticity, and the application of digital imaging techniques to several forensic subdisciplines is discussed. Finally, we had presented the comparative analysis and future research challenge in medical image processing.

References

Ali, M., Ahn, C.W., 2014. An optimized watermarking technique based on self-adaptive DE in DWT–SVD transform domain. Signal. Process. 94 (0), 545–556.

Ali, M., Ahn, C.W., Siarry, P., 2014. Differential evolution algorithm for the selection of optimal scaling factors in image watermarking. Eng. Appl. Artif. Intell. 31, 15–26.

Ali, M., Ahn, C.W., Pant, M., Siarry, P., 2016. A reliable image watermarking scheme based on redistributed image normalization and SVD. Discret. Dyn. Nat. Soc. 2016 (7), 1–15.

Anantharaj, N., 2014. Tampering and copy-move forgery detection using Sift feature. Int. J. Innov. Res. Comput. Commun. Eng. 2 (1), 2132–2137.

Ansari, I.A., Pant, M., 2017. Multipurpose image watermarking in the domain of DWT based on SVD and ABC. Pattern Recognit. Lett. 94, 228–236.

Araghi, T.K., 2018. Template based methods in image watermarking to avoid geometric attacks. In: International Conference on Research and Innovation in Computer Engineering and Computer Sciences (RICCES).

Araghi, T.K., Manaf, A.A., 2019. An enhanced hybrid image watermarking scheme for security of medical and non-medical images based on DWT and 2-D SVD. Fut. Gener. Comput. Syst. 101, 1223–1246.

Arney, D., Venkatasubramanian, K.K., Sokolsky, O., & Lee, I., 2011. Biomedical devices and systems security. In: 2011 Annual International Conference of the IEEE Engineering in Medicine and Biology Society. IEEE, pp. 2376–2379.

Arun Anoop, M., 2015. Image forgery and its detection: a survey. In: 2015 International Conference on Innovations in Information, Embedded and Communication Systems (ICIIECS), Coimbatore, pp. 1–9. https://doi.org/10.1109/ICIIECS.2015.7193253.

Bhatt, H.S., Bharadwaj, S., Singh, R., Vatsa, M., 2012. Recognizing surgically altered face images using multiobjective evolutionary algorithm. IEEE Trans. Inf. Foren. Sec. 8 (1), 89–100.

Carew, R.M., Errickson, D., 2019. Imaging in forensic science: five years on. J. Foren. Radiol. Imag. 16 (1), 24–33.

Coatrieux, G., Pan, W., Cuppens-Boulahia, N., Cuppens, F., Roux, C., 2012. Reversible watermarking based on invariant image classification and dynamic histogram shifting. IEEE Trans. Inf. Foren. Sec. 8 (1), 111–120.

Cozzolino, D., Poggi, G., Verdoliva, L., 2014. Copy-move forgery detection based on patchmatch. In: 2014 IEEE International Conference on Image Processing (ICIP). IEEE, pp. 5312–5316.

Gangadhar, Y., Akula, V.G., Reddy, P.C., 2018. An evolutionary programming approach for securing medical images using watermarking scheme in invariant discrete wavelet transformation. Biomed. Signal. Process. Control. 43, 31–40.

Ghoneim, A., Muhammad, G., Amin, S.U., Gupta, B., 2018. Medical image forgery detection for smart healthcare. IEEE Commun. Mag. 56 (4), 33–37.

Gupta, A.K., Raval, M.S., 2012. A robust and secure watermarking scheme based on singular values replacement. Sadhana 37 (4), 425–440.

Huang, H., Coatrieux, G., Shu, H.Z., Luo, L.M., Roux, C., 2011. Medical image integrity control and forensics based on watermarking—approximating local modifications and identifying global image alterations. In: 2011 Annual International Conference of the IEEE Engineering in Medicine and Biology Society. IEEE, pp. 8062–8065.

Huang, H., Coatrieux, G., Shu, H., Luo, L.M., Roux, C., 2012. Blind integrity verification of medical images. IEEE Trans. Inf. Technol. Biomed. 16 (6), 1122–1126.

Joseph, A., Deepa, S.S., 2015. An efficient watermarking based integrity control system for medical images. In: 2015 International Conference on Control Communication & Computing India (ICCC). IEEE, pp. 357–361.

Karakus, S., Avci, E., 2019. Application of similarity-based image steganography method to computerized tomography images. In: 2019 7th International Symposium on Digital Forensics and Security (ISDFS). IEEE, pp. 1–4.

Makbol, N.M., Khoo, B.E., Rassem, T.H., Loukhaoukha, K., 2017. A new reliable optimized image watermarking scheme based on the integer wavelet transform and singular value decomposition for copyright protection. Inf. Sci. 417, 381–400.

Mulla, A., Baviskar, J., Wagh, S., Kudu, N., Baviskar, A., 2015. Probabilistic triangular shuffling approach in DWT based image compression scheme. In: 2015 International Conference on Communication, Information & Computing Technology (ICCICT). IEEE, pp. 1–6.

Murali, S., Chittapur, G.B., Anami, B.S., 2013. Comparision and analysis of photo image forgery detection techniques. arXiv preprint. arXiv:1302.3119.

Myna, A.N., Venkateshmurthy, M.G., Patil, C.G., 2007. Detection of region duplication forgery in digital images using wavelets and log-polar mapping. In: International Conference on Computational Intelligence and Multimedia Applications (ICCIMA 2007), vol. 3. IEEE, pp. 371–377.

Nomir, O., Abdel-Mottaleb, M., 2007. Human identification from dental X-ray images based on the shape and appearance of the teeth. IEEE Trans. Inf. Foren. Sec. 2 (2), 188–197.

Pandey, R.C., Singh, S.K., Shukla, K.K., 2016. Passive forensics in image and video using noise features: a review. Digit. Investig. 19, 1–28.

Puech, W., 2008. Image encryption and compression for medical image security. In: 2008 First Workshops on Image Processing Theory, Tools and Applications. IEEE, pp. 1–2.

Sadeghi, S., Jalab, H.A., Dadkhah, S., 2012. Efficient copy-move forgery detection for digital images. World Acad. Sci. Eng. Technol. 6 (11), 1339–1342.

Sharma, D., Abrol, P., 2013. Digital image tampering—a threat to security management. Int. J. Adv. Res. Comput. Commun. Eng. 2 (10), 4120–4123.

Tang, C., Zhang, H., Kong, A.W.K., Craft, N., 2012. Visualizing vein patterns from color skin images based on image mapping for forensics analysis. In: Proceedings of the 21st International Conference on Pattern Recognition (ICPR2012). IEEE, pp. 2387–2390.

Thakur, S., Singh, A., Ghrera, S., Mohan, A., 2018. Chaotic based secure watermarking approach for medical images. Multimed. Tools Appl. 79, 4263–4276.

Vali, M.H., Aghagolzadeh, A., Baleghi, Y., 2018. Optimized watermarking technique using self-adaptive differential evolution based on redundant discrete wavelet transform and singular value decomposition. Expert. Syst. Appl. 114, 296–312.

Index

Printed in the United States
By Bookmasters